Regionalism and Globalization

Regionalism and Globalization

Essays on Appalachia, Globalization, and Global Computerization

2nd Edition
2011

Joseph J. Matvey, III, Ph.D.
Sociology, 1987, University of Pittsburgh

Contribution by Tsze Chan, Ph.D.
American Institutes for Research/John Hopkins University

Preface by Roland Robertson
Professor of Sociology
University of Aberdeen

iUniverse, Inc.
New York   Bloomington

Regionalism and Globalization
Essays on Appalachia, Globalization, and Global Computerization

iUniverse books may be ordered through booksellers or by contacting:

iUniverse
1663 Liberty Drive
Bloomington, IN 47403
www.iuniverse.com
1-800-Authors (1-800-288-4677)

Because of the dynamic nature of the Internet, any Web addresses or links contained in this book may have changed since publication and may no longer be valid. The views expressed in this work are solely those of the author and do not necessarily reflect the views of the publisher, and the publisher hereby disclaims any responsibility for them.

ISBN: 978-1-4502-2491-8 (pbk)
ISBN: 978-1-4502-2492-5 (ebook)

Printed in the United States of America

iUniverse rev. date: 5/4/10

For Lois

through the seasons

may i walk through life with you--
through the seasons?
can i hold your soft hand under the moonlight
and share a gentle kiss on an autumn night?

the seasons are soft
where you stroll
like the mist rising on summer mornings
across the foothills of western Pennsylvania

in winter
wood fired stoves heat rural homes
and bake cornbread
while elaborate quilts warm beds
and keep feet cozy
from the frost gathering on windowsills

and here now in spring--
i love you
when everything blooms
and i can see the flowers in your eyes

kittens purr softly around you
they sense your gentle spirit
and i--
i feel truly at home with you
comfortable in my thoughts and feelings. And
each gentle embrace
brings me closer to you.

you give meaning to my life
when you are away i am lost in the portals of nothingness
and it is your return that makes my heart beat again
how deep in my life you are
how you are such a part of me
how in love i am with you.

CONTENTS

POETRY

PREFACE

The contemporary study of globalization began to gain force in the early 1980s. One can find many previous examples of writing about it through the ages, even though that specific term was not used. In fact, the precise term, globalization, was not used at all until the period of the 1950s and 1960s and even then it was only used more or less casually.

Unfortunately globalization did not come into full public consciousness until the 1990s, as meaning the crystallization of the global economy and the steps that had been or should be taken to make the world free of regulation, public ownership, and protectionism. In other words, the hallmarks of globalization were seen as involving deregulation, marketization, and free trade. Among the major promoters of this view were, on the political front, Bill Clinton and Tony Blair – even though they both built upon the ideas enunciated previously by Ronald Reagan and Margaret Thatcher. The continuity between Thatcherism and Blairism is only now becoming fully recognized.

On the more academic front, the most well-known proponent of globalization was Anthony Giddens. Giddens became well-known in Britain through his work on what was called the Third Way and his contact with Blair and Clinton was fairly extensive. Here, it should be noted that the idea of the third way has had a long and unfortunate history and can be found in such doctrines as National Socialism. It was adopted not merely by Mussolini but also by Hitler, and the founder of the Turkish Republic, Ataturk. The Third Way involved an unoriginal – but dramatically promoted – offer of an ideological position "beyond" the conventional distinctions between Right and Left. To many intents and purposes this is what became known among some intellectuals, politicians and policy makers as constituting globalization. Moreover, it was the underlying basis for Giddens's *The Consequences of Modernity*, even though in that particular book he didn't explicitly use the term the Third Way. In other words, globalization had the strong connotation of the rendering of the whole world in capitalistic terms – in spite of people such as Blair, Giddens and, to some extent, Clinton, presenting themselves as men of the left! In the UK the particular political policy is known as PFI (Private Finance Initiative), one which has become increasingly controversial.

Meanwhile, in the late 1970s and early 1980s there had developed an entirely different approach to globalization, i.e well before the economistic meaning of the term as described above. It should be noted that, in principle, economic globalization could just as well have meant the road to global socialism as it could have meant the road to global capitalism. However, those concerned with the move in the direction of global socialism have tended to reject the idea of globalization, largely because of its association among policy makers with global capitalism. Needless to say, capitalism is under particular attack at this time even though few advocate its complete removal.

The multidimensional approach, giving special attention to cultural factors arose primarily at the University of Pittsburgh in the late 1970s and early 1980s, but it was also linked to work within the Theory, Culture and Society group at what was then the Teeside Polytechnic in the UK. This endeavor was mainly confined in Pittsburgh to the Department of Sociology. The first articles that came out of this development were delivered in the form of conference papers and, later, in various journal articles. This culminated in the publication in 1992 of my book, ***Globalization: Global Culture and Social Theory***. At the center of the latter was my own revised depiction of what I had previously called the global field. The latter term was intended to come to terms with the issue of the form or pattern of globalization over the past five hundred years or so. Much of this venture was a calculated endeavor to confront Wallerstein's very influential attempts to describe and analyse the crystallization of what he called the capitalist world-system. This was done from the same perspective that Max Weber had used in his famous book, ***The Protestant Ethic and the Spirit of Capitalism***. Just as Weber had said of Marx that it was as plausible to produce an idealistic theory of the growth of capitalism as it was a materialistic theory, so the same could be said of the course of globalization. This was the presupposition behind the work of what became known as the Pittsburgh School, the central members of this consisting, inter alia, of Frank Lechner, Michael Cavanaugh, JoAnn Chirico, Gary Abraham, Aysegul, Baykan, Juliana Martinez, Denise de Silva, Victor Roudometof and, of course, Joseph Matvey.

The book that follows, written by Joseph Matvey, should be seen as having arisen partly in this context, as the author makes clear in his early pages. Matvey's book is a wide-ranging approach to the theme of globalization, ranging from a focus in the early chapters on the coal mining area of American Appalachia and the appalling conditions of poverty in that region. (It is more than incidental that Arnold Toynbee described the Appalachian region as very backward in relation to Western civilization at large.) As Matvey's book moves from the issues of regionalisation and globalization to a more direct confrontation with globalization per se he attends to the contemporary significance of Japanese Buddhism, most particularly in its Soka Gakkai form. Soka Gakkai has been remarkably influential on a word–wide scale and Matvey interestingly explores its relevance to the study of globalization. Indeed, he rightly conceives of this form of evangelistic lay Buddhism as an important part of the overall globalization process.

At the same time he adds to the existing literature on globalization with particular reference to the study of global education. The later chapters are mainly concerned with the consideration of what is now often called connectivity, considered mainly from a computerization standpoint. Matvey also attends in his penultimate chapter to the very significant issue of glocalization, with particular reference to the importance of the cultural factor. Thus it should be noted that Matvey shifts from a primarily economic approach to one based on culture. In this particular sense, the book as a whole is an autobiographical statement involving an interesting and moving account of the changes in thinking of a particular author over a few decades, one who was intimately familiar with the Appalachian region and moved on to consider to situate Appalachia in a global context. What one sees in this odyssey is the way in which what used to be thought of in almost exclusively economic terms is now thought of in primarily cultural forms. In this transition Matvey implicitly acknowledges the importance of global consciousness, as well as global connectivity.

The most relevant term here is *economic culture*. For many years sociologists have spent much of their time worrying about the link between economy and culture. However from about the early 1980s it became increasingly apparent that the worrying wasn't necessary. Use of the term economic culture illustrates how a simple conceptual move can solve what seems to be an enormously substantive problem, as is best exampled by Matvey's use of the term subsistence culture. The same could be said of the way in which the use of the term glocalization overcomes the alleged problem of the opposition between the global and the local.

This is indeed a book of great scope involving the study of "locality" as well as a focus upon the entire world. The former is best seen in the chapters on Appalachia while the latter is most evident in the concern with humanity at large. This kind of daring perspective is necessary at this time when the complexity and confusion surrounding the fate of the planet is central to much of social science and other disciplines. Finally it should be remarked that when Matvey "returns home" he does not in fact return to the "same" home that he started from. Appalachia has "changed" simply because Matvey has now placed it in context.

Roland Robertson
Aberdeen, February, 2010

FORWARD AND ACKNOWLEDGEMENTS

Regionalism and Globalization represents sociological research—both qualitative and quantitative—spanning 25 years from 1985 through 2010. The three central themes of this volume are simply Appalachia, Globalization, and Societal and Global Computerization. Before we turn to the core components of the book though, a brief biographical sketch follows first.

Graduate school in Sociology at the University of Pittsburgh during the early 1980s was an exciting and eventful time to be engaged in the Academia. In early 1982 I graduated from Union College, a Methodist oriented and accredited Liberal Arts College in the heart of Appalachian Kentucky. At Union I majored and earned my Bachelor's with a double major in Sociology and Appalachian Studies and a minor in Economics. I must admit though, while I received an adequate and well rounded Liberal Arts education, I was taught in Sociology by two Marxian oriented Assistant Professors who were both very sincere educators, brilliant teachers, and whom both I still admire deeply, but the net effect was an intensified intellectual saturation in Marxian Sociology.

Nevertheless, I found myself at Pitt in Grad School with a Teaching Fellowship that essentially paid about 60% of my education while the rest of costs were made up with student loans. In terms of the Department, I was ill prepared for the diverse field of Sociology. I spent my free time in cubicles in the Pitt library trying to read all I could and play catch-up to the broad spectrum of Sociology. In my first year I was mentally scattered, which is probably normal for most incoming 1st year students, and after a time of teaching recitation classes in Introductory Sociology courses I gained my confidence and along with my extra-curricular reading began to feel more academically comfortable in my surroundings.

As I mentioned, it was a dynamic period at Pitt. While I did not realize it initially, later I came to understand that my mentor, Roland Robertson, who taught graduate courses such as Global and Cultural Change, was in fact, the foremost theorist on Globalization across the entire field of Sociology. By my 2nd Academic Year at Pitt, Roland and I formed a friendship. Due to my Marxian background, I was always focusing on the "economic" factor in our discussions while he would alert me continually to the influence of culture. Sometimes we shared the dialogue over Bass Pale Ale, an imported beer he introduced to me. I also recall helping him move from Shadyside to Squirrel Hill in Pittsburgh, and what I remember most were all his books in double papered supermarket bags. There were bags and bags and bags of books---it never ended. He tried to comfort my endless predicament by noting "I've always felt it was like a sin to throw away a book."

My specializations in Sociology were heavily influenced by the research orientations of both Roland Robertson and Patrick Doreian. Patrick was deeply involved in the Social Networking subdiscipline of Sociology. It is also not a stretch to say he is one of the foremost Social Network theorists in the field today, and perhaps busy achieving that status during my graduate school years. While Roland was fascinated with culture, Pat was grounded in the structural and relational influences on social reality. Consequently, my two areas of specialization in Sociology were narrowed to Cultural Change and Macro-structural Change.

What followed after my comprehensive exams--when I was told it was common for grad students taking their comps to walk around like zombies two weeks before and after these exams—I found myself gearing and focusing on my future dissertation. In 1985 I chose my doctoral dissertation committee with Pat as the Chair and Roland and Gil Shapiro also as members of the group. I followed my heart and chose a topic I knew best, a thesis on Appalachia. I prepared an overview and delivered and spoke on it on Halloween Day in 1985. Primarily I wanted to present a macro-structural history on the central Appalachian region and reveal how both structure and culture interacted to create ongoing patterns of subsistence practices in the mountains of Appalachia. Discounted was the notion that subsistence culture represented a state of cultural backwardness. Instead I theorized that a structural condition of regional economic underdevelopment fostered a dynamic and adapting culture of subsistence farming, craft, clothing, and food production practices within the confines of the modern Appalachian homestead. Such practices increased the value of income—income that was quite scarce in the mountains of central Appalachia.

In August of 1987 I successfully defended my Dissertation and earned my Doctorate. Less than a month later I landed a one year Assistant Professorship at Francis Marion College in Florence, South Carolina, teaching two sections of Introductory Sociology and two sections of Methods of Social Research. This too was an exciting time filled with bright promise. I engaged my students to do projects, demanding more from the Methods students than the Introductory Students. While the mid-term and final exams constituted 80% of the grade, 20% belonged to the projects in the manifest form of a 15 or more page paper and a class presentation. Two-thirds of the class time was devoted to teaching while the remaining one-third was set aside for class presentations. To me, and to the students, this was the most enjoyable time of the semester. The projects were fascinating and filled with creativity and sincerity of effort. I may have been a liberal grader, since few students in my classes got less than a C with many A's and B's—but I never failed to be impressed by the talent and academic skill of the Carolinian students. Most gained and learned much as was evidenced in not only their projects, but on the essay exams as well.

I enjoyed my first year at Francis Marion, and at the end of the academic year, ready to look for another teaching position, Lloyd Birch, Chair of the Department of Sociology, invited me back for a second year, and during this time I had many students from my Introductory Courses in the previous year now take my Methods Courses. More was expected of them to be sure, but a majority did their best and brought more exciting and uniquely new projects to the academic table. In addition, during my stay at Francis Marion, I had the opportunity to work with a colleague, Tsze Chan, a Pitt Alumnus from our grad school days. Tsze was teaching at the University of Maryland, and we decided to collaborate to develop theoretical research on the theme of Societal and Global Computerization. The result after several months of work manifested in a presentation on Societal and Global Computerization at Penn State University, during a snowstorm in the winter of 1988.

In addition, I continued work and research in the field of Globalization and also in 1988 I presented this research on the phenomenon of "Global Connectivity." My theory was quite straightforward and dealt with the growing trend in globalization of the horizontal linkages of *like* social groups, organizations, institutions, and societal sectors across societal lines and their corresponding emergence and legitimacy at the distinctly global level. The paper was presented in Atlanta, Ga, at the Association for the Sociology of Religion Conference in 1988.

In short, I was off to a promising career. I would have considered continuing to teach at Francis Marion but the Department had reworked my temporary-replacement position into a tenure-track position centered heavily upon a quantitative orientation and, at that time, I had few statistical or quantitative skills. Moreover, events would soon change and my career in the Academia would come to an unexpected end with the emergence of a debilitating illness in the late summer of 1989. I returned home to Pittsburgh, and in time began assisting my father in his commercial real estate and marketing business in the 1990s. Essentially, the position developed into a computer consultant for the JJ Matvey Marketing Agency. Much of what I used at that time were software programs such as Lotus, PFS, Quattro Pro and other spreadsheet and database applications. The work was far different than teaching, but it was through this particular type of skill that I gained knowledge in statistics and other quantitative areas.

After my father passed in 1997, my wife and I developed a home business of selling collectibles and cultural keepsakes. During this time however, I continued to do social research and in 2005 put several chapters together into a volume entitled ***Regionalism and Globalization: Essays on Appalachia, Globalization and Global Computerization.***

The Second Edition of ***Regionalism and Globalization*** represents three revised and redeveloped chapters as well as four new chapters, along with a collection of poetry inter-spacing the chapters of the book.

There are several notable mentions that go out to some of the people that influenced this second edition of ***Regionalism and Globalization***, and interestingly enough, they are all women. Lois, my wife, of course was the heart and soul of this project—she never made it easy on me and challenged me at each juncture to not only pursue the perfection of the manuscript but also to develop a poor man's marketing plan to stock the bookstore shelves. Audrey Daniels, my health professional, continued to challenge me, not specifically on the book but to look past my disabilities and develop the creative and dynamic areas of my life with vigor and determination. In addition, my mother Norma Jean and mother-in-law (the late) Nora Dilling also played encouraging roles in the development of this edition—with advice from my mother Norma Jean, and with Nora the central figure of the interview process in Chapter Two.

Some footnotes here…while I have not pursued employment in Academia, this research spanning 25 years--created, revised, reworked, redeveloped--has been a wonderful intellectual pursuit. It is not tied to the stresses of "publish or perish" in the university system, nor to the requirements of academic standards for tenure. It is, however, a valuable part of the creative process and of my cultural work ethic. I am a sociologist. It is a unique way of examining and understanding the global, societal, organizational, and individual dimensions of our sociality.

Another mention here…in the absence of a professional editor to smooth out the chapters, there may be some "choppiness" in the read as parts of this research began as early as 1985 while other chapters developed and were reworked in the 1990s, and finally, some chapters represent current research as recent as 2009. My writing has changed over this period. Also, Chapter Eight in particular represents spruced field notes from a conference presentation at Penn State University on Societal and Global Computerization in 1988.

Finally, while the chapters on central Appalachia could make for an historical volume on the region, in this book each Appalachian chapter is treated more as a collection of essays. While the first two chapters give consideration to northern Appalachia, we also get a glimpse of counties in distress in central Appalachia when comparisons between Major Coal counties are made between the two Appalachian sub-regions. In the third chapter we move toward a model of present-day underdevelopment in central Appalachia as a mineral export periphery. Once we examine "the way it is," in the chapters that follow we explore "how it got that way," and dig for answers in earlier eras. This is not a history book, then, but there are many historical lessons learned in focusing attention on essays of earlier eras of the region.

Joseph J. Matvey III
February 2010

Global Individuation

I)

For the past several weeks
there have been the rains with no storm
anticipation without desire
an aggregation of beings with no apparent community.

Even the birds have failed to return to my kitchen's
windowsill when clearly it is time they should.

What is in the Calm?

A puzzling unseen spawning from the lack
of what should be seen in the normality of things.
The why is bypassed
left unanswered and I am moved instead
to a vivid spirituality of sorts

as I now question artificialities
and breathe into the calm
creating wind
to form the horror of storm within my own mentality.

II)

and

sprouting from the awareness are a
variety of self-help therapists:
psychotechnicians
psychobiologists
psychoeconomists
and psychoanalysts
all involved in the great scientific pursuit
of looking out for number one...

...This ultimate end product collapses inward
upon itself
upon its universe
and we find billions of human worlds colliding.

Retreat.
withdrawing into its own analogue of life:

the mind
like Maillol's Night
alone
and quite desperate.

INTRODUCTION

What Is Globalization?

Many are under the impression that globalization represents a world social order where national societies or nation states wither away and in their place is a giant monolithic world government dominating the globe—a "global big brother," if you will. This is not globalization. It signifies, however, one legitimate view or perception of global social order held by a particular social group in the world today.

There are literally dozens of "perceptions" out there with regard to global social order. What we can say is that with globalization, individuals and social groups increasingly have and hold views and perceptions of how the world should be structured and ordered. Globalization, then, is what Roland Robertson coins as a ***growing awareness of the global.*** The perception above can be termed the Global Governmental view. There is, in addition to this perception, a Global Village perception intersecting with John Lennon's popular song *Imagine*. In *Imagine*, Lennon deflates images of national societies, religions and ethnic differences separating and compartmentalizing humankind, and conflates and heightens notions of brotherhood and humankind in what he calls a "brotherhood of man" where the "world will be as one." Unlike the Global Government model, however, *Imagine* represents perfect anarchy and communism in its purified Marxian ideal where the State has withered and we find ourselves within a single cultural utopia.

Now let's consider a third view of global social order, one based on and grounded in terror, jihad, and mass murder. The view from this extreme wing of Islam, pursues the creation of chaos and destruction in the social environments of the so called "infidels" of the West, carrying out its ultimate goal of purifying the globe for a fundamentalist religious social order given to and structured around a very distorted view of Allah. Interestingly enough, this is indeed a perception of global social order, and like the global village view it too sees a vision of a unified world—only the unification is based on the extreme and distorted vision of Islam.

Views and perceptions like these, along with several others, are heavily developed in Robertson's classic work, ***Globalization: Global Culture and Social Theory***, in a full- blown theoretical scheme we might entitle, for simplicity's sake, Global Gemeinschaft and Gesellschaft. Here, Robertson recasts Tonnies' original theory in a global context, and lists eight key perceptions or images of global social order.

Where is the bulk of the world with regard to its perception of global social order? Perhaps it is somewhere between the extremes of Lennon's model and the jihad view. It is fair to say most of human kind supports the notion of a family of nations and the corresponding legitimacy of those societal systems. Most, too, accept the UN as a legitimate international governmental organization coordinating the complexities of global social differentiation and global social problems such as poverty, housing, human health and disease, environment, pollution, global warming, as well as ethnic and cultural repression.

These then represent perceptions of global social order—they are properties of the globalization process but no single view constitutes globalization in and of itself. That individuals, social groups, organizations and nation states all hold views of global social order, no matter how divergent those views and perceptions are with respect to each other, the fact that they hold those perceptions at all is evidence of globalization.

Perceptions, however, deal with the "subjective." We are welcome to our views of global society to be sure, but these views tell us little of the objective structure of the globe at any given moment. They are, in other words, held cultural keepsakes, commitments and ideals for how the world should be ordered and structured but not the objective order and structure of the globe. What is the objective global condition at this particular juncture in civilization's history? Pretty much what I will term a State Federationalist structure.

The State Federationalist structure is what George Bush Sr. coined as the *new world order* comprised of a "family" of nations. As individuals are endowed with certain inalienable rights, so too are societies in this family of nations. Generally nations are viewed as equals, but most realize that a few strong nations dominate the playing board as well as international relations. There are in addition to this pluralistic family of nations, global governmental organizations such as the UN as well as a host of international governmental sub-organizations under the umbrella of the UN. Hence, objectively there are both state and international organizational forms coexisting. It is also clear that the trajectory over the last century has been an increase in global organizational formats and the global connectivity of like societal organizations on a global level. This, however, does not indicate either a weakening or withering of the nation state, for while global organizations are evident, we live in an objectively situated arrangement of vibrant and strong states comprising the global system.

Although I would contend that most, or at least a majority, of the world's population accepts the given structural arrangement of a family of nations and global coordinating organization such as the UN, this structure is not accepted by all social groups. From radical anarchist and environmental groups to jihad terrorists, their goals are to disrupt, destroy, and create chaos in the current structure to both get their point across as well as manifest their own particular views of global social order. Here then is the interaction between subjective collectively-held perceptions and objective global structural organization and conditions.

What is globalization then? It is at one and the same moment both the subjective and objective. In the interaction between subjective and objective, what occurs is the ongoing evolution of the current global system. Consider civilization's history. At one point the objective structure of the globe consisted of a number of world empires. These however, over time, gave way to the birth, development, and maturation of the national society or nation state system. There is no reason to think, however, that the state system will be with us forever. One might envision a future world dominated politically and culturally by major metropolitan cores and their surrounding peripheries. Or returning to an earlier example, we might find the manifestation of a global village. The fact of the matter is ***as*** various social groups and their corresponding perceptions of the global come into contact with the objective structure of the globe and with each other as well, the entire global social system evolves. This then is the heart and core of what globalization is all about.

The Intersection of Regionalism

The bulk of this volume is devoted to the phenomenon of globalization and global computerization. We explore theoretical globalization as well as empirical indicators of that process. Computerization is in fact, one indicator of globalization, but it is also an independent technological process with its own dynamics and patterns.

There are also the global social problems of hunger, poverty, inadequate housing, and socioeconomic distress. Consider the Third World. Global capitalism has been primarily responsible for the development of "core and peripheral" economic systems where profits from core-organized economic activity flow out of the periphery and back to the core's corporate elites and metropolitan zones. This flow of capital has become systemic over the years and is in large part responsible for the widening economic gap between the rich and poor at the global level. At this point, one-sixth of the global population is homeless with many others existing in conditions which lead to malnourishment, deprivation, poverty, and starvation. This is the effect of greed and greed-driven economic systems on the global stage.

In this book, however, we utilize the empirical example of this global social problem not in the study of regions of Africa or Asia or Central America, but in the socioeconomic conditions of distress right in the Core's very backyard: Appalachia--particularly, central Appalachia. The logic embedded in core and peripheral economic systems at various points across the globe is also a logic that *works* within societies as well as beyond their boundaries.

Theoretical Currents of Regionalism and Globalization

Conceptually speaking, the essence of this work deals with both Regionalism and Globalization as systems of patterned regularities. The theoretical tools here combine insights from World Systems, Global Integrationalist, Parsons' Model of Societal Differentiation and the Robertsonian Theory of Globalization. In this book, *Regionalism and Globalization*, two central theoretical constructs are utilized.

First, in the chapters dealing with the Central Appalachian mineral export economy, we are focused primarily on the economic sphere -- specifically economic underdevelopment. It is here that a Core/Periphery model is most appropriate. Central Appalachia is not a nation-state or even a colony but, rather, a region of persistent poverty and underdevelopment. A Core/Periphery perspective will be utilized to construct and move toward a general Model of Underdevelopment in the region. Culture will also be explored, and incidentally, not as a "yesterday's people" ethic, but rather a dynamic response to a continued and regenerating system of underdevelopment.

Second, in the chapters dealing with globalization, our concern is with differentiation within societal systems and the growing horizontal connectivity made at the global level by societies and their sectors.

In the chapters on Globalization and Global and Societal Computerization, the preexisting degree of differentiation of societies followed by integration through federationalism at the global level are crucial variables orchestrating the connectivity of like spheres and sectors.

The Spatial Expression of Economic Differentiation

Core and Periphery are theoretical constructs essentially referring to the spatial expression of global corporate capitalism. The Core/Periphery model will be utilized extensively in chapters on the Central Appalachian region. Here we are not speaking of "like" spheres or sectors integrating horizontally, but rather, capitalist ownership vertically expressed over physical space or topography. In the economic sphere, we find structures comprised of ownership, corporate institutional, divisions of labor, occupational, and organizational hierarchies. Primarily, the geographic clustering of top or elite roles in this hierarchy are termed "metropolitan" or "core zones" while bottom layer roles represent a peripheral status. It may prove useful with regard to the Appalachian chapters to define, distinguish and discern some of the major terminology utilized.

Undevelopment, Uneven Development, and Underdevelopment. These terms refer to the character of the regional economy. Undevelopment simply implies the lack of economic development and diversification -- a condition commonly utilized to refer to the state of the subsistence economy before the era of industrialization. Uneven Development generally implies inter-regional divergences in levels of development and economic diversification across a given geographic landscape.

Underdevelopment cannot be equated with undevelopment. Underdevelopment implies a depressed or distorted level of economic growth despite the potential for full development (Girvan, 1976: 30-31). This is analogous to the term underemployment. A class of workers may embody the potential for full-time employment but be underemployed due to structural constraints placed upon the full utilization of labor potential.

Underdevelopment can be revealed in various dimensions. On one level it can be expressed as depressed socioeconomic conditions among the regional labor force. On another level it can be revealed as the incomplete transformation of a regional economy to capitalist social relations -- thus, the persistence of peasant or subsistence economies alongside an industrial sector. Still a third dimension of underdevelopment can be defined as the lack of economic diversification and the dominance of a regional economy by a single industry.

Hinterland and Periphery. These terms imply a particular role that a given regional economy plays in a larger economic division of labor. Primarily, hinterland and periphery refer to the bottom layers of a particular production, division of labor, exchange or ownership hierarchy (Braudel, 1979b; Girvan, 1976:20-22; Bergesen, 1980: 6-11). Their polar opposites -- metropolis and core -- refer to positions at the top of these hierarchies.

The term "periphery" as it has been utilized in recent literature adds a dimension through implying levels of development at the core of the system are actually fueled by corresponding levels of underdevelopment in the periphery (Bergesen, 1980). Thus particular sets of hierarchies are not merely categories of role clusters but role clusters which operate in a symbiotic relationship with each other.

Typically, the term "hinterland" has been utilized to define a regional zone surrounding a particular metropolis, while periphery has most commonly referred to nation states at the bottom of a world politico-economic hierarchy. If we abstract the economic notions of hierarchy, roles in the hierarchy, and a symbiotic relationship it will prove useful to utilize these terms in defining Central Appalachia's role in particular economic hierarchies.

Mineral Export Economy and Mineral Export Enclave. Mineral export economy refers to the general character of industry in a given regional economy (Girvan, 1976: 25). It implies a particular type of production, namely, the extraction of minerals. Furthermore, mineral export economy points to a general dominance of this particular type of industrialization in the region (Girvan, 1976).

Mineral Export Enclave, simply defined, refers to the lack of integration of the mineral export sector with the regional economy. It defines a clustering of subsidiary units in the region, which has primarily been organized by metropolitan-based forces. Girvan (1976: 32) contends these subsidiaries are more integrated with the metropolitan corporate economy than the local economy, which in turn has implications on the manifestation of development potential in a given mineral export economy.

Subsistence Farming and Domestic Production. Subsistence Farming generally refers to the pre-industrial farm mode outside the social relationship of capital. It will also be utilized to define the farm class outside the capital relation during the industrial era. Central to the notion of subsistence farming is production for home consumption, although some level of community trade may also be evident.

Domestic Production characterizes a practice of producing use values for either home consumption or to be geared to the market. Domestic production is carried out by both the farm and non-farm population.

Globalization: Societal Differentiation and Global Connectivity

Along with technological developments, a theoretical current highly conducive to connectivity at the global level rests upon the pre-existing degree of differentiation in societies in general. Central to the concept of progressive societal differentiation is not merely the splitting up and compartmentalizing of the spheres of social life, but chiefly it is the institutionalization and legitimization of these spheres as specialized stages of authority in orchestrating particular sphere-specific affairs of social life. What occurs on an intersocietal level, then, involves the coming together; hence the term, global connectivity of "like" spheres. For global connectivity to proceed in the truest sense of the term, there must be a relatively standard level of intrasocietal differentiation of social spheres across societies. The past century and a half can be most accurately viewed as an era of standardization in intrasocietal differentiation across the globe. More recently, trends in modernity point toward an increase in the level of differentiation within what are primarily considered Eastern, Gemeinschaft, agrarian, and Third World societal systems. As Department of Education, Department of Environmental Resources, and a Department of Cultural Development, etc., become commonplace collective household terms in these societies, the commitment to the overall normative structure of modernity equips societies with a host of sphere-specific realms and representatives. In that modernity can be viewed as dual dimensional -- in the sense of having both societal and global functions -- a natural outflow of intrasocietal differentiation leads to the linking of societal specialists with global-oriented frameworks.

Hence, the prime mover in global connectivity is the horizontal integration of societies and sectors in global formats, institutions, organizations and rituals. This in accomplished through federationalism -- the drive to include not merely core but all societies in these international formats.

Regionalism and Globalization: Overview

The first two chapters deal with the coalfields of the Blacklick Valley in Cambria County, Pennsylvania — in the Northern Appalachian Region. In the first chapter, briefly examined are the production, concentration, and employment in the Appalachian Coal Industry. We then move on to comparisons of four study populations: U.S., METRO, MAJOR COAL COUNTIES and BLACKLICK VALLEY. In the comparative study, examined are the clustering and variance of socioeconomic indicators both within and across study populations. The chapter concludes with an historical examination of the Blacklick Valley.

In the second chapter, interview research is employed with a resident from the Blacklick Valley, Pennsylvania. The interview primarily deals with Nora Dilling growing up in the coal town of Nanty Glo and examines religion, the structures of everyday life, education, the Great Depression, history of Nanty Glo, and Nora's family and children born in Nanty Glo. Centrally, the interview fuses a personality onto the previous chapter, Chapter One. While statistics and socioeconomic indicators tell us much, the stories of a resident allow those statistics to come alive.

Chapter Three shifts our attention from Northern to Central Appalachia where the focus is on poverty, education, out-migration and general underdevelopment of the region in the modern era. In this chapter is the move toward a general model of Regional Underdevelopment in Central Appalachia.

In the fourth chapter we visit the pre-industrial 1750-1880 era and compare Central Appalachia with Southwestern Pennsylvania in Northern Appalachia with regard to economic development. Primarily examined is the development of "core" producing status in the Pittsburgh Appalachian Region and the corresponding peripheralization of Central Appalachia in the pre-industrial period. Methodologically-speaking, we compare four study populations: SOUTHWESTERN PENNSYLVANIA, OHIO RIVER COUNTIES, RIVER NETWORK COUNTIES and MOUNTAIN COUNTIES in terms of the degree of self-sufficient farming in these areas.

The fifth chapter focuses on Subsistence Culture in Appalachia, from its roots in the pre-industrial era to its persistence in the modern era. Offered is an explanation for the continuation of subsistence practices in Central Appalachia long after they have died out in other parts of the U.S. Examined here is the character of farming in the early industrial era and the significance of the Great Depression in preserving subsistence practices. This chapter closes with a look at the marketization of subsistence crafts and goods in the Era of Globalization.

Moving from regionalism to globalization, the sixth chapter opens by documenting the initial penetration of Buddhism within the U.S., mirroring the expansion of the Japanese community along the West Coast from the Pre-World War I period through the 1970s. This chapter introduces a three-pronged approach that follows the early penetration of Buddhism in U.S. society to its ongoing development in modern/postmodern U.S. society. In this chapter we compare Traditional Sectarian, Globalizational Sectarianism and Post Modern Syncretism in reference to some of the variety of ways Buddhism developed in the U.S. In addition, we briefly examine a variety of Buddhist forms, beliefs and doctrine, and conclude by looking at the growing appeal of eastern (particularly Buddhist) religions and organizations to youth in U.S. Society.

In Chapter Seven, a theory of Globalization is set forth. A five-pronged model examines the phenomenon of Globalization and the Globe as System. First, the concept of *Global Moral Density* is explored, followed by a focus on *Global Connectivity*. *Global Federationalism* represents a third prong, while *Global Culture* illuminates a fourth prong. Finally, in a fifth prong, theoretical considerations are given to the notion of the *Globe as System*. In this chapter two empirical processes are also considered, one being the emergence of Global Education at the University level, while the other centering upon the growth, dynamics, and increasing legitimacy of Global Organizations, with particular reference to the United Nations and its sub-organizations.

In Chapter Eight the global significance of Societal and Global Computerization is explored. We begin with the rationale for applying a model of computerization across the whole of modern societies, and following, we present a model of Societal/Global Computerization in a typology of societal and global structural parameters and ideal orientations. As a way of a conclusion, we focus on the globalization process and how it impacts upon societal computerization.

Chapters Nine Through Eleven all deal with aspects of the globalization process. Nine presents a visualization of the technological compression of the globe in a five-tiered ranking system of modern national societies. The disparities between the Top and Bottom of the globe are startling.

Chapter Ten represents a qualitative case study of the Pittsburgh Region with regard to Internet Chat. The contention is made that chat rooms are more than an association of individuals, with some taking on the dynamics of highly structured cyber social groups.

In Chapter Eleven we explore the Sociological Enterprise and how, as we move deeper into the Globalization paradigm, we face rewriting our Introductory Sociology texts to adapt to the changes brought on by Globalization.

Chapter Twelve revisits the initial development of Robertson's "Global Field" schematic and demonstrates the flexibility and broad scope of the theoretical research tradition in dealing with current problems and processes in the Global Human Condition. As one empirical aspect in conjunction with the schema, the author looks into the concept of global spaces.

Chapter Thirteen attends to some of the wisdom of The Christ with regard to how we make sense of and formulate symbolic meaning for our lives and cultural ethics as we proceed into the Global era. How appropriate that the Wisdom of The Christ is not outdated but speaks to each individual in each society in the Global Age.

Finally, in Chapter Fourteen, the epilogue, we explore yet another aspect of computerization's future in a globalized age with respect to the development and spread of desktop operating systems in an age where monopoly capital predominates computerization's market orientation. Some social forecasting is developed with respect to the growing popularity of the Linux Enterprise.

Appalachia

Every twenty miles or so
in the flat scarcities of the Cumberlands
rest markers of civilization:
Corbin.
Barbourville.
Pineville.
Towns known only to geographers.
Tourists.
Travelers.
And perhaps relatives
from some distant metropolis.

Towering skyscrapers?
The mountains appear high enough.
Concert halls?
They have festivals.

To tourists these hills are an awesome work of magnificence.
To coal operators they are obstacle after obstacle.
And ones who dwell here have no doubt held
both these sentiments.

Old men gather in bib jeans at the courthouse square
in noon day to trade pocket knives and speak of coal.
And they speak not of material substance as much as of
its symbolic significance.
Coal carried families through winters
sent children to school
put gravied beef on the table
and kept the dream alive.

There are zones of rurality here
where hands are more accustomed to the plow
than in the handling produce at the A&P.
Minds more patient in the process of quiltmaking
than in making a transactional choice over bedware at
the nearest urban department store...

Transactions take more time in the mountains.
Unlike the almost robotic metropolitan "next please"
Appalachians inquire of the farm, the family...
Attitudes, life stories, whole states of mind exchange.

Each community a microcosm unto itself
yet intricately bound to the wider cultural quilt
as evidenced in the parades of regional festivals.
Identity is secured to the whole.
One Appalachian noted "here you are raised something,
a Baptist, a republican..."

They have formed a groove
a patterned way of life and livelihood
within the mazed hollows of Appalachia.

CHAPTER ONE

The Culture of Coal: Coal and Ghost Towns in the Blacklick Valley, Pennsylvania

from No Pretty Song

...while it may sound simplistic, this is what I gotta say
anytime anywhere a man gets killed we should shut them all down for a day
and the next time the mine explodes we shouldn't load no coal
till the whole damn country's darker than the blackest Kentucky hole.

--Pete Zaharoff

Introduction: A Song of Appalachia

Zaharoff emerged from the coal towns and coal culture of the southwestern Pennsylvania fields and wrote "No Pretty Song" in 1977 as anthem of solidarity with his coal miner brothers in eastern Kentucky in the wake of the Scotia Mine Disaster, at Ovenfork in Letcher County, Kentucky in 1976 where 26 miners were killed in the 3nd worst coal mine explosion since 1970 in the Appalachian fields (USMRA). West Virginia, also, has not escaped from mining disasters in its history, as the Massey mine explosion killing 29 in 2010 proved. In fact, the Monongah Explosion in West Virginia in 1907 proved to be the worst mining disaster *ever* in the coal industry with over 350 miners killed (Ibid). And again in 1968, Consol's #9 mine in Farmington, West Virginia, claimed 78 lives in a mine explosion (Ibid). In addition, Hazel Dickens wrote "Mannington Mine Disaster" (referring to Farmington) in 1971 and sang

> "Now don't you believe them, my boy, that story's a lie,
> remember the disaster at the Mannington mine,
> Where seventy-eight miners where buried alive....."
> (Carawan, 1975)

Hence, "No pretty song" sings not just to the Scotia Disaster, or the "Mannington" song to some isolated incident, but the songs of Appalachia offer a glimpse at one of the more dismal aspects of *the culture of coal* among the miners throughout the northern and central Appalachian fields of Pennsylvania, West Virginia, Kentucky, Tennessee, and Virginia. From political dependency with Judges in the pockets of coal companies, to mine disasters and a lack of legal rights in light of those mine explosions and disasters, to the historical poverty-like conditions in shanty type coal towns, to instant and intrusive media attention on conditions in Appalachia, and finally to the shared sense of "powerlessness" that John Gaventa (1982) so eloquently spoke about in the mining culture of Appalachia in his award wining book, *Power and Powerlessness,* there has been a long history of human exploitation in the Appalachian Mines, regardless of subregion. Also characterizing the culture of Appalachian coal is an equally longstanding history of *boom/bust* in the mines followed by a withdrawal of capital from the region, particularly in the Blacklick region of Pennsylvania where a number of ghost towns have been created.

In addition to Zaharoff's *No Pretty Song,* there is also a song by John Prine (1971) called "Paradise," that speaks to the condition of the withdrawal of capital and subsequent making of a ghost town from coal town origins. In it he sings, "O daddy won't you take me back to Muhlenburg County, down by the Green River where Paradise lay? Well I'm sorry my son but you're too late in asking, Mr. Peabody's Coal Train has hauled it away." Peabody Coal does not operate in the Blacklick Fields, or points south in central Appalachia, nor has all the coal been hauled away, but the message of the song deals with the deeper more fundamental notion of once thriving coal towns now barren and ghostlike due to either resource depletion and/or other factors like wide boom/bust swings leading to the subsequent withdrawal of capital. Guy and Candie Carawan's *Voices from the Mountains,* first published in 1975, is filled with the song of Appalachia and more particularly, the culture of coal, including songs of the Appalachian mountains, the environmental tragedy of strip mining, out migration, coal miner solidarity and struggle, grass roots community efforts, black lung, and as well, the mining disasters and explosions.

A crucial yet implicit question emerging over the course of the next five chapters of *Regionalism and Globalization* is whether the central Appalachian coal fields specifically, and Appalachian coal fields more generally, will meet the same fate of the some of the ghost towns of the Blacklick Valley in western Pennsylvania?

The history of central and northern Appalachian coal has been a history of boom/bust. From 1990 to 2000 McDowell County, West Virginia, lost 22.4% of its population, while in neighboring Kentucky, Harlan County lost nearly 10%. In Northern Appalachia, the coal mines of the Blacklick Valley in Cambria County, Western Pennsylvania no longer operate at 100% capacity. From the late 1960s and on into the New Millennium, the region's coal production has shriveled to next to nothing. Some towns folded -- as did the coal and railroad interests -- and moved on to greener pastures, while other towns adapted to the absence of coal as the major employer in the Blacklick Valley.

In this opening chapter, the focus primarily will be on the Blacklick Valley in western Pennsylvania, northern Appalachia, but we will reference heavily, especially in the census data summaries, conditions not only in Blacklick, but Appalachian Metropolitan Statistical areas as well as the socioeconomically depressed central Appalachian coal fields, and finally comparisons will be drawn between the Blacklick fields and Pennsylvania and the wider U.S. Society as a whole.

The Culture of Coal: The Blacklick Coal Fields

The Blacklick coalfield is one of 9 major coalfields in the Western Pennsylvania Appalachian region. The largest by far is the Klondike field in Greene County producing close to 40 MST of coal per year. Blacklick in Cambria County, at this time, produces no coal. The Blacklick coalfield is located near the border of Indiana and Cambria counties in western PA. The field stretches beyond Cambria County into Indiana County, producing about 3 MST of coal in 2003, but the central focus of this report deals with Blacklick in Cambria County.

If we examine the Blacklick fields in Cambria, we find three major townships in Cambria County: Blacklick, Jackson, and Cambria Township. To the north of Johnstown and on the Cambria/Indiana border is Vintondale, while Nanty Glo is several miles east on the border of Blacklick and Jackson Township, and Ebensburg a few miles further east in the middle of Cambria Township, and also to the north of Johnstown. (Cambria County Pennsylvania Township Maps, Map: http://www.rootsweb.com/~pacambri/cambrimp/)

Examine Map 1.1 of the Blacklick Coal field. (Blacklick Field: Map at http://www.coalcampusa.com/westpa/blacklick/blacklick.htm) Note Ebensburg, the county seat of Cambria County, and the surrounding satellite towns of Nanty Glo, Colver, Revloc, and Twin Rocks. Some of these, and other towns such as Bracken and Wehrum, were built as company towns, while others, like Nanty Glo obtained a degree of independence early on and survived after the fall of the coal industry in the Blacklick fields. In addition, some mining towns like Wehrum and Bracken, once thriving single company coal towns, today are in fact Ghost Towns.

MAP 1.1

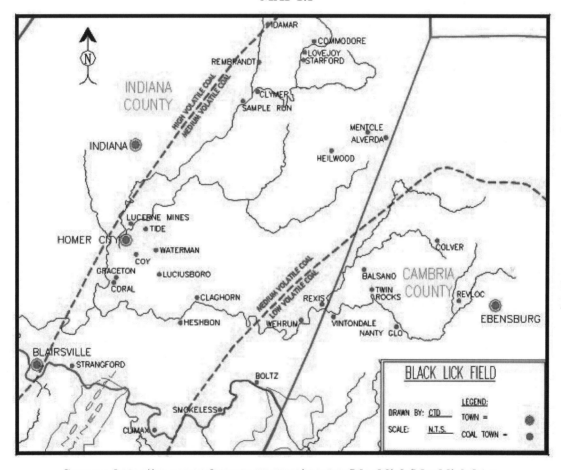

Source: http://www.coalcampusa.com/westpa/blacklick/blacklick.htm

The Early History of the Blacklick Fields

In the "Nanty Glo History Timeline" we find the early emergence of the coal town, Nanty Glo, which translated means "valley of coal." (<u>Life in the Valley: Streams of Coal,</u> p 9). Actually, before Nanty Glo was given that name it was a lumber camp called Glendale, and consisted of only a handful of houses. In 1896 the first mine opened, but it would not be until 1918 that Nanty Glo would be officially "incorporated" as a borough. Between 1896 and 1918 the area would witness the following developments. (**Nanty Glo History Timeline**, Timeline at ttp://www.nantyglo.com/frm8.htm)

*1896 First Mine opens in Glendale/Nanty Glo
*1899 Pennsylvania RR arrives near Glendale/Nanty Glo
*1900 Lincoln Mine opens
*1907 Emma Coal Company opens
*1915 Heisley Mine opens

During this period Nanty Glo witnessed a sustained growth in coal mining and population. As a major coal town with several coal companies and several major mines operating under various ownerships, we find Nanty Glo and its "coal patch" satellites flourishing:

> In 1900, the community had a population of 300. By 1920 the community had four major coalmines and the population had grown to 5,598, with residents from 15 states and 23 foreign countries. The population of Nanty Glo reached it's peak in 1940 at 6,217…..The end of World War II brought more closings with Springfield No. 1 in 1948 and Webster in 1949. (Life in the Valley: Streams of Coal, p. 9).

"Coal Patch" towns of 1000 or more residents thrived around Nanty Glo, but unlike the larger coal town, most of these were single company towns where one company owned all mines, stores, and housing. In this setting we find the mine operators control was absolute and mirrors company town and housing patterns found in satellite coal patches throughout the northern and central Appalachian coalfields.

What greatly fueled these developments and the subsequent rise of a number of other coal towns in the Blacklick Valley was the transfer of ownership of the Blacklick and Yellow Creek (B&YC) Railroad to investors Coleman and Weaver in 1911, which in turn renamed it the Cambria and Indiana Railroad. (C&I) In the years that followed, the C&I expanded, sporting several branches throughout the region. From "A Short History of the Cambria and Indiana Railroad" note the expansion of the Blacklick fields. (see source: Delano's Domain)

> "Construction began at both ends of the project in February, 1911. On April 20, 1911, the name of the Blacklick and Yellow Creek Railroad was officially changed to the Cambria and Indiana Railroad. In October 1911, the first shipment of coal over the C&I left Colver…….Not all of the coal originating on the C&I was to come from Coleman and Weaver mines - by 1919, 23 mines of various ownership were located along the C&I with others still to come." (Ibid at http://www.trainweb.org/cambriaindiana/history.htm)

A look at 1911 and the 1920s also reveals the substantial expansion of the C&I railroad throughout the Blacklick Valley

> "The C&I's first listing in **Poor's Manual**, a railroad directory, was in 1911. The line's length was 18.8 miles, from Rexis to Manver. At that time, the C&I owned four locomotives, three passenger cars, and 612 freight cars. It connected with the PRR at Rexis and the New York Central at Manver. Main offices were in Philadelphia. The 1923 volume of **Moody's Railroad Investments** shows that the railroad expanded to Colver, Nanty Glo and Revloc, all Weaver-Coleman enterprises. Total trackage, including sidings, was 59.15 miles. Rolling stock in the early 1920's included nine locomotives, three passenger cars, 2,497 freight cars and two work cars." (Ibid at http://www.trainweb.org/cambriaindiana/b&yc.htm)

Although a promising beginning in the Blacklick fields with the expansion of the C&I and opening of several coal towns, the coal boom days are now long gone. At one time, though, "during the 1930's and 1940's the C&I had the largest inventory of rolling stock in the western hemisphere" and "The C&I would become known in some circles for a time as the richest railroad in the country, generating the most revenue per mile of track owned." (http://www.trainweb.org/cambriaindiana/history.htm)

Blacklick, within Cambria County, was becoming a strategic coal producer in the western Pennsylvania Coal Fields: "…from 1910 through 1929, Cambria county miners produced over sixteen million tons of coal each year. As many as 50 new company towns or company built residential areas emerged during this period." (Life in the Valley: Streams of Coal, p. 31).

Blacklick Valley: Boom to Bust

In Blacklick in the early 1960s there "were only four mines left on the line." In "A Short History of the Cambria and Indiana Railroad" we find that "in the late 70s to mid 80s the mines at Colver, Nanty Glo, Stiles all ceased operation." (http://www.trainweb.org/cambriaindiana/history.htm). In Nanty Glo in the 1980s, Bethlehem Steel organized its subsidiary operations with "BethEnergy No. 31." (Life in the Valley: Streams of Coal, p. 31) and "when that mine closed in the mid-1980s, the era of coal mining as a way of life in the Blacklick Valley, came to a close." (Ibid).

In Colver we find that the "mine was closed in 1978," and by 1990 the rail stopped operations from Colver. In addition, the C&I Rail System would formally fold in 1994." (see source: **Colver Homepage**). What remains of the once thriving company coal town?

> "In 2001, the population is just over 1000 made up of approximately 430 families. The town (Colver) is essentially a retirement community and bedroom community for nearby industry." (Ibid at http://home.earthlink.net/~hilltj/index.html)

While Colver is one example, we find that other towns like Nanty Glo have hung on throughout the boom/bust phases so characteristic of the coal industry. The occupational structure of the town changed with the withdrawal of coal capital, leaving fewer jobs in the Managerial/Professional and Construction/Extraction sectors as well as work directly in "support" to the once thriving Nanty Glo mines. Nanty Glo and other towns in the Blacklick field that have refused to fold, represent a triumph over the death of community due to reasons that range from natural disasters to "Acts of God" to company shut downs. People hang on what is dear to them and adapt when the "winds of change shift." Something has endured to create a sense of place so characteristic of the Appalachian Culture. The "sense of homeplace" matters and finds ways to continue.

An important question before continuing is what has become of the Blacklick coalfields? Most of the mines, along with the railroad, are gone. Coal is no longer the saving grace of the region. Why? There are several factors. First, if you refer back to the Blacklick Coal Field map, you will note that much if not all of Cambria County Blacklick Coal is low volatile coal compared to higher grades to the west. This is not the only factor for why coal did not become king, and with the opening of the central Appalachian fields, high volatile coal seized the moment, so to speak.

Secondly, came the mechanization of mining from the late 40s through the 60s, unemploying not only the Blacklick fields, but fields across the Appalachians. In some cases towns went under and did not recover. From the 60s onward, we find strip mining growing in the Central Appalachian fields. By 1970 over 90% of the coal was mechanically loaded, with 30% being extracted by continuous mine technology. In the 70s about 30 % of the coal was strip-mined giving southern WV and eastern KY the competitive edge. (Matvey, J, 1987 *Central Appalachia: Distortions in Development*). All of these and other factors contributed to a decline in employment rates, particularly in the low volatile Blacklick fields.

There are a number of other factors at work, but we will conclude here by including the growth of Johnstown into a Metropolitan Statistical Area, which drew on the satellite towns and economies for labor. The Johnstown MSA encompasses the whole of Cambria County and portions of other counties such as Somerset. Coal production exists in the Cambria MSA but it is not central to Johnstown's economy.

Blacklick and The Ghost Trail

MAP 1.2

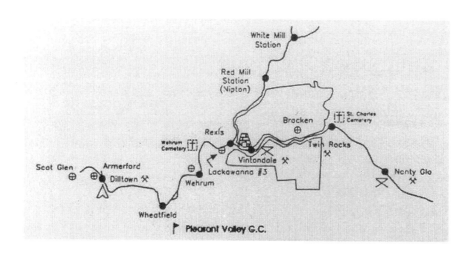

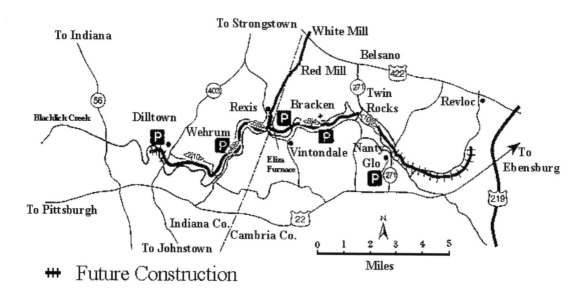

ⴕⴕⴕ Future Construction

Sources: http://cpcug.org/user/warholic/trailmap.html and
http://cpcug.org/user/warholic/morsels/trail.gif

A year before its demise in 1994, C&I donated "four miles of the former Blacklick and Yellowcreek Railroad known as the Rexis Branch." (**Ghost Town Trail** at http://cpcug.org/user/warholic/trail. html). This railway would become part of what is now referred to as the Ghost Town Trail, in tracks emerging at Dilltown in Indiana County and traveling east 3 miles to Wehrum, and then 3 more miles to Vintondale in Cambria County and finally 6 further miles east to Nanty Glo. Overall Nanty Glo was 12 miles east of Dilltown. This particular rail line has become a tourist attraction known as the Ghost Town Trail. In Map 1.2 note the entire line east to west, and moving due north from Rexis to White Mill Station. Several of the towns such as Wehrum and Bracken are now Ghost Towns. Also, after the closing of the mines, and closure of the C&I RR in 1994, several towns have continued to lose population and become the so called "retirement communities." (Colver Homepage at http://home.earthlink.net/~hilltj/index.html). Towns once thriving and producing thousands of tons of coal from the earth are now shut down. The towns and counties in other parts of Appalachia know the boom/bust character of coal all too well, yet we can all learn something from those towns which died out at the roots and from which no economic life would sprout again. Ultimately, while we find a message of hope from towns such as Nanty Glo that continue to adapt and change over the years without the mines, we should take heed and caution at the towns that are no longer with us. The Ghost Town Trail might be seen as a ritual or meditative act in that as we hike and bike we contemplate the limitations of capital and industry.

The Culture of Coal: Study Populations

We now turn attention to four central study populations utilized in this chapter to compare and contrast socioeconomic status. United States 2000 Census data from the U.S. as a whole is the first population, an Appalachian METRO sector as the second, a major COAL COUNTY zone the third (counties producing greater than 10 MST annually), and finally the BLACKLICK Coal Fields in Cambria County, where many of the mines have long since shut down.

The Table 1.5 Data Sheet encompasses the four study populations along with a comparison table for all 4 zones. In the following sections the four-prong study populations will be examined in three crucial areas: 1) education levels including high school and college attainment rates for the population over the age of 25; 2) median household and family incomes; and 3) poverty rates for individuals and female-headed households.

TABLE 1.1 DATA SHEET
CENSUS 2000 PROFILES
STUDY POPULATIONS

	US	PA	AVE
POP 2000	281,421,906.00	12,281,054.00	
HS Grad or Higher	80.40%	81.90%	81.15%
College Grad or Higher	24.40%	22.40%	23.40%
Median HsHd Income	$41,944.00	$40,106.00	$41,025.00
Median Fmly Income	$50,046.00	$49,184.00	$49,615.00
Per Capita Income	$21,587.00	$20,880.00	$21,233.50
Median Income, Men	$37,057.00	$37,051.00	$37,054.00
Med Income, Women	$27,194.00	$26,687.00	$26,940.50
Poverty FHSHD	26.50%	24.90%	25.70%
Poverty Individual	12.40%	11.00%	11.70%

TABLE 1.2 DATA SHEET
METRO APPALACHIA

	Ashland Huntington, WV/KY	Charleston WV MSA	Cincinatti, KY Portion	PGH MSA	Johnstown MSA	Lexington MSA	AVE
POP 2000	315,538.00	251,662.00	370,715.00	2,358,695.00	232,621.00	479,198.00	668,071.50
HS Grad or Higher	75.60%	80.80%	81.00%	85.00%	79.20%	82.10%	80.62%
College Grad or Higher	14.40%	20.40%	20.70%	23.80%	12.70%	28.70%	20.12%
Median HsHd Income	$29,415.00	$35,418.00	$44,848.00	$37,467.00	$30,442.00	$39,357.00	$36,157.83
Median Fmly Income	$36,619.00	$43,991.00	$53,192.00	$47,546.00	$37,413.00	$49,876.00	$44,772.83
Per Capita Income	$16,357.00	$20,378.00	$21,420.00	$20,935.00	$16,755.00	$21,237.00	$19,513.67
Median Income, Men	$32,017.00	$35,565.00	$38,195.00	$37,470.00	$29,033.00	$35,526.00	$34,634.33
Med Income, Women	$21,592.00	$24,051.00	$26,870.00	$26,121.00	$20,904.00	$25,963.00	$24,250.17
Poverty FHSHD	35.70%	27.30%	24.20%	25.00%	29.00%	27.30%	28.08%
Poverty Individual	18.30%	13.30%	8.60%	10.80%	12.20%	12.60%	12.63%
Coal >10mst		16,613					

TABLE 1.3 DATA SHEET
MAJOR COAL COUNTIES

	Mingo County, WV	Boone WV	Logan County, WV	Harlan County, KY	Pike County, KY	Greene County, PA	AVE
POP 2000	28,253.00	25,535.00	37,710.00	33,202.00	68,736.00	40,672.00	39,018.00
HS Grad or Higher	59.60%	64.00%	63.10%	58.70%	61.80%	75.70%	63.82%
College Grad or Higher	7.30%	7.20%	8.80%	8.90%	9.90%	12.20%	9.05%
Median HsHd Income	$21,347.00	$25,669.00	$24,603.00	$18,665.00	$23,930.00	$30,352.00	24,094.33
Median Fmly Income	$26,581.00	$31,999.00	$29,072.00	$23,538.00	$29,302.00	$37,435.00	29,654.50
Per Capita Income	$12,445.00	$14,453.00	$14,102.00	$11,585.00	$14,005.00	$14,959.00	13,591.50
Median Income, Men	$31,660.00	$34,931.00	$31,515.00	$29,148.00	$32,332.00	$32,189.00	31,962.50
Med Income, Women	$18,038.00	$19,607.00	$20,212.00	$19,288.00	$19,229.00	$21,332.00	19,617.67
Poverty FHSHD	46.30%	35.40%	41.80%	50.30%	45.50%	41.70%	43.50%
Poverty Individual	29.70%	22.00%	24.10%	32.50%	23.40%	15.90%	24.60%
Coal (ThShTons)	13,976	30,308	10,537	10,548	27,547	38,303	21,869.83

TABLE 1.4 DATA SHEET
THE BLACKLICK COAL FIELD

	Vintondale	NantyGlo	Blacklick Colver Twp	Jackson Twp	Ebensburg	Cambria, Twp	Total POP & AVE
POP 2000	528.00	3,054.00	1,035.00	2,200.00	4,925.00	3,091.00	6,323.00	21,156.00
HS Grad or Higher	67.80%	75.10%	69.70%	72.60%	82.00%	87.80%	70.60%	75.09%
College Grad or Higher	4.10%	8.70%	4.80%	12.60%	8.50%	26.40%	12.00%	11.01%
Median HsHd Income	$22,386.00	$25,500.00	$23,388.00	$31,504.00	$34,747.00	$32,628.00	$32,955.00	$29,015.43
Median Fmly Income	$34,688.00	$37,727.00	$28,421.00	$34,777.00	$40,400.00	$45,128.00	$41,031.00	$37,453.14
Per Capita Income	$11,689.00	$14,184.00	$12,219.00	$14,244.00	$15,790.00	$19,634.00	$16,868.00	$14,946.86
Median Income, Men	$25,000.00	$30,192.00	$30,114.00	$27,885.00	$31,706.00	$32,226.00	$28,778.00	$29,414.43
Med Income, Women	$11,908.00	$20,302.00	$16,944.00	$21,250.00	$22,660.00	$24,464.00	$22,772.00	$20,042.86
Poverty FHSHD	19.20%	35.00%	23.30%	29.40%	17.80%	21.30%	26.30%	24.61%
Poverty Individual	8.60%	13.80%	17.10%	9.80%	6.20%	8.40%	10.50%	10.63%

TABLE 1.5 DATA SHEET
STUDY POPULATION SUMMARIES

	US	AVE POP METRO	Total POP BLACK LICK FIELD	AVE POP MAJOR COAL	CORRELATION		PEARSONS	
POP 2000	281,421,906.00	668,071.50	21,156.00	39,018.00				
HS Grad or Higher	80.40%	80.62%	75.09%	63.82%	High School		High Schol IV	
College Grad or Higher	24.40%	20.12%	11.01%	9.05%	College			College IV
Median HsHd Income	$41,944.00	$36,157.83	$29,015.43	$24,094.33	0.891485389	0.986337336	0.891485389	0.986337336
Median Fmly Income	$50,046.00	$44,772.83	$37,453.14	$29,654.50	0.938217665	0.966947436	0.938217665	0.966947436
Per Capita Income	$21,587.00	$19,513.67	$14,946.86	$13,591.50	0.864813348	0.999200132	0.864813348	0.999200132
Median Income, Men	$37,057.00	$34,634.33	$29,414.43	$31,962.50				
Med Income, Women	$27,194.00	$24,250.17	$20,042.86	$19,617.67	0.788367016	0.993448472	0.788367016	0.993448472
Poverty FHSHD	26.50%	28.08%	24.61%	43.50%	-0.884818982	-0.550141205	-0.884818982	-0.550141205
Poverty Individual	12.40%	12.63%	10.63%	24.60%	-0.891255103	-0.543302264	-0.891255103	-0.543302264
Coal (ThShTons)				21,869.83				

TABLES 1.1--1.5 Data Sheet and Study Populations Summary Sheet: 2000 Census: Demographic Profiles.
http://censtats.census.gov/pub/Profiles.shtml

Population 1: The U.S.

The first tier of our study populations is simply the overall U.S. census statistics from the 2000 Census Demographic Profile Reports. The three other study zones will be compared and measured against these U.S. means. Since the central study of this report is the Blacklick Coal Valley it will be useful to include, alongside the U.S., statistical information from Pennsylvania, utilizing it as a referent point here for the Blacklick Valley.

Population 2: METRO/MSA Appalachia

The second tier of our four study populations will be termed the METRO zone. The Metro zone is comprised of 6 major MSAs, with all but two located inside Appalachia. In northern Appalachia, Pittsburgh and Johnstown, as Appalachian Cities, are included. Moving south we find Charleston and Ashland/Huntington located in WV/KY while the Kentucky portion of the Cincinnati MSA is considered along with the Lexington MSA.

Before proceeding it is important to note the inclusion of non-Appalachian MSAs in the METRO study population. For the most part, both the cities of Cincinnati and Lexington have been target areas for Kentucky Appalachian out-migration during coal bust cycles. Appalachian Kentucky sits on the fringes of these two central MSAs, along with the portion of the Ashland MSA that it is within.

In terms of West Virginia, both MSAs, Huntington and Charleston, are within state boundaries, as is the case for the Pittsburgh and Johnstown MSAs in PA. The METRO population zone employed here should not be taken as a sample of U.S. Metro zones. It is more the population of several Metro core centers within or in close proximity to the Appalachian region.

Metro: Data Analysis

MSAs outside the Appalachian region, such as Cincinnati and Lexington, fared very well in terms of education, income levels, and poverty rates. It is within the Appalachian metro centers that we see a significant drop in income medians in comparison to the U.S. medians. For example, while Lexington enjoyed a median household income rate of $39,397, Johnstown hovered at $30,442. Part of the problem here stems from the fact that Johnstown had the lowest percentage of its population with college-or-higher degrees. We also see the same pattern when comparing Ashland/Huntington to Cincinnati or Lexington.

If we turn to Charleston and Pittsburgh we find higher educational levels in those MSAs in comparison with both Ashland/Huntington and Johnstown. In fact, there is a significant convergence in several of the statistics between Ashland/Huntington and Johnstown.

The variance between some core zones is striking, especially in terms of the median income for households with a range from $29,415 in Ashland/Huntington to $44,848 in the Kentucky/Cincinnati core. Family median income mirrors household income at $36,619 for Ashland/Huntington and $53,192 for Cincinnati.

There is also a great variance in higher education. If we take the percentage of the population over the age of 25 with a college degree or higher, we find Ashland/Huntington at 14.4% while Lexington KY bettered the national rate at over 28%.

Finally in examining poverty levels among the Metro Zones, Cincinnati held the lowest rater at 8.6% compared to Ashland/Huntington at 18.30%.

Overall, while the means for specific Metro Zones do vary, they also give us a look at some of the things we would expect to find in a typical Metro Zone: High Educational rates in most cases, relatively higher income rates, and lower poverty levels.

Population 3: MAJOR COAL ZONE: Counties above 10 MST annually

The third tier of our four-pronged regional study is comprised of the coalfields in KY, PA, and WV — the three leading coal-producing states in the Appalachians. These counties include Mingo, Boone and Logan in southern WV, Harlan and Pike in KY, and Greene in PA. We term this population a Major Coal Producing Zone due to the fact that these individual counties produce greater than 10 MST of coal annually. Greene County PA was Appalachia's leader with over 38 MST yearly, while not far behind were Boone County, WV, and Pike County, KY, at 30 and 27 MST, respectively. On average, the six major coal counties under study produced 21.9 MST a year.

Kanawha, WV, is yet another major coal-producing county, but is placed with the MSA tier due to the fact that the county houses Charleston, which is both an MSA and state capital. All other major coal producing counties in WV are to the south of Charleston and they lack any MSA aside from Charleston. So we consider Charleston/Kanawha as an MSA, but throughout this report we will refer to it as a case example in comparison with other coal counties.

Another point worth mention is the fact that Greene County is not only a major coal producing county with over 38 MST a year, it is also the only county in Pennsylvania producing greater than 10 MST annually.

Major Coal: Data Analysis

Educational levels, in terms of those over the age of 25 with a high school degree or higher, ranged from 59.6% in Mingo and 58.7% in Harlan to 75% in Greene. The percent of the population holding college degrees or higher hovered at 7.20% in Boone to 12.2% in Greene.

There is also divergence within the population of major coal counties in terms of income medians for households ranged from $18,000 in Harlan, KY, and slightly over $30,000 in Greene County, PA. Greene also fared best in almost all categories, while one reason for Harlan's distress is the fact that it's poverty rate was double that of Greene County in PA. Even if we drop the "outlier" Greene from the study population, we still find a variance from $18, 655 in Harlan to $25,669 in Boone.

As was earlier noted, Charleston stands on its own as an interesting case. Located in the County of Kanawha it is both a MSA as well as Major Coal Producing County at over 16 MST annually. If we compare Charleston with the other coal-producing counties we find a sharp contrast in socioeconomic patterns with Charleston standing far above the Major Coal Counties. Let us then compare the outlier Greene County, PA, in the Major Coal zone with the MSA of Charleston. In education attainment at both the high school and college level, Charleston fared better than Greene. In fact, in almost every statistical indicator across the board, Charleston ranked above the outlier Green County, PA.

Charleston can be a beacon of hope in the hills or a lighthouse along the shores, reflecting its light to coal-producing counties across Central and Northern Appalachia in that it is possible to mix coal production with metro manufacturing along with public administration. The problem for many Appalachian coal-producing counties, and the reason why most of these fare so poorly, is that they lack what Charleston has in terms of a multidimensional occupational and industry structure.

Population 4: The Blacklick Fields

We turn now to the Blacklick Coal Valley of Cambria County. The Blacklick fields hold several towns and townships. While Ebensburg is the county seat, we find our study population also containing older coal towns such as Nanty Glo and Vintondale, while Colver and Revloc were completely company-built and -controlled towns. Aside from these, we find several townships such as Blacklick, Jackson and Cambria that have also been included in this study population.

One of the "outliers" in the Blacklick study population is Ebensburg relative to the other towns and townships in the Blacklick fields. First, note the educational level, sitting at a rate higher then the national average for percent of the population with college degrees or higher. This is primarily due to the fact that, as mentioned earlier, Ebensburg is the county seat for Cambria County, and generates employment in public administration at a level far greater than the surrounding coal towns of Revloc or Colver.

Several levels and rates in the Blacklick field are worth noting at this point. The percent of the population with high school degrees or higher ranged from 67.8% in Vintondale to 87% in Ebensburg — again, Ebensburg tops the national average. If we turn to the percent of the population 25 years and older with college degrees or higher, again we find Vintondale at the bottom with 4.1% of the population, while Ebensburg at 26.4% again tops the national rate of 24.4

Household income medians show a wide variance in Blacklick towns and townships ranging from a low of $22,386 in Vintondale to $34,747 in Jackson Township.

If we take the State of Pennsylvania as a referent point for the Blacklick coalfields, we find that across the board it diverges with Pennsylvania at significant levels. Only in the poverty rates do we find convergence between these two groups with poverty levels for female-headed households at 24.9% in Pennsylvania and 24.61% for Blacklick.

Inter-Population Comparisons

In rank ordering the four populations we have studied, we find a significant drop in socioeconomic status from U.S. to METRO to BLACKLICK to MAJOR COAL ZONES. We have, thus far, primarily focused on intra-zone convergences and divergences, along with comparing zone rates to the U.S. means and medians. In doing so, we have only half the story. At this point, we take the means from each population prong and examine the inter-zone convergences and divergences. In the Table 5 on the Data Sheet, population rates are presented for comparison.

First, note first the drop in high school graduate rates along with the percent of the population over 25 with college degrees or higher. The national rate for those over 25 with a high school degree is 80.4%. The Metro zone converges with the national, but we find Blacklick dropping to 75.09% while the Major Coal Zone levels at 63.82%. In viewing the percentage of the population over 25 with a college degree or higher, the U.S. rate is at 24.4%. We notice first, the Metro zone slipping to 20.12%, and Blacklick falling to 11.0% while the Major Coal Zone drops to 9.05%.

In turning to median income levels, we find a similar downward plunge from the U.S. rate through the Metro, Blacklick and Major Coal zones. Median household income ranged from $41,944 in the U.S. to $24,094 in the Major Coal Zone, while median family income varied from the U.S. rate at $50,046 to 29,654 for the Major Coal Zone.

In discussing the poverty rates across zones, we first turn to comparisons of female-headed households. Here we actually find convergence among all but the Major Coal Zones. Blacklick fared best with the lowest percent of female-headed households below poverty, while the rates jumped for the U.S. and Metro zones. Only the Major Coal Zone stood out with 43.5% of the female-headed households below the poverty level.

For the most part, the Major Coal Zone has done poorly on almost any and every statistical indicator studied. It should be noted, however, in terms of the poverty rate, this Major Coal Zone held double the number of individuals below the poverty levels in the other three study populations.

Conceptually Speaking: What about Appalachia?

Is there life after coal? One glaring finding is even **with** Coal life is hard when we examine the Major Coal Counties of central Appalachia. Their socio-economic status falls below the Blacklick Valley—and it **is** the Blacklick coalfield region that is partially comprised of several dozen ghost towns. On the other side of the next chapter we will explore central Appalachia's condition of distress more fully, and map out a model for regional underdevelopment in that sub-region.

What then has enabled the Blacklick Valley to exit beyond the era of coal? Here is the gem of a core/semi-periphery/periphery analysis. The Blacklick fields, along with the eight other major coal fields in southwestern Pennsylvania have benefited historically due to the core producing status of the Pittsburgh region, as well as the development of semi-peripheries such as and most notably the Johnstown MSA (very near the Blacklick fields) Greensburg, Washington, Butler and other city centers For our purposes here, the regional multiplier effect in both the Pittsburgh core and Johnstown semi-periphery drew labor from the Blacklick region within a variety of manufacturing specializations and pursuits. In other words, there was **work outside the mines**—as we will see that this was not the case in central Appalachia.

Thus, various types of employment are created by the spatial expression of capitalism, and Blacklick's proximity to the Pittsburgh Core and Johnstown's semi-peripheral zone rewarded the coalfield with employment opportunities in manufacturing that were generated as the result of a region-wide multiplier effect. In fact, a few chapters ahead we will ask and answer the question of why there was and is **no** region-wide multiplier effect in the central sub-region of Appalachia.

Hence, we are not painting a socioeconomic picture revealing the entire Blacklick region as a set of ghost towns. In fact, most towns still remain in the region and some such as Nanty Glo and Ebensburg along with the various Townships fare rather well as we found in the 2000 Census reports.

Is there any hope for the Major Coal Zone in central Appalachia? Although there is much socio-economic distress in this region, we might do well to return to Kanawha County, West Virginia as one county--on the border of the southern and northern coal zone in West Virginia--where manufacturing, public administration, managerial and professional, and coal production all coexist. Obviously, like Ebensburg is the outlier due to its county seat status, so Charleston in Kanawha County is the State Capitol. Not every county in central Appalachia can make the same claim so we find Charleston unique in drawing a wide range of government and public administrative employment. However, the interesting point for further analysis is the fact that coal employment co-exists with diversified economic development in Kanawha County. This, we will find is not the case among the Major Coal Zone in central Appalachia.

My Father's house

My father's house
I'm searching for
the root to which man is unconsciously bound.
The ongoing history of oneness
like a weathered oak
bearing leaves through many seasons.
But where is my father's house?
Surely not the farm.
That life passed with Studebaker's Golden Hawk
and forgotten Woody Guthrie ballads.

And now root consciousness
of my father's house forms
in endless stories related
in restaurants and real estate offices
in late night bars and on the road.
is this my father's house?

This life moves too fast Joe.
Its foundation is attached to ideas and data
and we are mere particles of light
speeding toward a destination
we forgot.
So with a few hours left before I part
on a Greyhound of contemplation
we talk and drown
time
with alcohol. Freed from it
we can see each other
and cram years lost into a night of conversation.
but there is more to my father's house.

Summers must be set aside for the days
when we can move away from the terminals
of inputs and outputs
and prime rates
to spend time in the mountains
and learn of our history.
Here they call a man by his real name:
Jozef the Czech.
Your name is tied to earth
to your father's house.

There must be a time in every son's life
when he returns to his fathers's house.

CHAPTER TWO

Growing Up North Appalachian: Nora Dilling, Nanty Glo and the Culture of Coal

Introduction

Socioeconomic indicators and census statistics, as utilized in the previous chapter, allow us to draw a schematic or paint a portrait of a given town, region or nation but they also lack a humanitic dimension such as a historical personality of a resident or residents who have lived through each decade. This chapter provides the humanitic dimension by integrating the life and times of Nora Dilling in Nanty Glo from the early coal boom days to the final coal bust era during the 1960s and on. Hence, we affix personality and personal history upon the statistical indicators of the previous chapter. Taken together, we move toward a more holistic understanding of the Culture of Coal in the North Appalachian region of Western Pennsylvania.

Nora Dilling was born in Cambria County, Pennsylvania, in 1920. The family moved to Blairsville, Pennsylvania, when Nora was approximately 3 months of age and moved back to Nanty Glo when Nora was 1-1/2. The family settled in the flourishing coal town of Nanty Glo, situated in the Blacklick coalfields of Western Pennsylvania. Nora's family took up residence in one of the company houses in the Springfield section of Nanty Glo. She grew up living in company housing and shopping at company stores since her father worked for one of the mining companies in operation in Nanty Glo.

Nora and her family were members of the Church of the Brethren, a Protestant religious order that practices the washing of the feet and restricts its membership from serving in combat roles in the military service or during war time. This absolute respect for the dignity of human life is a benchmark of the Church of the Brethren.

As Nora grew, church became the focal point of her life — not only in terms of worship but social life as well. She played piano at a very early age and also became part of the choir at her church.

During the first twenty years of her life, Nanty Glo grew as a key coal town in Cambria County and the Blacklick Valley. It was not a "coal patch" or single company town. Several different mining companies set up shop in and near the Nanty Glo area, and there was not one but a variety of mines offering employment. In addition, Nanty Glo not only hosted one, but also several company stores, and several company housing projects across the town's landscape.

Nora married George Dilling in 1938 and began a family. George, interestingly enough, built their house from scratch beginning in 1939 and one year later they moved into the house -- a day before the arrival of their firstborn, Peggy Dilling. George worked for the Post Office as a mail carrier part-time up until WWII and then he moved into a full time position. When drafted, George served in the Army as a conscientious objector in a medic role (due to religious constraints on combat roles he was stationed at a hospital in Missouri taking care of soldiers). It was during this time that he felt the call to begin preaching and after the war he preached at churches in the Western Pennsylvania and Northern Maryland area. By 1950, while he continued to work full time for the post office, he now took on complete preaching duties.

The Lord blessed the Dillings with 7 children, born throughout the 1940s and 1950s. All became active in the Church of the Brethren and several went on to Church of the Brethren affiliated colleges.

When the mines began their final "bust" phase from the end of WWII through the 1960s, somehow the town of Nanty Glo survived. Perhaps because Nanty Glo was not a coal patch owned by a single company, but a full blown coal town with independent stores competing with company stores, independent housing competing with company housing, with the growth of the downtown sector after WWII, and also due to the fact that the Johnstown MSA (metropolitan statistical area), drew from a regional labor force — where many from Nanty Glo found work. Other coal patches and single company towns withered and became ghost towns.

Nora and George moved from Nanty Glo in 1990 to Plum Boro, Pennsylvania, closer in locale to several of their children. They were blessed with 12 grandchildren and 9 great grandchildren. Sadly, George, in his mid-80s passed away in June of 2004. In his retirement, he was proficient with the computer and became very active with the Nanty Glo homepage, email list and bulletin board.

Nora continues to create value in her life. She is active in charity work for a teen pregnancy center in Monroeville, Pennsylvania, making baby afghans and baby clothes, and also making inspirational booklets for nursing homes for the aged. She is also very active in the local Methodist Church's prayer circle.

These days she enjoys visits from her primary and extended family during the summer months and over the holidays. This, then, is the story of Nora Dilling, from the 1920s and 30s in her school days to 1940s and 1950s in her family building years, and continuing on until her present years in the new millennium.

Nora Dilling: Childhood Memories

The Trouble with Brothers!

I remember going over to my neighbor's house…Mrs. Smith's. She was Hungarian and oh could she tell the stories. Ghost Stories, and stories about people. She was just filled with stories. The neighborhood children would be sitting around on her swing and porch listening, enthralled. I remember we were at her house and she said, "It's time to go home," because my mother had called us and said it was time to come home. I think it was 8 o'clock. So the boys ran on ahead of me -- my two brothers, Carl and Ralph, and there was a path there between our houses, and so on this path they were hiding and I didn't know. And as I came up the path they jumped out and said, "BOO." Well, I just collapsed. They ran in the house laughing and when I didn't come right away then Carl came to find me. I said, "You know what…I could have had a heart attack and died." "Yeah," he said, "we won't do that again."

Wintertime

I remember going to a neighbor's and whenever I was coming back it had rained on top of ice and snow and the road was icy and, oh, glittery ice and this rain was an inch or two on top of the road and I can remember skating. Going a little bit and then I'd walk and then I'd skate a little more… and, Oh! I thought that was great fun! Sled riding on the hill above our house was fun. But Ralph and I got cold so quickly, then we would go home.

Nanty Glo

I've always lived in Nanty Glo.... the section we lived in was called Springfield named after the Springfield Mines. Now, when we signed our mail it was always Nanty Glo because we got our mail at the post office.... a box number and our box number was 14. We had to go to the post office to pick our mail up and it was at least a mile away. I would stop after school to pick up the mail.

Resourcefulness

I remember they had a slag hill and when a coal car would break down they usually disposed of the car on top of the slag. My Dad got the bright idea to send my brothers up to the hill and retrieve the wood and iron from the dilapidated coal car. We burned the wood in our stove and the iron was sold for extra money.

Coffee Soup

Coffee soup was a slice of bread in a bowl and you pour hot coffee with milk and sugar and that was our breakfast lots of times. Well, we as kids thought that was delicious. I also remember the summer heat and if we were having a meal we still had to fire up the cook stove, so a lot of times we had coffee soup for breakfast and also for lunch so we didn't have to fire up that cook stove.

School

The first two grades were one room schoolhouse, and then after that I went downtown about a mile to go to third and fourth grade. And then I had to go across town about a mile and a half to go to fifth and sixth grade.... and then back to downtown for the upper grades and high school. No buses ran in those days...had to walk everywhere. And I had to go home for lunch. We had an hour for lunch, and then I'd have to be back.

1) The Primacy of Faith

What was the happiest memory of your Church during your school days?
I played piano for Sunday school and Church at age 13.
What was your Church like? How many services on any given week?
About how many people would attend a Sunday Service?
Our Church was an "alive" church: enthusiasm and love for God and Country. We had Sunday School at 9:30, a Worship Service at 10:45, and Evening Worship at 7:30 p.m., and then Prayer Meeting Wednesday at 7:30 p.m. About 150 to 175 would attend Morning Worship.
Would you say people were religious in Nanty Glo?
I wouldn't say "religious" but rather, they liked to get together for worship.
How many churches would you say there were back in your school days?
7 Protestant and 3 Catholic -- 1 Greek and 1 Ukrainian and 1 Roman.
Tell me more about your Church...was the congregation mostly mining families? What kind of people made up the congregation?
Our folks were sprinkled with mining families, but also business people, store owners — we knew we all were sinners saved by the love and grace of God through the shed blood of Jesus on the Cross. This was strongly preached most every Sunday.
At what age did you get involved with the Church?
Mother took me at age 2. I remember when I was about 19-20; an artist came and painted on the arch in the front, a picture of the Transfiguration. In the Baptistery he painted the Baptism of Jesus by John. These paintings had a big impact upon me — He, Jesus, did it all for me.
Would you say your parents/family was religious? Tell me about your family and Church?
No, but Mother taught us Bible verses and to ask a blessing at our meals and at bedtime. Dad always said, "Listen to your mother." He didn't attend services because of a bad experience as a new

Christian and said, "If that's being a Christian, I don't want to be one." Although I should mention he drove us to Church and waited till services were over to take us home, and in the late 60s and 70s, he would play the violin at special services like Christmas and Easter.

Would you say your parents were instrumental in involving you at Church?

Yes, very much so. If I hadn't gone when little would I have enjoyed the services and my participation in them when I was growing up… I wonder.

Would you say you were more or less religious than other teens around your age? More involved in church activates than other kids or about the same?

I would say I was much more involved. From Christmas and Easter, Children's Day, Mother's and Father's Day, Thanksgiving and in later years community worship with most of the other protestant churches.

How often did you get or were you at Church on any given week?

Three times at least for services and then there was choir practice on Thursday evening at 7:30 p.m., unless another Church event was taking place on practice night. Oh yes, Revival for every night for two weeks of the year.

How old were you when you began to play piano for the church choir?

I was 13 in April and started about that time in 1933. Choir came later.

When were you saved? What did that mean to you at that time?

I accepted Jesus at age 9 at a revival service. I remember getting out of my seat and walking down to the front of the Church and the pastor, Rev. Homer Hess, asking if I wanted to accept Jesus as my Savior and I said "YES."

I don't remember much about the baptism except being embarrassed to take off my wet clothes and putting on dry ones. Mother shielded me as best she could from the 3 or 4 women in the same room who were or should have been watching the others being baptized.

It meant total commitment to Jesus and winning others to him by the way I would/did live, my conversation, etc.

What other activities, besides playing piano, were you involved in at Church? You also mentioned the "Bible Study"…. tell me a little more about that?

My mother in the 1930s would lead a group of up to 25-30 youngsters to a field below our house. She taught us the 23rd Psalm, the Beatitudes, the Lord's Prayer, and so forth, as well as several songs such as "Jesus Loves Me." She also taught the group the song "Jesus Wants Me for a Sunbeam" – that song was actually my first solo at age 3 at the church where my grandparents attended in Lovely, Pennsylvania.

I taught Sunday School class for years as well as Bible School for 2 weeks in the summer. This is how the day would go, especially Bible School — be at the piano at 8:55 prepared to play the march "Onward Christian Soldiers" as the children and teachers marched into the sanctuary. Then, scripture and prayer by the one in charge; for many years the one in charge was one of my good friends, Mae Swartz and Isabelle Hakenan.

Did the Church ever have potluck suppers or dinners? Tell me about this?

No, our church never believed in having "suppers." The feeling was that money should come from each member as God had profited them and give 1 /10th of it – our Tithe. When I was about 12-15, they did have a project. The women would go to a member's house and make soup that they sold for 25 to 35 cents a quart. This was to help pay for remodeling, etc. I do remember that George [Nora's future husband] was the best seller and delivered most of that soup.

For a year or two the finances had hit an all-time low, so they decided to have chicken suppers in the church basement. It was an all-day job and my dad soon put a stop to it because my mother had a very bad heart and it was too much for her. She would be exhausted for several days after. Preparing, cooking, serving and clean up as usual were done by only a few.

We did have a small lunch at class meetings once a month, prepared by the host home.

Your Church has a tradition of the "washing of the feet"…was that just Church of the Brethren? Tell me about the practice? Did it humble people who participated?

Our communion was unique. We tried to keep to the pattern set by Jesus. We first had a meal of sop – bread or crackers in beef broth (lamb – mutton too expensive and very hard to get). We ate together, two persons to a bowl, each having their own spoon, glass of water, and one slice of bread cut in half and a slice of beef to be made into a sandwich. No butter, catsup or mustard – DRY! Good however. The sop was too soppy for me, but tasty. The sop was cooked on Saturday and hoped it wouldn't spoil until Sunday evening at 7 p.m. In the fall it was always cold and in such a big pot it couldn't be put into the fridge, which most folks didn't have anyway.

After the "supper being ended, Jesus took a towel and girded himself, and began to wash the disciples' feet." The deacons for the men and their wives, the deaconesses, for the women would have about 5-6 persons go to a back room, remove their shoes and stockings, and then sit down while a deacon (for the men)/deaconess (for the women) would wash one person's feet [the "washing" was scooping water from the bucket over the sitting person's feet while holding each foot one at a time; the apron was very long and this was then used to dry the feet of the person you just washed]. For the women there were usually 3 buckets/tubs so it would move faster. The person sitting would then wash the feet of the next person, and so on until the last three to have their feet washed were the ones who washed someone else at the very beginning. As each person was done, they exchanged a kiss of friendship, a handshake, and then the one who had finished washing the feet untied the apron from their own waist and tied it on the one whose feet they had just washed. Sometimes someone older would be unable to kneel [at the bucket to wash the sitting person's feet] – then the younger one getting their feet washed would hold their feet up high for the one washing to be able to do it more easily… [When a person had had their feet washed and washed the feet of another] then wash and dry hands, put shoes and stockings back on, and return to the sanctuary for the bread and "wine" (grape juice) [note – this was all done in silence with no music and no talking other than for instruction and the pastor guiding the communion with Bible reading, etc].

The deaconesses on the Saturday one day prior to the communion feast, would meet at one home to make the communion bread, with the exception of the deaconess cooking the meat. The communion bread was made of flour, butter and milk. You mixed and kneaded that dough until it "cracked." It was then placed on a cookie sheet and marked with "perforations" to a size of 1 to 1-1/2 inches long by about 1/2 inch wide, and then baked – but not browned.

At the communion feast, after the meal and the foot washing, the communion bread was presented on a meat platter with a special cloth. This platter would be held out to the person at the end of a sanctuary row and a long strip would be taken, each person broke off a piece for the one sitting next to them and passed the strip along the row until the last person came around to the first person to complete the circle. The pastor prayed and gave thanks for this broken body/bread and prayed and then we ate the communion bread. Then the grape juice - "wine" – we did not believe in strong drink – that was on the table in two place settings, each took one and held it until a prayer of thanksgiving for His shed blood for us, and then we drank. Then we were led in prayer for another opportunity to meet together to partake of the communion once again. We sang a hymn and went home, coming back the next day to clean up. [note – there were boards about 8 or 10 inches wide which could be attached to the back of a pew that were used for communion. These served as the table for the feast as well as had the cut out for the wine cups so that two holes for the tiny wine cups were between to spots for sitting, thus allowing two people sitting side by side to "share" the cup].

Oh yes – and for every service the women who were members [had been baptized] wore a white cap called a "prayer covering" for each service. During communion what a beautiful sight! At our baptism, each female was given one that we kept for life. In the late 1960s, more and more women refused to wear the prayer covering so that until I left [Nanty Glo] in 1990 there were only three of us. Now [2004] there is only one – Sylvia [Mountain]; Alice [Caldwell] died at 80.

Communion and feet washing was a beautiful experience. Humbling – yes.

2) Life in a Northern Town: Company Housing

What was it like living in Company Housing during your younger years?

Well the area we lived in was all company houses. 4 rooms…2 rooms upstairs as bedrooms and 2 downstairs, the kitchen and living room. Some had porches and some didn't. My dad put an enclosed porch on the back of our house so Mother put her washer out there and a stove. We used to play school out there and I always wanted to have the fire going when we played school.

The houses were all made the same…. there was no deviation and none of them were painted and it was just plain old wood and they weren't insulated. And the snow would come in on the winter nights because the roof boards had shrunk. When we awoke in the mornings, snow in 1 to 1-1/2 inch wide strips would be across the bed. The siding on the houses had worn apart in the middle letting in the snow. Needless to say, we always had lots of covers on to keep us warm.

Was all housing in Nanty Glo company houses? If not, what percent would you say were company housing?

About three-quarters of the housing was company houses and the other one-quarter was homes of the bosses, some owned by the company. It was similar to the company stores…Heisely Mines had its houses, Webster Mines had its houses and so forth. So, if you lived in a certain section of town they knew exactly who your parents were and where they worked.

There was housing for not only the workers' company houses, but also very nice and well-built housing for the company bosses.

What was the central heating system?

Heating was the kitchen stove and Dad put in a heating stove in the living room. He put a register in the ceiling so it would go upstairs. But it was just in that one area and had to spread through the entire house. We kept the stair door open so it would help with circulation.

Water system?

We didn't have water in the house, or a well, but did have a faucet out doors. And we had to let it run in the winter so it wouldn't freeze.

Mines and Mine Houses.

There were several different mines and mining companies in Nanty Glo. We were with the Springfield Mines but there was also the Webster, Lincoln and Heisley Mines. And outside of town was run by the Cambria and Indiana Railroad so they were called the C&I houses, so if you wanted to go in that direction, you just said the "C&I houses."

The mine bosses didn't live in the company houses…. they had large beautiful houses near downtown Nanty Glo. Beautiful brick buildings. The owners of course were absentee and didn't reside in Nanty Glo at all. Some I guess were from Johnstown or even Pittsburgh.

The standard of living for most of the miners was about the same across all the various companies. They all made about the same amount. They were not unionized when I was in school. They tried to unionize a couple of times, but the companies fought it.

The miners wanted an hourly wage, but before unionization they were paid by the piece. So if you loaded a car of coal you got paid but if you loaded a car of shale you didn't get paid. Unions wanted the miners to be paid for all work associated with the mines. In later years, the union wanted the miners to be paid "portal to portal pay," that is, starting the clock when going into the workplace until coming out at quitting time.

There was no electricity in the mines back then. They had their carbide lamps on their hard hats. In the olden days they had some canaries and they'd take them in to see if there was any methane gas in the mines.

They also used, in the early days, donkeys to pull the cars before the hoist was installed. So they were using the animals down there and the animals went blind because they never came out into the sunlight. They kept them in the mines all the time.

Many of the mines began to shut down in the post war era. The Heisely Mine stayed strong all the way into the 1960s, but the other mines and companies had closed up shop. The quality of coal was not very high. In fact, Springfield Mines, where my dad worked, the government said it was too filled with sulfur that they couldn't use it. This was in the early days of World War II.

Although we didn't, some families took in boarders to make some extra money.

What was the company housing like?

Most housing was like ours. No insulation, no attic, no basement, and just built on the ground. My father dug out a place under our house and built shelving so we had somewhere to put the things that my mother canned – green beans, tomatoes, pickles, etc. Also potatoes in boxes (we bought them by the bushel) and carrots. They kept very well there.

I remember when we lived in Springfield the snow coming in the cracks and onto the beds, because the boards had shrunken over the years. When we moved to Ivory Hill, which was about halfway to town from Springfield, the houses were better made. We did have an attic, a very small attic, and my dad worked with my brothers digging out a basement. Very hard work. There was no outside entrance, so all the dirt and stones had to be carried up steps, through the kitchen to the back part of the lot.

At Ivory Hill, the coal storage area for the heating coal for our furnace was under the front porch and we would have coal delivered. Whenever they delivered the coal they'd shovel it right in there. My father built this also and put a door on it to keep down the dirt and dust.

Now at Springfield, we had a regular bin for them to put the coal…we'd have to carry the coal buckets out and fill them up and bring them back to the house. Dad would do the buckets in the morning, and then Mother would have extra coal brought in when she would do laundry and the boys would get it before they were off to school. Also we'd check the bucket at noon, then after school and then after supper and before we went to bed. It was a task that required our attention several times a day.

3) Company Stores and Scrip

Did the coal companies operate a company store or stores in Nanty Glo?

Yes. Springfield, Heisely, Webster and Lincoln all had their own company stores. Webster closed but all were located in downtown Nanty Glo. Those who were in the Springfield Mines would shop at the Springfield Store, and those at Heisely would shop at Heisely Store, and so forth. My store was Springfield and I never visited any of the other company stores.

Did they pay in scrip or cash? Did the company store give credit?

They paid in money sometimes…. but whenever the mines were on strike there was no cash and you could only go to the company store. But because of the strikes you couldn't even get credit from the company stores. The company placed the amount the miners earned into the company store; therefore it was put on "the book." What was bought was deducted from "the book" reserve available. So unless my parents had saved some cash where they could go to the A&P where the prices were so much cheaper, then we just did without.

My parents were very, very frugal and Mother used to can a lot…lots of vegetables and fruit. Mother would make a lot of vegetable soup so that it stretched. So we had extras to eat beside the meat. There were times though when we couldn't afford the meats from the company stores and so we did without.

Well, I'm not sure about that [scrip or cash]. All I know is my parents saved money so they could buy at the A&P because the prices were too expensive at the company stores. The A&P was not connected with the company stores, and in fact was in competition with the company stores.

In the company store, they put it on the book, and then it was taken out of my dad's pay, so that we had to watch what we bought because you couldn't go over a certain limit. My dad wouldn't let us just buy…he always said we had to keep it at a certain level. He always would tell us to watch because this was the first of the month and "I don't want to go over this limit."

A&P did not give credit, but I have an interesting story. I went there one day and bought whatever Mother wanted and I said you can put it on the book because I thought I was at a company store, and when I got home they discovered it was A&P merchandise and they asked where I got it and I told them, and they asked how did I pay for it and I said I told them to put it on the book like we always do. They left me have the stuff…they didn't question me. …. But Dad said, "Oh No! That's the A&P. You don't get credit there…." and he went downtown right away to pay the bill.

What did Company Stores sell?

Oh they sold everything from soup to nuts practically. They had meat, they had yard goods, they had canned goods…they had very few fresh vegetables or fruits…they didn't have refrigeration in those days, so they had nothing to keep. And the meats they got in from Johnstown by the piece and when they sold that out if you ordered meat, well, you just didn't get any.

The miners could buy some things from the company store like gloves or buckets, but most of their accessories they got at the main mine office. For the most part the miners had to buy their equipment no matter where it came from.

Did the company stores sell clothes?

If they did I'm not aware of it. In those days most folks made their own clothes so most of what stores sold were yard goods rather than ready-made clothes. Those people who lacked the skill to make clothes would buy the yard goods and have others in the neighborhood make them the clothes. Sometimes in payment the women would offer the seamstresses extra yard goods instead of cash. In a way it was a barter system.

My mother was an excellent seamstress, and she made clothes for other families. I remember the minister of the church, when he was young he was crippled with infantile paralysis and his one shoulder was higher than the other, and my mother remade his suit jackets to where the lower one was padded and looked like a regular suit jacket.

4) Other Stores and Shops

Was there a department store in Nanty Glo?

In later years, but not when I was growing up. I also wouldn't call the company stores a department store because they were primarily geared toward food stuffs…. however once I went there and bought 3 skeins of embroidery floss for a nickel, and my dad said don't do that again because that's money we could be using for groceries. So that taught me a lesson.

Were there restaurants in Nanty Glo? Do you recall them? Were they independent or company owned?

When I was growing up and was in the fifth grade there was a lady by the name of Mrs. Hopkins who had a restaurant and I ate there for about week and then Dad decided that it was too expensive and I couldn't go back again, that I'd have to carry my lunch…. and that's how I started going to Mrs. Dilling's house for meals, where I met my future husband! I was so shy at that time, though, that I wouldn't go to the kitchen, but rather just stayed in the dining room to be by myself. I carried my lunch.

What about pharmacy's or doctor's or dentist offices?

Doctors, yes. There was a Dr. McAnulty, and Dr. Ebandjieff came in later. The doctors were associated with the mines. I don't remember when I was young if there was a dentist or pharmacist…. I think by the time I was in 8th grade, or 12 or 13. I remember Mr. Rinehart had a pharmacy at that time.

In terms of other shops besides the music and jewelry shop, we had an A&P and the post office. (They didn't start delivering the mail until right before the war started). There was at least one drugstore in the town. There were also several barbershops.

Was there a Theater?

Yes I remember we had a theater growing up. The "Grand" and the "Star" theatre were in Nanty Glo but I was never in either of them, but later they had the "Capitol." That was a grand one! It had beautiful drapes to cover the screen. That was independently owned and not owned by the companies. Mr. Tom Bello was in charge of the Capitol.

Stores in Nanty Glo, and The Victrola!

The main form of employment was the mines but there were a number of other businesses in Nanty Glo. Most people in Nanty Glo were connected with the mines, though.

There were stores, however. There was a jewelry store and a music store, and I remember going with my parents when they bought the Edison Victrola that used thick wooden records and a diamond needle. One record was "Uncle Josh Buys an Automobile." I also remember sitting in the car and Dad came out and said, "Well we bought it," and my brothers and I didn't know what he was talking about because all we knew was that it was a music store…but we didn't know why he went in there. Well pretty soon we had a Victrola in the house, and, oh, that was really something…. we were the only one in the neighborhood with one of those. We didn't even have a radio in those days. The neighbor kids would sit on the front porch and listen to the records.

What things did people travel to Johnstown for that they couldn't get in Nanty Glo? You mentioned a streetcar to Johnstown—was this heavily used by the people of Nanty Glo?

Johnstown had Glosser's and Penn Traffic department stores. And Bethlehem Steel owned Penn Traffic. Most of the time, though, if someone needed something and it couldn't be found in Nanty Glo, then people just did without. There was a streetcar from Nanty Glo to Johnstown and that is where I went to see the optometrist, but most did without unless it was an emergency.

So downtown Johnstown was where the doctors, restaurants, movie houses and other specialties shops served many outlying communities near Johnstown. Nanty Glo was one of those outlying communities. People didn't do a whole lot of traveling but they did have the streetcar that picked up in Ebensburg and maybe Colver and then Nanty Glo on the way to Johnstown.

What would you say the make up of the town was? English, German, east European, Italian?

The first wave was Welsh…. because Nanty Glo is the Welsh name for "streams of coal!" And the Welsh also settled Ebensburg. And after that came a lot of Eastern European peoples – from Hungary, Czechoslovakia, Ukraine, Latvia, Yugoslavia, Romania – and also other Europeans, from Germany, Italy, Greece, Austria, England, Ireland, and Scotland. I do not remember there being any Spanish, Portuguese, or French.

Did Nanty Glo have a city council? A school board? A police force? Were these company operated or were they handled through independent elections?

If there was a police force I don't' know… there were police that handled the weekend rowdies. When the Springfield Mines went on strike, Corporal Smith was on his horse with his billy club and gun at his waist and he scared most everyone. He was paid by the Springfield Company but I 'm not sure if there were other police that worked under him.

Did Nanty Glo hold anything for women?

Nothing! Just getting married, at age 14 or 15 they got married. They didn't even go to high school. If they were lucky enough they might get hired at the A&P and drugstore. The company stores had their own and didn't hire from Nanty Glo. The only other future for a girl was cleaning someone else's house.

I remember washing clothes and putting them on the line…. if it was winter the clothes would freeze and if you weren't careful in taking out the clothespins the frozen clothes would tear so you had to be careful. Then you'd bring the clothes in and heat them on the stove. They dried quickly once thawed out.

You also had to build the fire up for each meal and other tasks. Also you learned early how to cook, keep house, iron and bake and clean.

Friendship

Mother started a Sunday school. We would walk down past the railroad to an opening we called the Green Field. And some trees had fallen that we used for benches and she would teach us everything from the Beatitudes to the Lord's Prayer and in time we had up to 30 kids from Springfield who would participate. She would not only read scripture but also explain it to us and we learned so much!

I never had a real close friend but I was involved in a lot of group activities from choir to playing piano to attending the Sunday School. But never really had a special or best friend until later in life. Perhaps because I was so far out of town, and other than seeing kids at school, we just lived too far to become close.

I was also very busy when I was young. I started on piano when I was ten with a teacher from Ebensburg who would take the bus down to Nanty Glo and charge a dollar a lesson. So I put in at least an hour every day on my piano. When I got a bit better, my father would accompany me on the violin. After I started playing at church, Dad and I often spent 3 hours playing/practicing. Mozart, Beethoven, Handel, Hadyn, etc., was the program, and also Strauss waltzes.

This was probably another reason I didn't have a close friend… because I was playing the piano all the time in Church and didn't have time to socialize with the other kids.

The Church was the emphasis…. we didn't go out to the movies, dance or play cards and while at church I mostly played piano.

5) The Great Depression in Nanty Glo

What do you remember about the Great Depression?

I remember meals that were very skimpy…dandelion with warm dressing and onions, blackberries, cabbage and potato soup, vegetable soup, potato soup, pickles, chow chow.

Did it hit your family hard?

Because Dad worked at the mines in soft coal, and they were on strike for better pay and working conditions and the company store was to be used for groceries with only 1 dollar a day available while on strike, we couldn't buy much. Fortunately, Mother did a lot of canning — peas, string beans, corn, red beets, pickles, carrots, soup and huckleberries/blackberries and tomatoes. We also ate a lot of lima and soup beans. She and Dad were very frugal so that they were able to buy at the A&P things they wouldn't have purchased at the company store—as it was too expensive there. Being 9-13 I don't remember too much but do recall saying to Mother one day, "I'm so tired of pickles and blackberries" She replied, "I'm sorry, honey, but that's all we have." We also had jelly, but it was mainly for pancakes and most times there was no butter. There was no oleo then; that came during World War II.

What did most people do during the 1930s to survive and get by? (garden, craft, part time work, etc)

Most folks during this time either ate like we did or did without. We didn't do crafts to sell in those days — never thought of it and of course there was no available market nearby. Since all the houses had been built on slag from the mines, gardening was not much of an option. Dad went to the woods about a quarter of a mile away and came back with buckets full of dirt, then we planted a bit of lettuce, onions, some tomato seeds Mother had saved. Oh yes, I remember having rhubarb sauce on bread for a meal. We usually had oatmeal for breakfast. Also there was lots of free help given.

What happened to the families that were unemployed and couldn't get jobs? Did people leave for work in the cities, but keep their home in Nanty Glo?

Most families were like us "scraping the bottom of the barrel" and did without or had husbands leaving home to find work and if found would send money home.

Did the Govt. distribute food and food goods to those who were hit the hardest?

The Government/Uncle Sam did not give free food, welfare, etc., until after the Second World War started in 1941. Then we received ration books with stamps for purchasing meat, poultry, sugar, cheese, gasoline, kerosene, and also eggs making the money go a bit further. This was also when oleo was introduced — looked like lard with a packet of yellow food coloring to be added at home. It couldn't be sold colored! The packet resembled the Mrs. Grass' Noodle Soup mix we have now to be added to the soup.

Also during this time, we had a lot of out of work men — bums they were called — who would ask for something to eat. That's how a lot of them survived and hopping freight cars to find work in other cities and towns. Mother always gave them a sandwich of bread alone, and tomato and onion if she had it, and if not maybe jelly bread. The men were always grateful. George (Nora's husband) and I did the same, often inviting them in to join us for a meal, skimpy though it was, because George was only working part time until 1944.

When we remodeled our house we found chalk marks on the steps — on the inside of the risers, to tell the next fellows, this was a home that shared.

How did the church inspire hope among the congregation during the Depression?

The pastors of the church would encourage us by telling us it will get better...now we have a saying "this too shall pass." Of course, our faith in God was the biggest inspiration.

What did you do to stretch meals during the Depression? Was it difficult to get meats during those years?

Meat was plentiful, but no one had money to buy it during the Depression.

Would you say more people returned to the Church during those years looking for hope and inspiration or was it just too hopeless and hard for most families?

No, I don't think most people attended Church—they blamed God for all the misery.

What did you think of the world at this time? Did the Great Depression humble people?

George and I would pray "thy will be done." Not like the rush to church during 9-11-01. In fact some people quit coming to church because "if God caused all this, I can't worship him" "A loving God wouldn't have let this happen"

6) The Structures of Everyday Life: High School Years

What was the happiest moment of HS for you? Most difficult?

I don't know about "happy." I felt more "grown up" then. In high school, math was my most difficult subject. I especially liked English, history, geography and learning about the planets and stars.

What was your high school like? What were the class sizes during HS? About how many students in HS?

Our high school in Nanty Glo was on a hill. Oh, how hard walking up the hill in the icy wintertime! There were about 100 students in all 4 grades with about 20-25 in each class broken into 2 classes of commercial and academic, so our classes were small.

What was a typical weekday like for you....tell me about your day during a typical week during your school days?

Class started at 9 a.m., then noon till 1 p.m. for lunch, and back to school from 1 p.m. to 4 p.m. We changed classes, so only had about 50 minute periods with usually study hall periods when we did our homework or fooled around getting into trouble as some of the boys did. Changing classes was a hard lesson for me to learn. Some classes were on the main floor, others on the 2nd floor and study hall in the basement. Hurry! Not to be late or you stayed after school.

Were you involved in any activities or clubs at High School? If so, what kinds? Any clubs?

We had Girl Reserves to which I belonged from 6th grade on, winning points for my embroidery and quilting and making me eligible to go to camp for a week. The first time away from home and I got homesick both for home and the piano. I don't know how much the camp cost. I think the boys had a ball team in the summer.

Did you play piano at all for school, like school plays?

No, but I was in the school chorus in 7th grade.

If you had to say, do you think you were more drawn to Church activities or School activities?

Church, by far!

What was your favorite subject? Teacher?

Geography. My all time favorite teacher was in 4th grade: Miss Sealy, a beautiful [hand]writer and I wanted to write like her! Help! – my writing now is getting shaky and I don't remember how to spell very well [85 years old].

Where you an avid reader? What kinds of books did you read? Did you like the HS texts?

Yes, all and anything to read. The books at school were most interesting.

Did you have friends who attended both school and church with you?

Yes, 3 or 4 but not really close friends. Dorothy (Goughnour) Rupe I guess was the closest, and Marie Schlosser. She died when 16.

Did your HS have a library? Did you spend much time there?

No library so with only a dictionary to help I had to look elsewhere for reading material—The Bible!

7) The Structures of Everyday Life: Chores and Free Time

What was your happiest memory of your home life during your school days? Aside from School and Church, what was you typical day like?

Playing marbles, ball hopscotch, tag and campfires in the evening, roasting whole potatoes with my brothers and friends usually in our yard at the ash pile and telling stories. I also remember our trip to South Carolina and buying a whole big watermelon from a man right out in front of the field for 50 cents. No other melon tasted so good.

What was your home like? Bedrooms? Living Room, outdoor bath? Were there lots of chores to be done?

Our house had 2 bedrooms, a living room and a kitchen heated by wood/coal stoves. In the back yard a toilet — summer, phew! Winter too cold, one hurried to get back from outside. There was no water in the house until about 1937-38.

To do laundry, my Dad and brothers helped carry water before work/school. Needless to say we conserved and built a room on the back porch enclosed — then Mother did the washing there. He put a hole in the side with something that looked like a trough where she emptied the wash, rinse, and bath water. We bathed once a week....Saturday night. I was always first since I was the cleanest (Ha

Ha). We all used the same water. My dad, working around the mines, bathed in the tub each day. I remember him looking in the mirror to clean around his eyes. He looked as if he had a mask on before washing around them; put on his dirty clothes and went back to work the next day.

My brothers and I had two outfits…one week we wore one, while Mother washed the other clean for Sunday. Those we wore all the next week. But then, so did everyone else…so we all looked and smelled the same except the kids who had been eating garlic or onions. Sometimes that's all we had to eat—onion sandwiches.

Did your family keep a garden? If so, what did they grow? Did most homes keep gardens? Was there any difference in the size and scope of the garden during the Depression Years?

We had a garden, very small. Tomatoes (seeds saved), onions, lettuce, sometimes beans and potatoes. After we had a car about 1930-32, we visited my grandparents about one time a year where we would help reap their garden. We would be loaded down going home. Then Mother would can beans, beets, pickles, cabbage, carrots, and potatoes to store in the cellar area my Dad had dug out and put up shelves. This is where we placed the filled jars until needed.

This was all done during the Great Depression. Some neighbors had gardens but most didn't — and they wouldn't have known how to can them. Mother helped some of the neighbor ladies, but most found it too hard and time consuming. I was given the task of hulling nuts, cutting corn off the cob, peeling potatoes and beets — the usual things.

It wasn't hard keeping the house neat. Mother always kept it clean. I dusted, but each of us were responsible to make our beds, putting our dirty clothes in the clothes basket on Saturday night after bath time….We didn't have much of anything like now days.

Aside from gardening, did you have many chores to do around the house? If so, what kind of chores kept you busy? Did you have enough study time or did you find the chores left you without enough time for studies.

I finished up my homework rather quickly. We didn't get much in grade school. I started piano lessons in August of my 10th year at one dollar a lesson and our books were 35 to 50 cents. My Dad played the violin and helped me over many a rough spot. When I got a bit more proficient, we often played 3 to 3-1/2 hours at a time after supper. It was hard seeing by lamp light…Then we got electricity: I remember a hanging globe in the middle of the room, then the music was easier to read. I was always anxious to get supper over and the dishes done so we could have some music.

We had an Atwater-Kent radio — tubes before the electric came, but there was only one station that came in clear…KDKA, Pittsburgh. Sometimes we could get New York, WXYZ, I think; Boston WBZ, Chicago, but there was so much static that we didn't use it much. KDKA started about 1920-22. In the 30s we listened while Dad was at work to "The Cisco Kid" then Gene Autry, Roy Rogers, "The Lone Ranger," etc. Mostly on Saturday morning while making the beds and cleaning

Once a year Mother cleaned house — curtains, rearranging furniture, living room carpet. My job was helping move furniture and beating the carpet with a broom, then we got a wire carpet beater. The curtains were stretched on two pieces of wood that had nails sticking out. You hooked the curtain on the nails until they dried. Till then the windows had been cleaned, floor swept and scrubbed, furniture dusted and finally, the curtains hung. Dad didn't care for house cleaning so we hurried to get it done before he came home from work.

Did you ever cook meals for the family? If so, what did you make? What were some of the dishes you made while still in high school?

I never had to cook a full meal but rather helped to get it ready and the cleanup afterward.

Did you ever have any thoughts of getting hired at the five and dime or a restaurant in Nanty Glo?

27

No. I never thought of working. The law was you had to be 18 to be hired so even the boys had little opportunity. I always wanted to either be a teacher or a nurse. My eyes were very bad. While in high school, I had to quit in my junior year. I went back the next year again as a junior but couldn't finish.

8) The Structures of Everyday Life: Sense of Place

Before you got married, or during your High School, did you make any trips to other towns? If so, which? Johnstown? Pittsburgh?

I went one time a year from age 5 to the ophthalmologist by streetcar to Johnstown. Other than once or twice to take the children to the zoo, I was never in Pittsburgh until Rosemary and Dick (daughter and son-in-law) were married and we visited. My, what a long trip!

When you visited, did any other places spark your interest? Like maybe you might like to live there one day? Is Nanty Glo a special place to you? What was special about Nanty Glo?

Nanty Glo will always be HOME. We didn't have to lock our doors even at night! In the summertime the doors and windows were wide open. Dad didn't like the flies so he made screens for both doors and the windows. He kept the fly swatter handy and was constantly at hand.

Can you think of anything different about Nanty Glo compared to other places?

Most neighbors were friendly and always Hello's and How are You's were exchanged.

Did the town decorate for Christmas?

The town as a whole never decorated for Christmas. Now they do. Santa Claus wasn't pushed like it is now. It was Jesus' Birthday so gift giving was at a minimum. The most that my brothers and I got were three things: socks, underwear and shirt or a dress. Once I got a pen. I don't think I had ever had an actual doll until my Grandfather Geiyer (Mother's Dad) bought me one but I really wasn't allowed to play with it much. One day it disappeared, never to be seen again. I always hoped it was given to a little girl who needed it more than I. I don't remember asking where it was. I do remember having an old sock filled with rags. Mother embroidered eyes, nose and mouth on it and it was tied closed with a string. This was in my very early childhood.

9) Nanty Glo in the 1940s

The decline of the coal industry

After Roosevelt and Social Security came it helped out the older folks in Nanty Glo. The young ones often looked for work outside of Nanty Glo in cities such as Johnstown and Altoona. I guess about 7000 people lived in Nanty Glo during the boom years, but after the mines closed there were only 2500 in the city proper. A lot of people went out of town for work during the Depression years and post war years. When the mines began to close it affected the town in a major way as other stores and shops were forced out of business….it was like dominos falling when coal companies went out of business. This store would close and that store would close. Everything was so dependent upon the mines. We did see the opening of the Nanty Glo Journal, the town's newspaper, in the 30s, located where there used to be a jewelry shop.

Employment…. Did a lot of boys go into the mines?

Before the Great Depression some of them went in at seven years old. They stayed until they got black lung, or were injured in the mine and lost a leg or an arm.

Many came back from the war and had seen things that Nanty Glo just couldn't provide. Some of them left the area for good, while others got jobs in other cities close by and worked and maintained their residence in Nanty Glo.

Would you say the town of Nanty Glo grew or declined after the War?

After the War it declined because the mines were closing down, but on the other hand we had lots of soldiers coming home to family. But there was very little work at the time, even in the Johnstown area, so the guys began traveling further away from Nanty Glo for employment.

To your recollection, when did the coalmines begin shutting down? How about company stores?
Most mines shut down after the war to the best of my recollection.

Company stores? Do you recall when they closed?
Webster closed first because the mines petered out. Then Springfield fell next, I believe in the 1950s, and then Heisely was up until 1960s.

What do you think kept Nanty Go going even after the shutdown of the mines?
People tried to make do with what they had, and didn't expect things on a platter. Well those who were working in Johnstown or driving to Pittsburgh would drive back and forth each day or spend the weekdays in Pittsburgh and come home for the weekends.

Many of the soldiers who stayed in Nanty Glo would find work in not only Johnstown because it was close, but also Pittsburgh and Altoona and other cities and in some cases they would carpool to work

People's own initiative and cohesiveness and when times got hard we started neighboring and pulling together and building up each other and finding a way even without the mines.

Did you see that movie, the Dollmaker…well that was a lot like how we lived growing up in Nanty Glo.

What were the major changes to early Nanty Glo and modern Nanty Glo?
I would say there was a shift with the company stores going downhill even before the war, and about that time some Jewish investors came to Nanty Glo and opened up stores and even department stores. I remember going one year to the department store to get a coat.

Restaurants didn't do so well in pre- or post-War. Some would open here and there and then close. I think it's because we had a large population of east Europeans and many of them liked to eat at home, as did we.

The main employer in Nanty Glo, since the mines closed? I don't know if one stands out. There are grocery stores, pizza parlors, the newspaper, and so forth. Many people now commute from Nanty Glo to other towns and cities.

The mines began to close one after another starting in the 1950s and by the late 1960s all of the mines had shut down. One major reason for the mines shutting down was the quality of coal in the Blacklick Valley…. it was low grade coal that they said they couldn't use.

10) Courtship, Engagement, Marriage and the Early Years.

Before you married, were you looking forward to settling down someday and raising a family? Was it a dream of yours?
I wanted to be a teacher or nurse, but I didn't finish high school, so there was nothing left but to get married…or be an old maid. I did think I would like to be married and have a family. It was important to me.

How did you come to meet and eventually marry your husband, George? Describe your courtship and wedding?
Well we met at church…although he was 4 years older than me; we were in class meetings together and prayer meetings together. So, it just was such a natural thing that we didn't plan it—it just happened! At choir practice he would sit on the piano stool with me.

When did he give his life to the Lord?

When he was 9.

You gave your life to the Lord when you were 9 too?

Yes, but I was four years younger so when he gave his life to the Lord, I was only 5.

Where was George employed during your courtship? After you were married?

Well the courtship was going to church. He would meet me at the church and then he would walk me home. Usually there were six or eight boys with us. We were all in the choir together and I played the piano. George was in the choir and had a beautiful tenor voice. Unfortunately, someone told him he couldn't "carry a tune" and after that when he was aware that he was singing, he did sing off-key! After that criticism, George decided he would sit on the piano stool with me. Well that was fine with me—I didn't mind, but Chalmer (George's older brother) raised the roof. He said, "You're interfering with her." And George said, "Do you want me to get up and leave?" and I said, "No, you sit still."

When did George propose to you?

We had been to a class meeting and began to realize there was something between the two of us, and in about six weeks he gave me my first kiss, and it just bloomed after that.

So he proposed to me about a year after that. We were in Johnstown, maybe for an eye doctor appointment, and he said, "here" and he had his hand down by his side and he said "here", and there were guys lounging around at the park and he said, "here, here...take it", so I put it in my hand and realized it was a ring box. So I put it on my finger and that was our engagement! And then we were engaged about a year and half before we got married.

The wedding?

Our wedding was very simple, and I did not have a white wedding dress. I wanted a dress that I could wear later, and so we got it from Sears and Roebuck Catalog for 10 dollars. There were about 15 people in my parents' living room as witnesses. We had no music.

11) Employment and Calling

I know that George was a postal carrier—when was this? Before or after your wedding? Was he primarily in delivery or Sorting?

He began working at the Post Office after he finished high school. He graduated in May and started working in October for the Christmas mail season—at Christmas mail all the catalogs were coming and that's when he was hired. He worked part time for the Post Office from after high school up until after the Second World War. After he came back from the service he was put on full time. He was a mail or foot carrier from the start.

When did he begin preaching at the Church of the Brethren? Did he eventually become a full time minister? When?

He didn't feel the call to the ministry till he was in the service—somebody asked him to lead a prayer service. Somebody was supposed to have a prayer meeting and they didn't show up. And so they asked George if he would do it and he said, "Well, yeah" And it was while he was teaching the class that he felt the call of the Lord to be a minister.

So he was making 25 dollars a month when he preached. But it wasn't until 1950 before he went in to full time [every Sunday] preaching. He never really had a pastorship because he would fill in for a church whose pastor had resigned, and he would stay several years till they hired another pastor. So he was preaching full time because he was busy but as far as having his own church—no. Full time preaching for George was preaching at weekly services, attending necessary church meetings, performing minister-related duties, and so on. Some of the weddings he presided over were in the church he was preaching at and sometimes the bride and groom came to our house!

I heard that he preached at not only one but also several Church of the Brethren churches. Did you travel with him to the other western PA churches? What was that experience like?

He preached sometimes at several different churches both when he preached part time and full time. He also was at Dubois for four years. And then we went to Maryland, near Grantsville. There were actually three churches in Maryland and he and his brother Chalmer and another gentlemen would preach at those churches and each week they took turns preaching at each one.

Oh yes, there were times when I traveled with Dad…not always, though, because of my health and because of the family.

12) 1939-40 The House that George Built

Another interesting thing I heard was that he built you both a house! When did he begin that task and when was it finished?

We got marred in 1938 and he started on the house in 1939 and the first floor was complete and we moved in the day before Peggy was born in 1940.

So it took him about a year to build the house?

And the reason it took so long was he wasn't making much money and he couldn't buy the lumber in a whole load—he had to buy it a couple pieces at a time.

So Mr. Ragley, who owned the lumber yard, said, "George you're a good fellow, take whatever lumber you need and you can pay me as you can pay," so we owed him money for a long time.

Tell me about the house he built… what was it like? How long did you live there? What did you use for heat and was there indoor plumbing? What were some of the other features of the house you can remember?

The house had a kitchen and a bedroom/living room in 1940 and was one floor at that time. We had electricity but no water so George dug a well and then we got water in the house, but we were still going down back to the toilet [outhouse in the back of the house].

Before we moved into our house, we lived with my mom about 4 months, and then with a couple who had a large house, and finally to George's mom's for several months. After that we finally settled into the house George built.

How was the house heated?

George had gotten a large furnace and dug out — we didn't have a basement, but he dug out enough to have a cement block underneath and put the furnace on top of that and it had one big register for the two rooms. It was a coal furnace and George built a coal bin inside the newly dug out cellar and the deliveryman would shovel it through an opening into the little room.

Family Life in the Early Marriage Years

The early years were busy with Peggy born in 1940 and Donna born in 1941, and one thing that made it a lot easier was that I got an electric washing machine—had to hang the clothes outside as there was no dryer. We didn't even know anything in those days about a dryer. And we had kerosene stove that I cooked on.

When you were growing up you had a wood-burning stove, so this was an improvement?

Oh yes, kerosene was advancement.

Looking back, were those early years of family building a happy time for you?

Oh yes, we were busy at the Church and we walked everywhere—we didn't have a car. We didn't go on any trips because we didn't have the money.

13) 1941 and WWII

How did people get by during the WWII era? In terms of income?

Well the army would take a little out of their pay each month—maybe 10 dollars and give it to the men. However, the bulk of the money was sent home to us so we lived on that. I got about 29 dollars a month.

Also they gave foodstuffs through the food stamp program. But you had to watch because they didn't give out all too many stamps and because things were so expensive you'd run out of stamps quick.

We really couldn't buy sugar or butter because of the war. If we could buy meat it was very scarce and it cost so much, so we very seldom had meat. We ate a lot of macaroni and spaghetti and filling things.

So the major income during WWII was George's pay from the Army and the food stamps?

Yes. Yeah, I thought we had been getting good wages because from 25 dollars a month at the post office to 29 dollars a month from the Army, well, I felt rich!

What about the mines in WWII. Were there a lot of people still working in the mines in the war era?

Yes, and some people were deferred because they were working in the mines. And they were making good money in the mines at that time.

Was there ever a time in your early marriage when the cost of living seemed out of control? Did you, in other words, ever go through some hard times financially in the War and Post-War era? How did you make do?

No, I felt the Lord was taking care of me and my money stretched like you wouldn't believe! As soon as I got my money from the Government I paid my tithe...10% right off the top—whatever was left we used, and it just seemed that the money stretched and stretched like elastic.

No, I never had a real hard time like some folks, and I didn't buy a lot of stuff. A lot of folks went into debt. I never was one for buying "things"...as you can tell our home is not fancy. It's home, but it's not fancy.

I had heard George served in WWII, but in a non-combat role due to the beliefs of Church of the Brethren about taking another's life. What then did he do for the service during the WWII years?

Yes he was a conscientious objector, but he did have to go through basic training with a gun, and go under the barbed wire and everything. He never went to a CCC camp like a lot of the guys did when they felt that way.

Where did they place him?

They placed him in the hospital—taking care of patients. I remember when he was on his way to Missouri. They got on the train in Harrisburg and took the train to Missouri where George was going to be stationed. Someone had gone AWOL and the Sergeant came along and picked out George and said, "You see that guy stays in his seat," and George didn't know anything about it and said, "Why do I have to do this" and the Sergeant said, "Because he's away without leave and he's under arrest." And George said "Well I don't know how to do that," and he said "Yes you do" and George then took care of it and the AWOL man didn't try to get away from George. He had cuffs on his legs so he couldn't run and he was handcuffed to the seat.

14) A Family Grows

The 40s were a family building time for you? Tell me about the development of your family during the 1940s. What was life like during that decade? When were Peggy, Donna, and Posie born?

Yes. Peggy and Donna arrived one year apart in the early 1940s, while Posie and Ken were two years apart in the mid to later 1940s. We didn't get indoor plumbing until after Ken was born. George dug a cesspool out in the yard and put in a bathroom.

George put a porch on in the 40s so I did the laundry out there. Then he added onto the house—4 rooms downstairs, and upstairs but the upstairs wasn't finished. Living room, kitchen, bedroom, and dining room were all on the first floor at that time.

While George was still in the service Mr. Tom Davis, an elderly gentleman down the road, before Ken was born fixed up the upstairs and made three rooms upstairs. So we moved the beds upstairs.

We also remodeled the dining room and living room to become the new living room and the areas in the back that we used for a bedroom became the dining room. And upstairs the boys shared a bedroom and the girls shared a bedroom.

I did a lot of embroidery at that time—embroider a bedspread, and tablecloths and stuff like that and that kept me busy. And the department stores came into Nanty Glo but that didn't mean anything to me because I was at home—whatever shopping we needed George would get downtown when he was at the Post Office. So he would bring home groceries or whatever we needed from downtown, so I didn't get downtown unless I had to go through downtown to go to church.

What about George's first car?

I believe he purchased a Model A Ford, but this was at some point while he was still in the Service.

What role did God play in your early Marriage—obviously you and George were strong believers in Church of the Brethren doctrine. How did you ensure that God would be a great part of your children's lives?

Oh, it was God first, and us second! Church twice every Sunday, and prayer meeting on Wednesday night. We also got the children involved in Church as early as we could…I remember Peggy and Donna's first duet at the church…they recited a little poem at Christmas "My sister and I aren't so very big, we have so much to say, we just like to tell you how glad we are that Christ was born on Christmas day." And then for Easter they would say "..how glad we are that Christ rose on Easter day!" Rosemary and Ken recited the same poem when it was their turn.

What about your parents and George's parents? Were you close with them and how was the in-law relationship? What about your family? Did you continue to have a close-knit relationship with them after you were married? How long did they all live after you started your family?

We were on good terms, but we were busy with our immediate family. We didn't really have extended family get togethers except on the holidays. Sometimes for Thanksgiving or Christmas we'd get together, then after my parents got older and George's mother got older we would have my parents for Thanksgiving and Mother Dilling for Christmas. And the following year we'd switch families at holidays. George's father died before Peggy was born.

15) Modernity and Modern Things

The family building continued on into the 1950s.

Yes, in the 1950s… Richard was born in 1952, Lois in 1955, and 1959 was Nancy. George was preaching full time in the 1950s.

Here we are in the 1950s, the decade of Modernity promoting everything from television sets to kitchen appliances to laundry appliances to make life easier…. did you experience some of this so called "modernity" in your own house?

Well, we already had the electricity in, and we got the phone service in before Rosemary was born, and George was in the service. My mother said, "I think you need a phone, in case we need to get to the hospital." And since he was in the service I got to have the baby at the hospital for free.

We were able to get a refrigerator from my mother—the old General Electric with the motor at the top. It had one space for a freezer with containers of ice. We got that shortly after WWII.

When did you purchase your first TV?

Before the birth of Richard in 1952, I was bed-ridden and George got me a TV. And you ought to have seen how he had that fixed up… the TV was across the room so he hooked it up somehow so I could turn it off and on right there at the bed. I had my bed in the dining room then.

We also got rid of the kerosene stove in 1946 or around the time Ken was born and George got us an electric stove. We didn't get a dryer until the late 1950s, and about that time or soon after we purchased a freezer.

Were there things on the market that you wanted for your family but just could not afford? Did it make you feel poor or inadequate not to have any of these products?

No, I didn't see things like that. If they were there for sale I didn't go into Johnstown that often and I didn't know they were for sale. It wasn't like I was "gimme gimme gimme" — we weren't like that.

What about others at this time—how did they fare?

A lot of them were okay, but there were a lot who were spending more than they were making. We could afford some of the major appliances as they become available, but by no means were we wealthy.

Was there poverty in Nanty Glo in the 1950s?

No not really. During the time I grew up, yes there were many poor, but not at the time of the 1950s.

I know coal was closing shop in this era, but was it still the dominant form of employment at that time?

Heisley Mines was still going very very well, but Springfield had closed, Webster had closed, Lincoln had closed. And then they put in a coal cleaning plant, they called it, in Ebensburg, so a lot of the folks went up there for work.

What about the company stores and housing in the 1950s.

Well the mines sort of dwindled out and the company stores closed one after another, but other stores like the American Store (Acme) and A&P took their place. As far as company housing, the company house my parent's lived in … they were able to buy for 500 dollars and there they lived until they died.

16) The Trip Across America

What do you remember most about your famous trip across America?

We packed up food and clothes and with friends we started off from our house and I remember when we got to South Dakota and saw Mt. Rushmore and the Black Hills. That was a tremendous thing for us to see. We saw where there had been gold mines and silver — you could see where the openings were in the hills.

We went to a church conference for a week in Oregon. They put us up at a college and I had my own dorm room.

We went down to California to a friend's and stayed overnight with them and in their yard was all sand and they were filled with ant mounds and you could look down in them and see how busy the ants were.

We were elated at the many wonders we saw—especially Yellowstone National Park for the first time and all the wildlife. And when we got Yosemite we saw Bridal Veil Falls. I just kept thinking I couldn't believe it — all that water coming down. And the Giant Redwoods -- it was something!

What was the thing that stands out most about the trip?

Seeing the ocean for the first time! The Pacific! Just beyond there was Japan and Hawaii and I just couldn't believe it.

On our way back we stopped near Indian reservations and saw the crafts sellers and glass blowers and clay makers…. I had never seen anything like this before.

17) 1960s: Decade of Dissent

Here it is 1960—Lois is 5 years old and Nancy just turning 1. What was going on with family life at this time?

Well, George was preaching Sundays at the Montgomery Church of the Brethren in Indiana County about an hour or so from where we lived. Most times I went with him. We stayed all day and so we were very busy. Sometimes some of the youngsters would go with us, and sometimes not.

A family by the name of Mr. and Mrs. Small would have us for lunch after services. Usually there were people in the hospital that needed visiting so George would go with Mr. Small and visit, while myself and Mrs. Small would visit at their home.

In those days during the week was cooking and cleaning and washing and ironing — in those days you ironed a lot because you didn't have permanent press. And the uniforms George wore to deliver mail, I had to do his shirts and pants—lots of ironing to do. And then he came home for lunch so it was cook lunch and then supper—so I was a busy person.

In the 1960s Peggy was in nursing school for 3 years, then she went off to Juniata College, hired as a college nurse, while she earned a degree in Psychology. Donna, a year younger, also enrolled in Juniata College, but then took a job at Penn Traffic, a department store, and worked there 2 years. Donna then went on to study in Kansas at the Brethren Church affiliated McPherson College majoring in elementary education. Rosemary graduated high school in 1963 and went on to Clarion University in Pennsylvania and majored in secondary education in social studies. Ken and Richard both went on to McPherson and Ken majored in secondary education/music, while Richard studied chemistry.

You had such a big family—did the housework ever seem overwhelming to you while your children were growing up?

I wouldn't say overwhelming no—it was a job that had to be done and I knew that I had to, as soon as the meal was over I had to get in the kitchen and get the dishes washed, and then start something else. Usually I was busy thinking after breakfast what I was going to have for lunch and then after lunch I was thinking on what to have for supper. So whatever I was doing---that's what I was thinking about.

I listened to the radio while I was working, usually music—while I was cleaning and ironing and doing the laundry and hanging the clothes out to dry. I didn't have a dryer till Nancy was born. Music kept me going.

In 1963 do you remember where you were at when President Kennedy got shot?

Yes, I had the flu and Rosemary was home from college for Thanksgiving. They called me and said, "Oh Mom, you have to see this…the President is in a car and riding down the street." So I got downstairs and into the living room. I saw the shot from the grassy knoll. I saw a flash and saw the President got shot. They said it was from the tall building but I saw a flash from the grassy knoll and I knew that was the place from where he was shot.

What about the Vietnam War era? Some say it really tore this country apart and set sons and daughters against fathers and mothers. How did you feel about the war?

Well we were not in favor of war to begin with, but if our President felt it was necessary then we would go along. As far as protesting, we would of never done that. But I felt bad that our soldiers had to go over there because that war as well as the Korean War were wars we couldn't win. I feel the same way now about this war in Iraq. My thoughts are that we are living in the last days and the Lord said these things will come.

What about the Civil Rights Movement in the 1960s?

They wouldn't let Black Americans into the schools or let them drink from the same water fountain or use the same rest rooms—all that was so sad.

What was your Church's orientation? If you had a black family would you have welcomed them?

35

Yes we would have welcomed them just like we welcomed the immigrants who came to Nanty Glo – all are God's creatures.

I remember when Peggy and Donna were at Juniata and were coming home for a weekend and they invited a Kenyan student to come and stay with us. And the fellow across the street — Oh, he talked so dirty and said "Why do you have that nigger there for? He's no good. He's not like us." We tried to tell him God made him a special way and God made us a special way. Back in the 1920s the Klan was active in and around Nanty Glo for a time…we could look out the window and see them marching with their torches and white sheets and white hoods and carrying the burning cross. All I know is that was "not" Christianity.

Also in the 1960s was the lunar landing? How did you feel about that?

Oh…that was a big one, yes. To see the TV and to see him come down out of the capsule and then jump. That was a tremendous thing to see. It was impossible to think that he could go to the moon, much less for us to see it.

We looked at it as if it served a greater purpose, then, yes, it was worth going there. But if the only purpose was to see that we could do it, then we would have felt differently. I feel the same way if we ever go to Mars—what purpose will it serve?

18) "Teach Your Children Well"

When did you begin to paint?

I got into painting somewhere around 1968 or so. I used Artex paints and they were liquid in a tube with a tip like a ballpoint pen, and I did pillow cases, and tablecloths and painting for others…I painted a horse on a mountain and made it look like his mane and tail were blowing in the wind. And I sold that for 75 dollars.

So there was a future in it, but the thing was Artex and Tri Chem were competitors and Tri Chem bought the other one out, and I couldn't use their paints because that's when I discovered I had asthma…I also tried using oil-based paints and thought I could go that way, but I wasn't wise enough to use a fan and again I found this bothering my asthma. So I gave up on it….I considered watercolor and tried a little, but that didn't seem to be for me.

I taught painting also before the asthma to students in the local library. I taught till about 1978 or so. I painted quilt patches on cloth material.

Did you find enough time to do your paintings given household chores?

Well I sandwiched the paintings between things—while I was waiting for the potatoes to boil I would get my paints out and paint a little bit. Also in the 1970s a lot of the kids were gone and I wasn't as tied down as I used to be so I pursued it.

What else did you pursue during this time?

I also taught piano in the 1970s in my home and had several students. I taught from the early 1970s till we moved from Nanty Glo in 1990. And during this time I got an organ and I was also teaching organ as well — I had 15-20 students at a time. I started out asking for a dollar per lesson. Some folks said "You're not charging enough" but my main goal was teaching others to learn rather than starting a business.

I was also very involved with church all my life….in the later years during the holidays I was there to play music for the youngsters to do their skits and other plays. And during this time I also was involved in church activities on Wednesday, choir on Thursday, and several services on Sunday—I practically lived at the Church!

Did Church ever tire you out? What was it like to sit through the same sermon on a Sunday?

Well no, it wasn't the same….the evening service was completely different so the pastor had to have two sermons. One was for morning and another one was for evening—and no, I never got tired. And in the summer time we had Revival and I also did all the music for that as well. Busy, Busy, Busy.

What about household appliances in the 1970s?

Well when Lois came home from school one day, she urged us to get a microwave but I didn't see any use for it, but she was persistent telling us how they had made meatloaf in it in such a short time. Well I don't know if I ever saw one or heard others talk about them, but I finally changed my mind and got one.

I remember you telling me how you went from wood-fired to kerosene stove, and now you go from electric to microwave---during your life doesn't technology just boggle the mind?

Boggle the mind, Yes! It' like going from a horse and buggy, to a Model T to a Model A to what we have today. I also remember feeling the same way about the dishwasher when I first got one—I felt I would never use it. And then I tried it and changed my mind about that as well.

Did you ever say "I wish they would have invented these back in the days when I started my family?"

The automatic washer and dryer…Yes. Dishwasher, Maybe. Because I had Peggy, Donna, Rosemary, Ken, Richard, Lois, and Nancy .. they were my dishwashers!

What else was going on with your family in the 1970s?

Much the same as the earlier decades…washed on Monday, ironed on Tuesday, baked on Wednesday, cleaned on Thursday. On Friday I kind of took it easy. Saturday was bake and clean days. And Church on Sunday, along with Church activities on Wednesday and Thursday nights.

Ken had finished college and taught music at a school district and then made his way out to California. He also was very interested in jewelry and made the females of the family rings and other jewelry keepsakes.

Many of our kids had either finished college or were in college by the 1970s. Only Lois and Nancy were home, and Lois went off to college in 1973.

Did you find the burden of kids lifted in the mid 1970s?

I had so much free time I hardly knew what to do with myself. It was here where I painted for as long as I could and taught piano and organ, and embroidery ….I had many problems with my back at this time though, and I had back surgery around this time too.

19) Empty Nest

It was just Nancy, but she went off to college in the late 1970s and so it was just George and I in the 80s. She started at Clarion but finished her degree at University of Pittsburgh at Johnstown. George had retired from the Post Office in those years, but still was busy preaching every week. I still taught piano and had to keep the house clean for the students, so I found things to do despite the empty nest.

How did you feel about the hostage situation in Iran?

We were very hurt by that---not angry, but hurt that other people would do that to fellow human beings. We were never angry—just hurt.

The Berlin Wall

I was over at a friend's house back in the 1960s and we were watching the TV and the Soviets building the Wall in East Germany and we were shocked that they would do such a thing. I remember crying about that. When they finally tore the Wall down I was elated then because that was going to be gone and I had felt that it had been up so, so long.

Would you say in your feelings about communism that it was an evil or misguided philosophy?

It was misguided but there was evil with it as well.

Tell me about your vacations?

Our church sponsored a week long vacation/retreat in Somerset County, called Camp Harmony near the place where Flight 93 went down. We'd pack up and had a cabin to ourselves because our family was so large. The kids could go hiking and swimming and had campfires---and we also had church gatherings all week long. Some of the kids worked for the camp in the summer for teen camping get togethers, and when it was family week they would join us.

Did these vacations bring your family together?

I don't know if it brought our family together but I can say that it brought our Church Family together.

What was the reason you finally decided to relocate from Nanty Glo after all those years?

Well a couple of reasons. First the winters were too cold and we found we had problems in digging ourselves out each winter. My back was bothering me something terrible and we lived in a 2 story house and I could hardly get up the stairs. And so in 1990 on my birthday we finally moved to Plum. I had turned 70.

(In November of 2009, Nora Dilling passed on at age 89)

State of Mind

And now I miss you Appalachia like coal trains
and a thousand crickets dawning on the outskirts
of memory. Memory?
My mind has become an analog of eroding mountainous
landscape--a topographical maze only fiddle tunes and
men from deep earth understand.

Where are you Cambs two years ago on a
Friday afternoon? Trips to the 'legger past
two hundred trailers, twenty six farms and fifteen
strip mines and sat up cooling off those hot Kentucky
nights on cold Budweisers.

And where are you Julip with your backroad-county
girls in denim cutoffs and checkerboard cotton shirts?
I speaking urban phrases like "whadda'ya names?" in the
presence of sweet dialects running smooth from the lips
of iced tea smiles.

It's quiet now Appalachia
Your mines quiet in the bust.
Your hills quiet in the night.
Mam'aw gathers up the young ones like farm eggs
and lets them snack on hushpuppies and RC

while here watching barefoot undergraduate girls in white bikinis
from urban dreamland fire escapes
I wash down calzone with cold Iron City

and think about when Jimmy passed on how half the county
came to pay their respects to one whose death was as
unpredictable as the mine explosions and floods those
Cumberland mountains have known over the past century
and a half

thinking about the time during pledging when Byron
and I tore that big old Coke sign down off the side
of a hill on 25e and packed it off on the roof of
Ditillio's Monte Carlo

thinking about how Boyd took us out-of-state college
boys in as his own--
would loan us a twenty like second nature
and always end a conversation with a "drop on by anytime"

and thinking about how Appalachia wraps itself
around you like the aroma of Chelsie's cornbread
and you begin to think of it as home
from a thousand miles removed in one mind.

CHAPTER 3

Central Appalachia:
Toward a Model of Regional Underdevelopment

Structural/Relational Analysis and Central Appalachia

Appalachia as a Social Hierarchy

There is not one Appalachia, but several. In fact, perhaps several dozen. The problem with the conceptualization of "Appalachia" as with the conceptualization of terms such as "region," and to a lesser extent "nation," is they usually contend to comprehensively capture *all* of social and economic life contained within. The history, in fact, of the Appalachian Regional Commission has been a history of classifying and reclassifying the Appalachian region to account for substantial variation in the region. We thus have historically evolved from notions of Appalachia with the connotation of "poverty" to notions of northern, southern and central Appalachia. Over the years, it was central Appalachia that became the sociological as well as political defining point for poverty and socioeconomic deprivation that was previously applied to Appalachia as a whole. Central Appalachia's infrastructural and structural grid revealed a region dominated by the extraction and export of minerals within a densely packed cluster of mountains. Topographical constraints were viewed then--and corresponded to--a condition of poverty, and this ideological position dominated most theoretical models on central Appalachia's socioeconomic plight from the 1950 period through the 1970s.

Harry Caudill in the early 1960s offered a radically different explanation. In *Night Comes to the Cumberlands*, Caudill suggests the reason central Appalachia was poor was not due so much to topographical constraints as it was to an outside coal industry bent on siphoning out not only the minerals but wealth of Appalachia as well. It was not, however, until more than a decade later, in 1978, that a major theoretical model in an academic account of relational analysis on the region would emerge with Helen Lewis' *Colonialism in Modern America*: *The Appalachian Case*, whereby the central Appalachian region was schematized as an colony of rich northern capitalists. Here then was a fundamental shift in theoretical and methodological thinking from topography to the *social relations* between the region and absentee and larger (colonial) culture and economy. Walls, however, contributed a chapter in Lewis' work entitled "Internal Colony or Internal Periphery" where he called for a drop of the "colonialism" baggage and to rightly view central Appalachia as an internal periphery in the larger US capitalist system. Hence the relational analysis further advanced. Almost ten years later, I (Matvey: 1987) continued to develop both Wall's initial thesis of internal periphery along with Girvan's (1976) theoretical model of *Corporate Imperialism*, heavily grounded in organizational structure and hierarchical relations, and produced a dissertation on a macro-structural history of the peripheralization of central Appalachian region from the frontier period through the modern era. I further tracked the development of underdevelopment in central Appalachia by examining the network of relationships between core-centered institutional parents in metropolitan areas and their corresponding subsidiaries in Appalachia. Hence central Appalachia's condition, and indeed, its socioeconomic deprivation was mapped out as the result of bottom level relational positions within a variety or organizational, institutional, production, exchange and division of labor network hierarchies with a number of US metropolitan core zones.

Ultimately poverty in central Appalachia was the result of not merely its exchange of minerals for manufactured and technological goods from the core producing centers, but in addition, from its symbiotic social relationship where the capital, profits, royalties are systematically siphoned from the region into the core-based corporate parent and financial institutions.

The Variation of Social Networks in Appalachia

At the outset, I claimed there was not one but potentially dozens of Appalachias. I stand by this statement for even within central Appalachia there is variation. This region can only be partially considered a single industry mineral export enclave as defined by Girvan (1976). There is a Major and Minor coal zone in central Appalachia. Poverty for the Major coal region is often the result of the boom/bust character of the coal industry, while in the Minor coal zone, coal does not employ a majority of the work force and much poverty here is due to the instability of minimum wage work and underemployment.

West Virginia is also peculiar in that while southern West Virginia approximates the Major coal zone of central Appalachia, it is the northern half of West Virginia where core-owned mineral extraction and manufacturing activity have co-existed. The problem then for northern West Virginia, is not merely the boom/bust character of coal as in central Appalachia, but the shifts in the global economy where core based transnationals are heavily investing in manufacturing in the less developed world that in turn is de-industrializing, deskilling, and under-employing the manufacturing base. In addition, the fact that large transnational oil and energy conglomerates now own and control coal fields not only in Appalachia but at points across the globe has added two dimensions of deprivation in the region: 1) an intensification of boom/bust cycles, and 2) global competition of coal production that has exerted a downward push upon wages and production in the Appalachian coal fields. As Bob Dylan sang in *Workingman's Blues #2*, "the buying power of the proletariat's gone down…it's a new path that we trod" and "they say that low wages are a reality if we want to compete abroad." (Dylan, 2006).

Yet another Appalachia emerges in the Pittsburgh region. Here are all the characteristics of a core metropolitan zone with a substantial headquartering of corporate firms in the downtown area of the city along with a clustering of large financial firms. Again, we find not only a large high level managerial class, but a scientific technical class ranging from employment in robotics and technological medicine to substantial corporate law, advertising, and business services in the region. The manufacturing base has long since withered from the shut down in the steel industry in the 1980s due to shifts in the global economy and the emerging and unchallenged position of Japanese based steel in the world economy. The downsizing and restructuring of the Pittsburgh steel industry sent reverberations through the manufacturing sector and the entire process lent itself regional de-industrialization, and underemployment for the Pittsburgh manufacturing class.

What is fascinating however--and this again reveals the power of a structural/relational network analysis--is that the shutdown in steel and manufacturing did not generate an elimination or flight of the corporate headquarters in and from the Pittsburgh region. Most corporate firms, restructured, divested, reinvested, redeveloped, and merged with other transnationals. Hence we must distinguish between what might be called the *geo-productive* core, heavy in manufacturing and traditional industries, and the *geo-corporate* core which is primarily based on organizational and institutional ownership and calls forth a scientific-technical, advertising, corporate legal, advertising, and business services class of employment. It was thus possible for firms, maintaining their headquarters in the Pittsburgh region, to divest, downsize, and de-industrialize from various manufacturing interests, and restructure their capital investments and expansion into high tech industries. Pittsburgh Appalachia witnessed a collapse, to be sure, in its industrial and manufacturing occupational structure, but the financial core emerged leaner and meaner, so to speak, and was fundamentally restructured, bringing forth a host of new occupational categories.

If we move to the east of Pittsburgh, toward the Johnstown semi-periphery, we find a situation akin to northern West Virginia, where both manufacturing and mining investments have fallen apart at the same time, creating socioeconomic distress in its wake. This short qualitative history of central and northern Appalachia, however, should be viewed as a way to understand the variation of the region. Hence core financial ownership and traditional manufacturing networks operated in the Pittsburgh region, while subsidiary organizational nodes existed almost fully in the central Appalachian coalfields. There are rhythms and drives that not only affect various networks in particular ways, but these networks themselves are differentiated from each other.

Hence Appalachia itself--while it may be easy to refer to it as "region"--is actually a clustering of a variety of dynamic economic networks of ownership and organization. Mapping these networks is the key to not only understanding the differences between various geographic points, but predicting the potentials and possibilities ranging from regional distress to opportunity.

Empirical Indicators: The Problem of Central Appalachia

Where is Central Appalachia?

Driving along the coal truck battered asphalt back roads through the hollows of central Appalachia is a beautiful scenic treasure. Stopping to talk and chat a bit outside a general store while enjoying an RC cola, I kind of feel like William Least Heat Moon in his book <u>Blue Highways</u>. Moon travels through rural town after rural town, occasionally stopping to visit and stepping into a cultural wonderland. For myself, central Appalachia is quite rural as well as rich in culture. I used to ask my students in both Pittsburgh and in the lowlands of South Carolina, "Where is Appalachia?" and most replied somewhere in Kentucky or West Virginia. Indeed that is the popular and in some cases sociological definition of central Appalachia, focusing primarily upon eastern Kentucky, southern West Virginia, and smaller portions of western Virginia and northeast Tennessee. Central Appalachia, in particular, eastern Kentucky and southern West Virginia, although rich in culture as well as natural resources, has been one of the most concentrated zones of poverty in the U.S. throughout the modern and post modern eras. The Appalachian Regional Commission, a regional governmental unit designed in 1964 to channel aid and modernization projects throughout the entire 13-state Appalachian region, termed central Appalachia "hardcore Appalachia" precisely because of longstanding and comprehensive unemployment, out-migration, and poverty. The Appal Mountain Lore Emergency Fund documented the fact that over 500 people died of starvation in the state of Kentucky from 1960-1966.

Since the 1960s, poverty has persisted with almost system-like regularity, crossing each generation. In fact, we will contend the problem of poverty in central Appalachia is part of an economic system comprised of capitalist ownership and institutional hierarchies as well as core-to-periphery relationships that regenerate underdevelopment from one generation to the next.

Turning to Tables 3.1 and 3.2, we find continued high rates of poverty and low educational attainment levels in the region. The pervasive issue with central Appalachia is not merely poverty and unemployment, but a region-wide system of underdevelopment, which relegates the region to the bottom layers of the capitalist hierarchy of ownership. Central Appalachia, in addition to high poverty, unemployment and low educational attainment levels, also suffers a poorly financed educational system and poor infrastructural services such as transportation, water, sewer and drainage systems. The region is also classified as a medically underserved area with reference to the number of doctors, nurses and health care personnel. The industrial sector of the region is primarily a single industry economy subject to boom/bust phases, which we will turn to shortly. The banking sector in the region is financially depleted. It lacks the capital to facilitate private investment conducive to economic development and diversification. The local and county governments also lack capital to provide infrastructural resources and social services to the inhabitants. The combination of these conditions we term "regional underdevelopment."

Table 3.1
Poverty Rates 1980-2000

	1980	1990	2000
Appalachian Kentucky	26.0	29.0	24.4
West Virginia	15.0	19.7	17.9
Appalachia	14.1	15.4	13.6
US	12.4	13.1	12.4

Table 3.2
% Completed High School and College
1980, 2000

	% Completed High School, 1980	% Completed High School, 2000	% Completed College, 1980	% Completed College, 2000
Appalachian Kentucky	40.4	62.5	7.4	10.5
West Virginia	56.0	75.2	10.4	14.8
Appalachia	57.3	76.8	11.2	17.7
US	66.5	80.4	16.2	24.4

Source: ARC Regional Data and Research. www.arc.gov Data based on 1990 and 2000 Census

Mapping Central Appalachia for Socioeconomic Analysis

It is difficult to pin a model of underdevelopment upon central Appalachia. Throughout the entire 13 state Appalachian region are stark contrasts in terms of economic activity. Indeed, even within central Appalachia we find intra-regional differences county by county. However, it is clear that within a cluster of central Appalachian counties in eastern Kentucky and southern West Virginia that coal production for export is the central and most crucial form of economic activity.

If we turn our attention to Eastern Kentucky in Table 3.3, we find not one Appalachia, but several. First is the ARC-defined region known as Appalachian Kentucky consisting of 51 counties. Within this cluster are 32 non-coal producing counties. Another cluster is the coal-producing zone consisting of 19 counties, and this cluster can be further subdivided into 10 Major Coal Producing counties (over 1 million tons) and 9 Minor Coal Producing counties (under 1 million tons). In Table 3.3, poverty levels are given for these distinct economic zones in Eastern Kentucky, and here we find the highest rates of poverty in the coal-producing region. Poverty levels in the coal-producing zone converged near 31%, while outside the coal-producing zone the poverty level hovered at close to 25%. In West Virginia, the only state fully encompassed within Appalachia, the data is broken down by state and also by the ARC-defined central Appalachian subregion. As a state, Appalachian WV's poverty level was 17.9% in 2000, and this figure only drops to 17.0% for the 28-county non-coal zone of the state. In the Major Coal zone, the poverty level climbs to 22.3% -- including both northern and southern West Virginia. If we follow the ARC-defined boundaries of central Appalachia only 9 counties qualify, with 6 as major coal producers and 3 as minor or non-coal counties. Here we find the poverty level climbing to 27.2% in the major coal-producing region of southern West Virginia, a rate nearly equaling the poverty levels of the major coal-producing zone in Eastern Kentucky.

Table 3.3
Poverty by Sub-Region, 2000

Region	Number of Counties	Poverty Level, 2000
US		12.4%
Appalachia	406	13.6%
Kentucky		15.8%
Appalachian Kentucky	51	24.4%
Non Coal Appalachian Kentucky	32	23.2%
Coal Appalachian Kentucky	19	30.8%
Major Coal Appalachian Kentucky (over 1 million tons)	10	30.8%
Minor Coal Appalachian Kentucky (under 1 million tons)	9	30.9%
Appalachian WV	54	17.9%
Non Coal WV	28	17.0%
Coal WV	26	21.3%
Major Coal WV (over 1 million tons)	20	22.3%
Minor Coal WV (under 1 million tons)	6	17.7%
Central Appalachian Southern WV	9	24.8%
Central Appalachia Southern WV non coal	3	20.1%
Central Appalachia SWV Major Coal	6	27.2%
The Central Appalachian Mineral Export Economy	***19 Eastern Kentucky 6 Southern WVA***	***29.0%***

Source: **ARC Regional Data and Research.** www.arc.gov **Data based on 1990 and 2000 Census West Virginia Office of Miners' Health Safety and Training**
2000 Coal Production by County Kentucky Department of Mines and Minerals, Annual Report, 2002.

In Table 3.4 we examine some of the characteristics of coal producing counties in eastern Kentucky and southern West Virginia. Among these counties listed, all are major coal counties, producing well over 1 million tons a year. In addition all have poverty levels much higher than the levels of their respective States. Finally, these counties represent some of the greatest losses of population in West Virginia and Kentucky from 1990-2000 with the exception of a small number of counties in western Kentucky.

Note for instance, Pike, Letcher, Leslie and Harlan -- all major coal producers and all suffered losses in population at over 5%. In West Virginia we find most of the major coal counties all losing more than double digits in population from 1990-2000, with the exception of Raleigh and Lincoln counties. Even in the heart of the major coal-producing zone in Central Appalachia, we find waves of out-migration, which we will turn to shortly in our focus on the single industry coal economy.

Table 3.4
Population Change 1990-2000
In
Major Coal Producing Counties of Central Appalachia

	Population Change 1990-2000	Coal Production 2000 (Millions of Tons)	Poverty Level, 2000
West Virginia	**0.8**	**169.4**	**17.9**
Raleigh	3.1	10.2	18.5
Lincoln	3.4	2.5	27.9
Wyoming County	-11.3	9.6	25.1
Logan County	-12.4	8.6	24.1
Mingo County	-16.3	22.0	29.7
McDowell County	-22.4	4.5	37.7
Central Appalachian, Southern WV (6 counties)	**-9.3**	**57.4**	**27.2**

Table 3.4 (cont)

	Population Change 1990-2000	Coal Production 2000 (Millions of Tons)	Poverty Level, 2000
Kentucky	**9.6**	**131.8**	**15.8**
Pike County	-5.3	34.1	23.4
Letcher County	-6.4	10.0	27.1
Leslie County	-9.1	6.5	32.7
Harlan County	-9.2	10.2	32.5
Major Coal Counties, Appalachian Kentucky (10 Counties)	-3.9	102.7	30.8
Minor Coal Counties, Appalachian Kentucky, (9 Counties)	9.1	2.3	30.9
Coal Counties, Appalachian Kentucky (19 counties)	**2.3**	**105.0**	**30.8**

Source: http://quickfacts.census.gov/qfd/states/00000.html **West Virginia Office of Miners' Health Safety and Training**. Kentucky Department of Mines and Minerals, Annual Report, 2002. ARC Regional Data and Research. www.arc.gov Data based on 1990 and 2000 Census.

45

Let us be clear then, as we move toward a model of regional underdevelopment, our focus is primarily upon eastern Kentucky and southern West Virginia, and in turn, the coal-producing zone of those state regions. This includes 19 eastern Kentucky coal-producing counties, and 6 major coal-producing counties in southern West Virginia. This 25-county region is slimmer than the ARC's definition of Central Appalachia, especially with regard to eastern Kentucky, but the map here is drawn along the coal-producing economy. We will term this zone as the Central Appalachian Mineral Export Economy.

This regional coal producing economy may only consist of 25 counties, yet, as a central industry, it has implications for surrounding non-coal counties in terms of a region wide multiplier effect and also diversified economic growth in the region. As hundreds of millions of tons of coal leave the Appalachian coal fields each year we ask "what, if any, is the spillover?" We will now turn our attention to offering an explanation as to why there is no multiplier, diversified growth, or spillover.

Central Appalachia:
Toward a Model of Regional Underdevelopment

In Chart 3.1, we find a model for regional underdevelopment. The first column [A] offers four basic structural prongs or patterns producing a set of economic dysfunctions [B] contributing to a continued condition of regional underdevelopment. The output or impacts of these dysfunctions are listed in the third [C] and fourth [D] columns.

The Structural Base [A] contains the particular nature and character of the Central Appalachian economy. First it is not only a mineral export economy, but also a single industry economic enclave centered upon coal production. In addition, a second dimension of the mineral export economy rests with the core based character of corporate capitalism in the region with the bulk of industrial units being mere subsidiaries to the larger transnational corporate parents headquartered in core metropolitan zones. Third, is the concentration of corporate and absentee patterns of land ownership. Again corporate parents owning and controlling vast amounts of land are primarily core-based transnational corporations. Finally, this Structural Base develops a condition of political dependency whereby local and state elites assist the absentee corporate owners, sometimes at the expense of the local inhabitants.

The particular character and nature of the Structural Base in Central Appalachia engages several Dysfunctional Mechanisms [B] distorting any real possibility for economic development and diversification in the region. Dysfunctional Mechanisms essentially "impact" upon three realms of the Central Appalachian society [C]: the Regional Labor Force, the Regional Economy, and Modernization Potential. Finally, we find further effects [D] of underdevelopment leading not to economic development and diversification but, rather, a regeneration of the entire system of underdevelopment through historical time. In the following sections we provide a detailed but brief description of the structural base, dysfunctional mechanism and the resulting impacts upon the inhabitants.

CHART 3.1
CENTRAL APPALACHIA
TOWARD A MODEL OF REGIONAL UNDERDEVELOPEMENT

A) The Structural Base: The Mineral Export Economy	B) Dysfunctional Mechanisms	C) Impacts Upon	D) Further Effects
		1) Regional Labour Force	
1) Single Industry Coal Economy	*Boom/Bust Phases	*High Unemployment	*Waves of Regional Out-migration
	*Mechanization of Coal	*Sporadic Employment	*Welfare Dependence
	*Lack of Inter-Industry Competition for Labour	*Regional Underdevelopment	*Subsistence practices as compensatory income
	*Inability to employ majority of regional labour force	*Low Per Capital Income	
		*Low wages/High Poverty	
		*Blue Collar Occupational Dominance	
		2) Regional Economy	
2) Absentee Corporate Institutional Relations (Parent/Subsidiary Relations)	(Forms of Profit Drain) *Subsidiary Profit Drain	*Low regional capital accumulation	
		*Decapitalization	*Lack of a" regional multiplier effect"
	*Corporate Acquisition Drain	*Conservative Lending Policies	
		*Inability to facilitate diversified growth.	
	*Coal Royalty Drain		*Regeneration of Single Industry Dependence
		3) Modernization Potential	
3) Absentee Corporate Land Ownership Patterns	*Concentration of Land in few hands	*Lack of prime development land tracts	
	*Corporate Absentee power over land development		
			*Inability to attract Diversified Investment
4) Political Dependency	*Minimal taxation upon absentee held lands.	*Lagging Infrastructure	*Continued topographical and physical barriers
		*Inadequate Transportation Network	*Lagging Modernization
		*Poor Social Services	*Underdevelopment
		*Educational system deficiencies	

Single Industry Coal Economy

Central Appalachia has not only suffered a long history of boom/bust phases but the industry was subject to intense mechanization in the modern era which unemployed tens of thousands, creating waves of out-migration from Appalachia to northern cities such as Cincinnati and Detroit. There is also associated with single industry dominance a lack of inter-industry competition for labor, which, in turn, works as a downward push upon wages. In Central Appalachia not only is there no alternative employment, but also the coal industry suffers from the inability to employ the majority of the regional labor force. Moreover, in a single industry economy, a coal bust phase will not only unemploy the industrial sector of the regional labor force, but also reverberate through the wholesale, retail, and service sectors to plunge much of the entire regional labor force into the realm of what the French historian Fernand Braudel calls "non-economy."

Joseph J. Matvey, III

What are the impacts? Upon the regional labor force we find periods of sporadic employment, high unemployment in bust phases, the underdevelopment of the regional labor force, along with a low per capita income, low wages, and high poverty rates. Further effects are basic collective reactions to the coal industry's instability, including waves of out-migration, welfare dependence, and continued cultural subsistence practices as compensatory income.

Absentee Corporate Institutional Relations (Parent to Subsidiary)

Problems in the Central Appalachian regional economy extend beyond the boom/bust character of the coal industry. The corporate economy in Central Appalachia is primarily core based with the huge transnational energy corporations controlling several dozen large subsidiary units in Central Appalachia. The parent exercises total control over its subsidiaries. Here we find the majority of parents headquartered in core metro zones while the bulk of industrial units in Central Appalachia are mere subsidiary units.

Norman Girvan recognized that a condition of "dependent underdevelopment" was perpetuated through the given structural character of these economies:

> ...And the mineral industry consists of a small number of subsidiary firms that are vertically integrated with large, oligopolistic transnational corporations. Dependent underdevelopment in these economies can therefore be analyzed with reference to (a) relationships between the subsidiary firms and their parent transnational corporations, and (b) relationships between the subsidiary firms and the host economy...(1976: 25)

> ...mineral industries in the peripheral countries have conspicuously failed to act as a catalyst for the generation of self-sustaining growth. They have remained economic enclaves within host countries, better integrated with the outside world than with the domestic economies of the periphery. They give rise to growth without development, and typically, when the boom conditions in the mineral industry come to an end, the economy faces the prospect of endemic stagnation, while the transnational corporations, fattened but still growing, move on to newer and greener pastures (1976: 25).

Subsidiary Profit Drain

The central problem with the character of Parent to Subsidiary relationships is profit or surplus drain on the regional economy. There are three forms of drain in Central Appalachia, two of which we will discuss now. The first form of drain is simply **profit drain**. Profits made in the mining industry by subsidiary units are siphoned out of the region at the discretion of the parents. While some will surely be reinvested in the coal industry, the point is decisions like these are in the hands of the parent rather than the subsidiary.

In West Virginia, members of the finance sector realize the importance of locally based ownership, especially as it relates to capital availability in the region. Gilmer Hines, then President of the Castle Rock Bank in Pineville, West Virginia, stated:

> ...a large percentage of them (coal corporations) have their homes offices in Pennsylvania. Most of them in Pittsburgh. All of the money from West Virginia coal ends up in the Pittsburgh banks. The only benefit that the people of West Virginia get from it is the salaries that are paid to the men...When a miner gets paid here for working two miles up the road, he's paid with a check drawn on the Pittsburgh bank (Coogan, 1980: 12).

Corporate Acquisition Drain.

In addition to profit drain, is another form of drain, which will be termed **acquisition drain.** Particularly since the 1970s, oil corporations have increasingly integrated into coal, acquiring a number of large native Appalachian firms. What occurs through acquisition is a reorganization of the acquired firms' financial accounts, centralizing capital and accounts within the metro-based headquarters of the parent firm.

Again, Hines gives an example of the loss of lending power when a company that merely kept their payroll in his bank shifted their accounts to the corporate headquarters:

> ...That payroll money was money that we could lend to our customers. We would depend on it; we knew that money was going to be here. They would keep a very good balance at all times, and the day before payday they would make a large deposit. So we would have several hundred thousand dollars that we could loan out. When they pulled that money out, it meant that much money we could no longer lend our customers (Coogan, 1980: 11-12).

The process where capital begins to accumulate on a regional level and provides the finance sector and local economy the potential for development is largely eliminated. Independents are transformed into subsidiary units. In effect, this process continues to replicate and reinforce Central Appalachia's role at the lower layers of the corporate institutional and ownership hierarchies.

What are the central impacts of drain upon the regional economy? **Low regional capital accumulation** -- The bulk of the profits or surplus ends up in core-based financial sectors. Over historical time we actually find **"decapitalization"** with capital only reinvested in the subsidiaries. There is also **conservative lending policies** in a capital starved region and the **inability to facilitate diversified growth** in the economy.

Corporate Land Ownership Patterns

Due to the character of coal as an energy commodity in the global economy and the ownership of that commodity by transnational oil and energy companies, along with corporate parents' drive for accumulation and expansion, corporate landownership patterns have tended to concentrate large and vast acreages of land and mineral rights into a relatively small number of absentee hands. Girvan notes

> These objectives frequently lead to possession of holdings far in excess of what is used by the firm over a long period of time. Such holdings significantly reduce the actual or potential national acreage held or used principally for purposes of agriculture and forestry. The same is true of the use of associated natural resource such as water and local building materials (1976: 43).

Many studies in the 1980s found both land and mineral ownership was in either absentee individual or corporate hands. In a report on land ownership in eastern Kentucky, compiled from the Appalachian Land Ownership Study by Robert Garrett of the Louisville Courier Journal, it was found that "ten large absentee corporations, all but one of them based outside Kentucky, owned 736,921 acres of surface or mineral rights, or about one-third of the combined surface-mineral land surveyed in the 12 county study." (Garrett, 1981: A-1). Again, in eastern Kentucky, over one million acres are owned by a mere 25 corporations and individuals in the 12 coal counties surveyed. Absentee ownership is a standard in eastern Kentucky, as local individuals only held 21% of the surface land. (Garrett, 1981 A-1)

In turning to West Virginia, we find a similar pattern with "50% of the surface land and about 75% of the minerals are owned primarily by absentee and corporate interests." In addition, "these companies pay only 16% of the property taxes collected." Further in West Virginia we find that "over 400,000 acres of land are owned by nine oil companies, (while) 10 million acres are leased by oil and gas companies." (Appalachian Land Ownership Study).

Hence, absentee individuals and corporations control and own much of Appalachia's mineral wealth, and two more dysfunctions in the regional industry are the **concentration of land in few hands** and **absentee corporate power over land and development.** The impact of these two dysfunctions is centrally the **lack of prime development land tracts** in the region suitable for industrial parks or industrial diversification. In a global economy, one must also take note that ownership of the mineral wealth must be free of any economic, commercial or residential development on the surface land above those minerals. In Garrett's report on the concentration of land ownership, he noted that most of the 1.02 million acres of east Kentucky land….was "devoid of development of any kind and being held for strip mining." (Garrett, 1981: A-1).

Both the concentration of land in few hands as one dysfunction, and corporate power over that land as another dysfunction has had major impacts upon decisions about the land available for future economic development. Girvan found the same problem regarding the bauxite industry in the Caribbean.

Royalty Drain

Earlier we introduced the notion of drain upon the regional economy. Two types discussed were corporate profit drain on the one hand, and corporate acquisition drain on the other. A third form of drain that spans the realms of the Parent to Subsidiary Relations and Corporate Land Ownership Patterns is royalty drain. Many of the individual landowners in Central Appalachia are not involved in coal production, but lease out vast acreages of their land to coal corporations for a fee, or **royalty**, upon every ton of coal mined. Again, we find capital, which could enrich the regional economy siphoned back to major metro-core zones. These royalties do not accumulate in the region, but again enrich the core metro financial sectors where many of the corporate and individual landholders are headquartered. In other words, a region rich in resources does not translate into an enriched financial sector. Rather, over historical time, Central Appalachia faces decapitalization.

We have now discussed three forms of Drain: Profit, Acquisition, and Royalty Drain. A synergistic impact upon the Central Appalachian economy from the combined effect of these forms of drain is simply the lack of a regional multiplier effect. The idea shared by many in the mainstream of economics is that as an industry grows and matures in a given region the outcome will be a positive reverberation through the various sectors of the society and calling into being a pluralistic array of other vertical and horizontal support industries, and finally giving rise to diversified economic development. How can we possibly hope to have a multiplier effect in a region where Profit Drain, Acquisition Drain and Royalty Drain all operate to negate any regional capital accumulation? In a nutshell, Drain operates in conjunction with the other dysfunctions and their impacts to regenerate the entire structure and system of regional underdevelopment from one generation to the next.

Political Dependency

> …The absentee owners are aided in underdeveloping the region by an infrastructure of dependency which is created through a coalition of interests involving the absentee owners and the local elite. The local infrastructure acts to protect its own and the absentee owner's interests…(Arnett, 1982: 26)

Due to the alignment of the governmental elites with institutional elites of transnational oil and energy conglomerates, we find the political sphere often serving the interests of corporate capital. Eastern Kentucky, for instance is basically a **tax-free zone for absentee individuals and corporate**

landowners. The impact here is there is a lack of monies to update and upgrade the infrastructure, social services, the educational sector, and transportation network.

In the Appalachian Land Ownership Study it was found that Pocohontas Kentucky Corporation -- which is not a Kentucky firm despite its name -- owns over half the surface land in Martin County, yet paid only 76 dollars in property taxes to the county in 1978. This is a recurrent pattern throughout the 12 county study--how is it allowed to continue? Douglas Arnett suggests a political climate of Dependency where the local and state elites work to create a climate attractive to the coal corporations. Again, returning to the land study, of the top 25 owners of more than 1 million acres of land, they paid on average, 27 cents per acre of land in taxes. (Garrett A-1).

It should be noted there have been attempts to arrest this process and try to reverse it. Despite the call from the conservative right and also in libertarian circles, if devices are left to themselves in terms of power resting with the states, we end up with a tax-free zone of dependency in central Appalachia. The ARC (Appalachian Regional Commission), however, as an attempt at "regionalized" government, accurately recognized the multidimensional "drain" problematic and instituted a severance tax on every ton of coal mined to form a base for economic development and diversification projects in local development districts of the region.

As the ARC developed in the 1960s, it followed a pattern similar to many state systems in mineral export economies of the Third World. Girvan (1976: 42) documents this pattern as attempting to use a taxation policy "structured around the resource flows from the mineral industry" to recover a percentage of profit that is consistently exported to the transnationals and their financial institutions in core zones. Sound familiar? Furthermore, the peripheral government would then utilize revenues gained from taxation to motivate expansion in the manufacturing and agricultural sectors through "heavy infrastructural expenditures designed to support and stimulate private capital" (Girvan, 1976: 42). The infrastructural expenditures included the creation, improvement, or modernization of roads, power and utility facilities, water and sewage systems, and the health and educational sectors.

In the long run, however, severance money in Appalachia was channeled into "greatest potential growth" areas rather than "greatest potential needs" areas and worked ultimately to reinforce the "drain" problem in what the ARC itself terms as *hardcore* Appalachia (Primack, 1978: 297-300). Primack contends that most residents in the region "predicted long range ineffectiveness" of the ARC "because it chose to ignore" key issues of land ownership, and the absentee based control of the region's economy (Ibid).

Compounding the dependency problem is the fact that multinationals own and operate production subsidiaries not only in central Appalachia and the U.S., but increasingly across the globe. Hence what globalization means for central Appalachia is that the region is thrust into competition with other regions in the Third and Fourth Worlds for capital investment in coal and energy production. These decisions, however, do not reside with the subsidiary firm operating in the periphery but with the corporate parents headquartered in U.S. core zones. Areas where production and labor costs are cheapest often become target zones of expansion for global corporate capital. This in turn creates a political climate approximating a "dependency" in the political sphere where elites are pressured to offer virtual "tax free" zones to the multinationals to attract capital investment (Arnett, 1982). The end result is a lack of general revenues in the political sphere for comprehensive modernization, social services and education.

Central Appalachia, then, still suffers with some of the nation's lowest educational attainment levels, skyrocketing unemployment rates, highest poverty levels, and also some of the highest out-migration rates in the nation. This then is the structural landscape of underdevelopment that the people of Central Appalachia confront generation after generation.

Conclusion

For the most part, the preceding model of underdevelopment is not applicable to Appalachia as a whole as we have previously discussed the pluralization of Appalachian in its variation even within subregions. However, this particular model is useful for mineral export peripheries in that they oft times reveal similar economic structures and social network relationships and roles. Is it useful to call the Major coal zone in central Appalachia a "periphery"? I think so, as long as the term periphery is not theoretically and methodologically deified. We must keep in mind that what is crucial in understanding regional histories is the historical spatial expression of capitalism and the clustering of various structures, networks and social relations over a given territory, and these then influence its poverty or prosperity.

In concluding, while I have called this essay a move Toward a Model of Regional Underdevelopment in central Appalachia, it is clear the future research strategy of Structural/Relational Analysis in Appalachia leaves the door wide open for much quantification to compliment more theoretical and qualitatively descriptive accounts of the subregion. Particularly in the area of the analysis of the units of industry and specifically in terms of parent and subordinate subsidiary unit relationships, there is much available for tracking and measurement. Additionally, both single industry enclave dominance and industrial instability can be measured. Surplus, Acquisition, and Royalty drain can all be statistically demonstrated. Core-based Elite, Financial, and Corporate entities can be empirically verified in terms of the amount of land and mineral wealth held. Intrafirm shipping, directed by corporate parents among their subsidiaries can also be easily mathematically captured for analysis. Finally, the financial networks can be mapped and charted, revealing the ties within the subregion to larger global financial networks. All in all, there is great promise for future Structural/Relational Analysis and Social Network Analysis in not only central Appalachia, but across the entire 13 state region—including all of its social and economic variance.

Notes from Deep Earth

[I]

Who left the miner's face black
and unattended. Under tons of carbon
unknown and to be dug up years later
sold under long-term contract
to Southern Power and Light. Rich
Coal.

[II]

I watched Consol organize an
entire human ant hill
and shook mam'aw from her sleep
when it caved in one afternoon.

[III]

Let me go down
and hear not that sound aloud
the one you know only as the ringing in your ears
and nothing more.
Let me go down and hear not that sound aloud
the one I have heard before from the outside
and wept the long Appalachian night away
over the Cumberland
and felt her hand on my shoulder in morning
saying "Come on, it's time to go."

[IV]

Sometimes in early morning
there's a soft mist rising from these hollers
that makes you think this is all a dream--
that none of it really happens
and you're just a character from the local color
of some novelist's romanticisms. Then sometimes
there's another kind of mist-- a thicker mist
rising from the womb of the mine
in the early morning of the aftermath
and you wish to God none of it really happened.

[V]

Jimmy used to bootleg Strohs out of Baker's
Holler on the side. The Sheriff knew
the Baptists knew and half the county knew.
We all know how things operate around here.
What we didn't know was that the roof would cave in
last Saturday out at the number seven mine
up at John's Creek and steal my cousin's life.
And now the Sheriff knows and the Baptists know
and half the county knows.
And we all know how things operate around here.

CHAPTER FOUR

Subsistence and Surplus Trade in the Appalachian Region, 1750-1880

Introduction

This book is not formatted historically with each chapter representing a neat series and sequence of events and developments in Appalachia. The previous chapter laid out a Model of Underdevelopment in central Appalachia's present day mineral export economy. The first two chapters, on the other hand, dealt with northern Appalachia in the southwestern Pennsylvania region, particularly the Blacklick Valley. Census statistics reveal the "central Appalachian" region as the most depressed and distressed socio-economic area with regard to its respective population. Even some of the "ghost town" zones in northern Appalachia faired better than the central Appalachian region. Aside from examining current statistics that allow us to draw comparisons and conclusions between central Appalachia, northern Appalachia, and metropolitan areas as well as the U.S. as a whole, it also begs the question of "How did it get this way?" Why did central Appalachia follow a path toward underdevelopment and peripheralization, while northern Appalachia seemed to survive the fall of the coal industry in the Blacklick Valley and other coalfields of southwestern Pennsylvania? A large part of the answer has to deal with the development of core producing status in the Pittsburgh region as well as the urbanization of nearby Johnstown region as a semi-periphery. Both these zones had a positive impact upon not only their own urban populations, but their regional populations as well. In southwestern Pennsylvania, there was a vibrant regional multiplier effect that worked historically to develop the entirety of the region.

The following two chapters look back, so to speak, to map out and provide an understanding as to the spatial expression of economic development and underdevelopment at particular geographic points. Hence, the central concern of this chapter rests with the emergence of the Central Appalachian region as a periphery from its frontier era in the 1700s until the late 1800s. The term "periphery" as utilized in this era is largely defined through the general character of **exchange** relationships between Central Appalachia and U.S. city zones. The character of these relations implies a difference in the types of commodities exchanged between these two zones, primarily agricultural goods characterizing peripheral production while manufactured goods and processed agricultural goods characterized city or core production.

Not only did Central Appalachia emerge as a periphery, but also within the region, geographic patches remained unaffected by the evolution and trade networks developing in the larger economic system. From the pioneer era of the mid-eighteenth century through the close of the nineteenth century, a sizable portion of Central Appalachia remained in the realm of self-sufficiency or "non-economy"[1] and was characterized by a pattern of small scale family farming. This pattern thrived and perpetuated itself unhindered until the penetration of metropolitan capital and the region's subsequent incorporation within the industrial system as a mineral export economy. Those portions of Central Appalachia remaining untouched also had implications in limiting the development of local towns and reinforcing the peripheral status of the region throughout the 1800s.

In order to answer the question "what caused the peripheralization of Central Appalachia," however, we must examine the general character of the economic formation surrounding the Central Appalachian region during this era. Southwestern Pennsylvania--or the Pittsburgh Region--provides one comparative case study. From 1750 to 1790 the general character of economic and social life throughout the entire Appalachian region converged. It was largely a mountainous hinterland sparsely populated with independent homesteaders involved in subsistence farming. However, toward the close of the eighteenth century, Pittsburgh developed and emerged as the principal producing and commercial center west of the Appalachians. Patterns of farming in the region witnessed a dramatic social and economic transformation where subsistence agriculture or `homesteading' broke down and was replaced with an agricultural farm economy based primarily upon surplus trade. The central methodological concern of this chapter, then, rests largely with comprehending the historical, geographic, and economic forces which operated in the Appalachian region from 1750-1880, caused intraregional divergence, and consequently geared the southwestern Pennsylvania portion of Appalachia to a developed status in the U.S. in the early 1800s, while Central Appalachia was maintained in an undeveloped peripheral state throughout the 1800s.

For instance, French historian Fernand Braudel observes, "on first sight the economy consists of two enormous areas: production and consumption..."

> ...But between these two worlds slides another, as narrow but as turbulent as a river, and like the others instantly recognizable: exchange, trade, in other words the market economy...Men's activities, the surpluses they exchange, gradually pass through this narrow channel to the other world with as much difficulty at first as the camel of the scriptures passing through the eye of a needle. Then the breaches grow wider and more frequent, as society finally becomes a "generalized market society" (Braudel, 1979: 25-26).

Once the market is established as the primary mode through which production and consumption are guided, it should not be assumed that a "generalized market society" depicts a system where all geographic areas are subordinated to the market. Braudel notes that even after a market society is firmly in command that "on the margins, and even in the heartlands of active economies, there may still be pockets, large and small, virtually untouched by the movement of the market" (Braudel, 1979: 224 -26). They are recognizable in form by characteristics such as the absence of currency, weak or few links with vital trade centers, and by a general reticence with the market economy.

A look at the principal causes of economic divergence in the Appalachian region during the 1800s allows us to approach a more comprehensive understanding of how uneven development crystallized through time and over geographic space before the era of industrialization in the region. First, we briefly examine the general economic expansion of the eastern seaboard centers in the late 1700s, setting the tone for a discussion of the general character of the Appalachian regional economy during this era. Second, the processes of development in southwestern Pennsylvania Appalachia encouraging core producing capacity in the Pittsburgh region will be highlighted. Once these processes have been mapped out, attention can be given to Central Appalachia to inquire as to whether the processes

---

1   "non-economy": Braudel speaks about how in the lack of trade and exchange there is no economy in the classic sense of the word and further notes that a number of English economists have referred to this type of self-sufficiency as "a form of life embedded" in the realm of "non-economy."

which encouraged growth and development in the southwestern Pennsylvania region were blocked, absent, or hindered in Central Appalachia. Along with this, we can then look into relevant additional factors, which may have perpetuated small scale farming over market trade and development in Central Appalachia.

Development on the Eastern Seaboard, 1750-1800

During the latter half of the eighteenth century the northeastern seaboard of Colonial America witnessed the rapid commercial and economic development of a number of city zones such as Philadelphia, Boston, New York and Baltimore (Chase-Dunn, 1980). In Philadelphia, for instance, the process of development crystallized with the emergence of the timber and iron industries as producers of raw materials. Although the primary trade flow of raw material was geared toward the European core, which in turn would flow back to Philadelphia in the form of European manufactured goods, the initial development of these industries laid the foundation for Philadelphia's later rise to a central producing status in the early 1800s in the fabricated wood and metal product industries (Stevens, 1964: 77-84). Aside from the raw material export industries, Philadelphia took the lead in the fur trade, raw and processed food exports, and in a host of other pursuits until the city ranked as the third most crucial commercial zone of the British economy; "overshadowed only by London and Liverpool" (Stevens, 1964: 77).

Key manufacturing activity emerged in the New England Colonies as early as 1770 with the development and expansion of the shipbuilding industry. This crucial factor enabled New England's cities to emerge as competitors with centers in Europe and England. The fact that "an estimated 57% of the shipping tonnage built in the colonies during 1769-1771 was sold abroad," confirms the fact that New England was far more than a commercial depot site or producing zone for the export of raw materials to the core (Chase-Dunn, 1980: 196-97).

Chase-Dunn argues that the initial development of core producing activity in the shipbuilding industry in New England resulted in capital accumulation among both merchants and producers in the colonies and subsequently laid the foundation for "the later rise of the United States to core status and world hegemony" (1980: 189).

In the hinterlands surrounding the eastern seaboard centers, the economic activity was predominately subsistence farming. The fact that a majority of the east coast rural farmers were involved in production primarily for home consumption, however, should not be confused with the notion that this class existed in isolation from the larger world economy or was "untouched by the movement of the market." Mutch's (1980: 859-60) documentation of the rural northeast emphasized the crucial role of the merchant in linking farm community to the world economy and to other farm communities as much of the hinterland surpluses gathered by east coast merchants were utilized by peripheral producers and in overseas trade. He concedes that most merchants were marginal "to the lives of the individual producers who made up the majority of the population," but he also notes that they made not only the network possible between a farm community and England but also formed the relation between city zone and hinterland. For instance, in eastern Pennsylvania, small town centers such as Lancaster, Reading, and York were connection points between local farmers from the back country and Philadelphia in the exchange of furs and surplus foodstuffs for European manufactured goods and imported articles that could not readily be obtained in self-sufficing rural farm communities (Stevens, 1964: 84). A relationship, however slight, did in fact exist between the eastern seaboard core zones and the surrounding hinterlands. As commercial development boomed on the eastern seaboard, ties with the hinterland zones were strengthened through the vested interests of local merchants and international traders in the city zones. Ultimately, the surpluses generated in the rural farm communities strengthened the volume of trade provided by merchants in the Colonies to the European Core. Later, as the import replacing process would sweep the entirety of the northeastern seaboard cities, the self-sufficient mode would increasingly break down in the rural east.

Appalachia: The Currents of Self Sufficiency, 1750-1790

Appalachia could be said to be an extension of the east coast centers' hinterland, but a more accurate analysis reveals it more as a frontier zone quite disconnected from the trade networks of the east during the 1750-1790 era. Unlike commercial development and the initial emergence of manufacturing capacity in the east, economic life at the western foothills of the Appalachian Mountains more closely approximated the realm of complete self-sufficiency (Lorant, 1980: 48-50). Paralleling the eastern seaboard, a rugged stretch of mountainscape virtually left the frontier in isolation from the east coast centers of Philadelphia, Baltimore, Boston and New York. In southwestern Pennsylvania, aside from the tri-rivers junction at Pittsburgh where a mere 400 inhabitants resided in 1790, much of the landscape existed in a self-sufficient mode while intracommunity trade acted as the primary mechanism of exchange (Lorant, 1980: 74). Farm acreage averaged close to 200 acres per farm family in the region, yet much of this was in forest with only 30-40 acres in cultivation at most (Buck, 1967: 266-67). Corn and wheat were the staple crops, and a variety of livestock were utilized in the self-subsistence setting. Buck's (1967: 271-72) figures indicate "little increase in the stock to population ratio" during the pioneer era, and with the fact that for "every hundred people in the region there were about forty horses, eighty-five head of neat cattle, and ninety-three sheep," little or no livestock were raised for market or export during this period.

The pattern of small-scale self-sufficient agriculture predominated the Appalachians. Striking similarities existed between the subsistence farm systems of southwestern Pennsylvania, western Virginia, and the eastern portions of Kentucky and Tennessee. Existing research on the characteristics of mountain farms in these portions of Appalachia indicates convergence with respect to farm size and average acreage in cultivation; in crops harvested and livestock tended; in handicrafts produced on the homestead; and in essentially weak links to eastern market centers (Lorant, 1980; Buck, 1967; Eller, 1982).

In the case of southwestern Pennsylvania, the isolation conferred upon the region by the Appalachians insured a subsistence orientation. This mode was so predominant during the pioneer era that no continuous market network existed between southwestern Pennsylvania and the east coast core producers, let alone the rest of the world economy. Intermittent market campaigns to Philadelphia were organized to combat isolation by launching expeditions on the local and village levels where gathered Pennsylvania surpluses were hauled by wagon across the mountains and exchanged for manufactured goods, spices, and other products from the east and Europe which were unobtainable in western Pennsylvania (Buck, 1967: 281-82). The isolation, intermittent market campaigns, and unstable nature of such campaigns acted in a way to spur a higher degree of self-sufficiency in western Pennsylvania than the degree of self-sufficiency witnessed in the rural northeast. Central Appalachia also converged in this respect with southwestern Pennsylvania Appalachia. Thus, before 1790, it is clear that the Appalachian frontier had yet to experience the development of any sophisticated market network through which production and consumption would be guided.

Southwestern PA Appalachia: From Subsistence to Surplus Trade and the Development of Manufacturing Capacity, 1790-1860

As early as 1800, southwestern Pennsylvania Appalachia began to diverge rapidly from the domestic production pattern that had characterized it in the latter half of the 1700s. Manufactories emerged in iron, textiles, boat building, leather, wood, brick and stone, brass and tin, and glass with an estimated product value of 350 thousand dollars (Lorant, 1980: 72). Thirteen years later in 1815 the valued product of these very same industries had risen to a little over two million dollars (see Table 4.1). In examining agricultural developments in the region, "customs records" from New Orleans reveal that close to 19,000 barrels of flour, originating in western Pennsylvania, reached New Orleans during the first six months of 1807 (Buck, 1967: 297). By 1826, the total manufactured product value of the Pittsburgh region was 2.6 million dollars, and by mid-century the predominance of the

Pittsburgh region as a principal producing and trade zone west of the Appalachians was undisputed as its manufactured product value was estimated at 27 million dollars (Lorant, 1980: 88). It is clear that from a frontier village of no more than 400 inhabitants in the late 1700s, dramatic social change had not only swept through the Pittsburgh region, but also swept through its entirety in a very short period of time.

TABLE 4.1
ECONOMIC CHANGE IN THE PITTSBURGH REGION, 1803-1815
[VALUE OF MANUFACTURED OUTPUT]

Industry	1803	1810	1815
Iron	$57,000	$95,000	$764,000
Brass & Tin	15,600	25,000	250,000
Glass	13,000	63,000	235,000
Leather	34,000	81,000	215,000

Source: Manufactured Product Values for Pittsburgh in selected basic industries are compiled from Lorant's (1980: 72-77) general findings.

One can detect two dimensions to the social and economic transformation in the Southwestern Pennsylvania Appalachian region. The first was one, which witnessed greater amounts of farmland under cultivation and a radical shift from production for consumption to production geared increasingly for export. Around this transformation, the rural farm population came less to resemble "homesteaders" (involved in all of the tasks of domestic production). Increased market dependence upon domestic commodities and other products of livelihood rendered the homesteader a "farmer" specializing solely in cash crop production.

A second dimension to the economic transformation was the development of Pittsburgh as a major manufacturing zone west of the Appalachians, supplying both travelers and new market areas in the west and south with processed foodstuffs and manufactured goods such as farm implements, glass items, and iron-related goods.

Popular as well as academic accounts focus much attention on Pittsburgh as a "Gateway to the West" and the unique tri-rivers location as the prime movers in the development of western Pennsylvania (Baldwin, 1980, 1981; Lorant, 1980). These factors along with isolation from the East, the expanding West, population changes, mineral rich surroundings, as well as other factors were the key geo-economic forces at work. What is important here, though, is how these forces or processes combined and interacted in such a way as to propel the transformation of the region.

Isolation and Traffic Flow

Isolation from the developing east coast was not sufficient reason in and of itself to either encourage the development of a manufacturing center in Pittsburgh or explain the shift from subsistence to surplus agriculture. At most, isolation was the crucial ingredient that **reinforced** the initial patterns of domestic home production. Regional isolation would, however, work with a number of other forces and aid in the transformation of the Pittsburgh region. The first of these forces to both entice the development of manufactories and a surplus pattern of agriculture was the steady buildup of migration traffic through the region after the Indian Wars in the 1790s (Buck, 1967: 286). As the westward expansion originated primarily in the east, the foodstuffs and other commodity necessities utilized by migrants were largely dwindled by the time they reached the Pittsburgh junction (Buck, 1967: 286). Milling merchants and processors of crude foodstuffs quickly sprang up in a relationship with the local farm population and gathered local surpluses at trade depot sites for travelers passing through the region (Buck, 1967: 301-303). Imported goods from Philadelphia and European core centers, otherwise unobtainable in the region, were exchanged by merchant travelers for grain and other food goods. Thus, population flows were not geared merely toward settlement patterns in the Pittsburgh region but in a flow-through traffic pattern which sustained a continual demand for local farm surpluses. Along with these developments, Pittsburgh also became a principal producer and supplier of basic manufactured goods such as nails, wagon implements, and boats that travelers desired. Isolation as a factor worked harmoniously with an increased and sustained demand by migrants for immediate needs incurred on the journey.

The River Network and Expansion in the West

Flowing from increased traffic in the region was an ever-expanding West as towns along the Ohio and Mississippi Valley areas soon became settled and populated quickly during the early 1800s. This demand, like the demand from traffic-flows, was continual and sustained, but unlike the demand from migration movements, town and community life in the Ohio Valley required a different set of commodity goods. Key **backbone industry goods** such as bar-iron, iron-related goods, farm implements, glass, stone, processed timber goods, and others were all essential to both the settlement and expansion process. Pittsburgh was well situated to act as a key supplier of these commodities due to its initial economic head start in the Ohio Valley from migration flows, isolation from the east, and easy access to these emerging market zones (Lorant, 1980: 72-77).

The expansion of the West not only enticed numerous merchants to establish themselves in the Pittsburgh region, but it also brought capital, chiefly from Philadelphia, and local branch banks soon emerged. In 1814 the Pittsburgh Manufacturing Company became the `Bank of Pittsburgh' and was largely owned and controlled by local capital (Buck, 1967: 299). The establishment and accumulation of capital in the Pittsburgh region provided the essential ingredient for manufacturing capacity which had been lacking in a primarily self-sufficing trade-by-barter region, and with regional capital formation two crucial developments emerged: First, the investment in boat building activities would tightly interconnect southwestern Pennsylvania Appalachia with its market zones along the Ohio River and river tributary regions; and, secondly, investment would flow into the emergence and expansion of infant manufactories in precisely the key backbone manufactured products demanded in the structural settlement and expansion of the West and South.

Boat building, as a key activity in southwestern Pennsylvania Appalachia, dated back to the 1790s when the Tarascon Brothers --"merchants from Philadelphia" -- set up facilities in Pittsburgh (Buck, 1967: 300). Throughout the early 1800s, flatbeds, keelboats, and even ocean-going vessels were constructed at Pittsburgh and acted as a crucial incentive for the local farm population in gearing increasing amounts of crops for export.[2] Buck (1967: 294) notes "merchants known as Kentucky Traders began to acquire stocks of provisions and other merchandize in western Pennsylvania, float them down the Ohio on flatbeds and dispose of them to the new settlers along the streams." Agricultural surplus trade, while facilitated through the stable establishment of merchants in southwestern Pennsylvania Appalachia, was also aided in part by the initiative of the local farm population. For instance, during the off season, a number of farmers exchanged part of their surpluses for boating gear and traveled the Ohio as far as Louisville to trade the remainder of their surplus (Buck, 1967: 293). This phenomenon should not go unmentioned nor should it be underestimated as a factor propelling the subsistence

---

2   Keelboats were long narrow craft some forty to sixty feet in length with a carrying capacity in between fifteen and fifty tons. Flatboats were similar in carrying capacity, while barges were much large, often measuring in between seventy-five and one hundred feet and capable of hauling much heavier loads (Lorant, 1980: 69).

oriented economy toward a transition to an agricultural trade economy in that scores of keelboats and flatbeds often manned by western Pennsylvania farmers, filled the Ohio River waters in the early 1800s--even well after the development of the steamboat in 1811 (Baldwin, 1980: 46).

At higher levels of commerce, milling merchants, as a crucial force in economic change, centralized in Pittsburgh and took advantage of both farm surpluses as well as the expansion of the boat building industry. The most notable of the early merchants to arrive in the Pittsburgh region were the Gratz Family and the Reede and Forde firm which held extensive connections with merchants at strategic points along the Ohio River Valley in Kentucky and Ohio (Baldwin, 1980: 33-34). Aside from these merchants was James O'Hara who had opened trade routes as far west as St. Louis (Baldwin, 1980: 34). The merchants, many of whom were also involved in boat building pursuits, provided the key link between an increasingly surplus oriented farm mode and the markets beyond the Pittsburgh region.

Some 600 recognized grain mills were in operation in western Pennsylvania in the early 1800s and much of the flour produced was then exchanged for commodities with regional milling merchants who entered into numerous trade networks with points as far south as New Orleans (Buck, 1967: 303). During the same era, Baldwin has documented the fact that as many as 10,000 young men were leaving Pittsburgh yearly for Louisville and points south on boats stocked with "flour and pork." (Baldwin, 1980: 4-6).

The expansion of boat building also greatly set the stage for the development of linkage manufacturing industries. As steamboat building capability emerged, the emergence and expansion of steam engine manufactories facilitated the growth of iron making and iron fabrication in the region as a vital linkage industry to boat building. From the production of the first steamship in the region in 1811, some fifty steamships were constructed in Pittsburgh between 1812-1826 and fifty more between 1826-1830 (Lorant, 1980: 89).

Manufacturing Capacity through Geographic Protection

The importance of the river network becomes even more crucial as this mechanism for the facilitation of trade was aided by the rugged geographic barrier of the Appalachian Mountains which separated the eastern seaboard from western Pennsylvania, protecting Pittsburgh's infant industries and allowing them to mature freely. A head start over other expanding cities such as Cincinnati, Louisville and St. Louis, and unhindered by any potential competition from the east, Pittsburgh was placed in a prime position to capture an extremely large market zone in the Ohio Valley, Appalachia, and the Mississippi Valley.

To be sure, when Pittsburgh infant industries emerged in the early 1800s, east coast core producers were not only matured but also engaged in competition with key European core centers. The expanding West was important in that it represented a new market to the east coast and neither distance nor terrain stopped east coast centers in their bid to capture such a market. In Philadelphia for instance, as early as 1790 pressure was put on state political elites to subsidize a turnpike to improve traveling conditions between Philadelphia and Pittsburgh (Stevens, 1964: 148-49), and yet, even with the completion of the Pennsylvania Turnpike in Pennsylvania by 1820, transportation of bulk goods to the West by overland wagon remained rugged relative to the steamship river transportation Pittsburgh enjoyed, and thus both risk and costs maintained themselves at higher levels for the east coast producers. The same proved to be true in improvements in roads from Baltimore to Wheeling with the completion of the National Road in 1818.

On the other side of the coin, Pittsburgh was free from the experience of harsh overland transportation and through the river network, could reach the western market with ease and at a cost so low that emerging competition from Wheeling, Cincinnati and St. Louis interfered only to a minor extent. In essence, the mountains acted as a tariff on eastern commodities, which might compete with Pittsburgh's infant industries, and thus allowed these industries to develop cleanly and efficiently. Census records underscore how manufacturing capacity matured in the farm implements industry in Pittsburgh. While plows "were made and exported in considerable quantity at Enfield, Connecticut," before the 1820s, Pittsburgh was well insulated to command that market thereafter. Per the U.S. Department of Commerce, Bureau of the Census of Agriculture, 1860, Introduction:

> One of the largest establishments in this or any other country, devoted chiefly to plough making, was established in Pittsburg, Pennsylvania in 1829. In 1836 it made by steam-power one hundred ploughs daily, of patterns adapted largely for the lower Mississippi, and cotton and prairie lands of the south and west...Another steam-plough factory in Pittsburg made in 1836 about 4,000 ploughs annually, including wood and cast iron ploughs, and a great variety of other kinds. These two factories together, made 34,000 ploughs yearly, of the value of $174,000.

Not only was plough making enjoying an unchallenged position in the Pittsburgh region, but the manufacture of scythes, sickles, hoes, shovels and numerous other agricultural implements were also manufactured and exported from Pittsburgh, with the Fosters and Murray Company a principal producer of such goods in the region (U.S. Department of Commerce, 1860: Introduction).

Other than farm implements, many of the commodity goods the West desired that Pittsburgh provided were bulk goods such as bar iron and glass which virtually extinguished any threat of competition for eastern producers in these industries due to problems in overland transportation of these goods. Pittsburgh, as a result of its competitive edge in these industries, would experience dramatic jumps in its manufactured product value from $350,000 in 1800 to 30 million dollars in 1850 and to 60 million dollars by 1880. Furthermore, during the early to mid 1800s specialized trade networks were strengthened between the east coast, Pittsburgh and points west and south -- another factor allowing Pittsburgh's manufacturing sectors to expand unhindered and facilitating the growth of surplus agricultural trade.

The predominant form of the trade network emerging in light of Pittsburgh's advantageous position to the West did not significantly differ from the pattern which operated during the frontier era of 1750-1800. Commodities not readily available in the Pittsburgh region, which were usually luxury items and imported goods from European centers, were brought over the mountains from the east and exchanged for bulk semi-processed agricultural goods and manufactured goods at Pittsburgh. These goods, along with some of the imported commodities, were then sent down river, either exchanged for raw agricultural surplus goods at points such as Charleston, Pikeville and Lexington or sent directly to Louisville where they were then transported to the New Orleans market. The international character of this trade network emerged when New Orleans commodities were then shipped to the West Indies where they would be exchanged for valued spices and other products, "that could profitably be imported at Philadelphia" (Buck, 1967: 293).

The trade network not only insured connection between Pittsburgh and the larger world economic system surrounding it, but it was also structured in a way that was clearly non-competitive to basic manufactories in the Pittsburgh region. With the coming of the railroads in the mid-1800s many of these circuits were disrupted while others were reinforced. Railroad transportation greatly eliminated the harshness, risk and cost of overland transportation, but the first set of tracks did not arrive in the region until 1851 and by this time the iron-related manufacturing industry in the Pittsburgh region shifted from a regional market zone orientation to a national scope as it began to lay much of the material structure of the rail system in the nation. At least 30 large foundries were in operation in the region by this time, and the advanced technology allowed Pittsburgh iron makers the flexibility to shift with the product demand establishing itself during that era (Stevens, 1967: 161).

Ultimately, while the riverways no doubt played a vital role in facilitating Pittsburgh's economic development, the overarching factor of protection from competitive center zones to the east due to the Appalachian barricade insured that demand from the West, isolation from the East, and the river network would interact unhindered to allow Pittsburgh to emerge as a crucial core producing zone in the U.S. and also encourage surplus trade patterns of agriculture among the southwestern Pennsylvania Appalachian farm population.

Indicators of Development and Interregional Divergence

By 1860, the economic divergence of the Pittsburgh region with other sectors of Appalachia was highly significant in terms of the producing status in basic manufactories. Data from the Census of Manufactories in central and southwestern Pennsylvania Appalachia in 1860, as compiled in Table 4.2, shows southwestern Pennsylvania experienced significantly heavier investments in all industries given (U.S. Department of Commerce, Bureau of Census of Manufactories, 1860). Eastern Kentucky on the other hand, while fully meshed in agricultural farming patterns, lacked any investment in the agricultural implements industries as late as 1860. The producing status of the southwestern Pennsylvania region, in that the region acted as a principal supplier of these goods to it own farm population as well as peripheral zones, is also indicated by number of establishments in these basic manufactories in 1860.

TABLE 4.2
DEVELOPMENT AND REGIONAL DIVERGENCE IN APPALACHIA, 1860

NUMBER OF MANUFACTORIES

Region	Black-Smitheries	Agri-Implements	Iron Related	Leather Goods
SW PA	151	48	106	240
Western VA	22	3	3	34
East KY	6	0	13	18

CAPITAL INVESTED

Region	Black-Smitheries	Agri-Implements	Iron Related	Leather Goods
SW PA	$72,000	$283,000	$7,000,000	$1,000,000
Western VA	7,665	5,500	20,000	143,000
East KY	2,550	0	915,000	66,000

Source: US Bureau of the Census, <u>Census of Manufactories, 1860</u>,
Washington: Government Printing Office.

Development in southwestern Pennsylvania Appalachia in 1860 can also be demonstrated by documenting the deterioration of the homestead pattern in southwestern Pennsylvania Appalachia. In constructing a 156 county data base from 1860 agricultural census data and comprised of counties in Pennsylvania, Virginia (which area would become West Virginia in 1863), Kentucky and Tennessee, an indicator of domestic manufactured production relative to total farm value was devised.[3] The

---

3   The homemade manufactured production reliance indicator is expressed in the following equation: (total county value of homemade manufactured good/total county farmvalue)*10,000. This is not a complete

population of county values was then applied to a boxplot analysis by state to compare intraregional rates of reliance on home production for domestic and capital goods in the Appalachian and Ohio Valley Region.[4] In Table 4.3, the results of the boxplots indicate the lowest rates of home manufactured production relative to total farm value in the southwestern Pennsylvania Appalachian region, which are solely comprised of counties in southwestern Pennsylvania.

TABLE 4.3
REGIONAL DIVERGENCES IN HOME MANUFACTURED PRODUCTION RELIANCE
BY STATE, 1860

HOME MANUFACTURED PRODUCTION RELIANCE

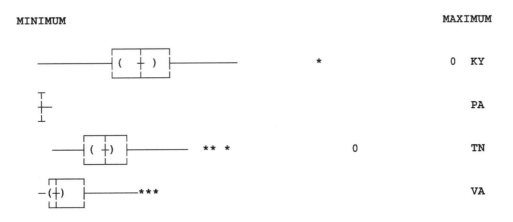

TABLE 4.4
HOME MANUFACTURED PRODUCTION
OHIO RIVER COUNTIES AND APPALACHIAN COUNTIES
1860

HOME MANUFACTURED PRODUCTION RELIANCE

```
    MINIMUM                                                 MAXIMUM

          _____
         |   (  +  )  |_____     *         0        (A)
          -----------

          ___
         |+ +|    *                                                    (B)
          ---
```

(A) ALL APPALACHIAN COUNTIES
(B) OHIO RIVER COUNTIES

---

indicator of self subsistence in that the indicator does not take into account the amount of food produced on the farm which was consumed by the residents and livestock, but it does however, provide an insight on a **homestead-type** domestic structure where use values other than food were produced within the confines of the family unit.

4   Boxplots utilized in this paper represent the median case (designated as a + symbol) for particular population groupings. Parentheses around the + indicate a confidence interval at the 95 percent level. The box itself represents the middle 50 percent of the cases. Divergence between two or more population groupings can be confirmed when the parentheses of these groupings do not overlap.

As independent manufactories expanded in the Pittsburgh region, comprehensive homestead production was limited to merely crop and livestock production for trade and export, and the farm population increasingly turned to the independent manufacturing sector in the Pittsburgh core for domestic necessities as well as capital goods required on the farm. Thus, the division of labor grew more pronounced in the southwestern Pennsylvania Appalachian region during the 1800s, and farmers became less involved with comprehensive home production and increasingly marketized, which in turn acted as one of the prime movers in promoting the increased expansion of commodity producers in the region.

Central Appalachia: Peripheral Trade Status in the Ohio Valley and Localized Development, 1790-1880

Pre-industrial Central Appalachia has consistently been characterized in popular and academic literature as a rugged mountainous region largely isolated from the world economy (Fetterman, 1970; Jones, 1975). It is here that a Robinson Crusoe family-farm stereotype has had its most successful application. While it is undoubtedly a fact that high rates of subsistence were evident in Central Appalachia throughout the 1800s, often overlooked in generalized accounts of comprehensive self-sufficiency in Central Appalachia is the crucial importance of the Ohio River trade network. Access to trade flows on the Ohio River Valley had a great influence on the breakdown of reliance upon the subsistence mode in those Central Appalachian counties that bordered the Ohio River. A prime indicator of this is expressed in Table 4.4 where counties bordering the Ohio River in Kentucky and Virginia are compared to **all** other Appalachian counties (including counties in Pennsylvania) in the 156 county database on the basis of the domestic home manufactured production indicator. The results of the boxplots in Table 4.4 indicate a general convergence with the findings in Table 4.3: lower rates of reliance on home manufacture in Kentucky and Virginia Ohio River counties. The findings also imply a greater dependence on the **general market**[5] for manufactured goods utilized on the farm and in the home place in the Ohio River case group compared to the general population of Appalachian counties as a whole.

Interregional Trade

Despite the images of isolation, there was substantial interregional trade between the Central Appalachian region and key city centers on the Ohio River. While the highland counties of Central Appalachia experienced a high level of household and intracommunity self-sufficiency, the counties bordering the Ohio River and its tributaries had access to commodity flows on the Ohio River network. For instance, in the river towns of eastern Kentucky, a number of flatboats and steamships traveled the Big Sandy River to Pikeville and Whitesburg, where manufactured goods and imports were exchanged for agricultural surpluses, ginseng, and other mountain herbs (Eller, 1982: 15).

The peripheral character of trade in Central Appalachia in relation to U.S. city producing zones emerges when one examines newspapers such as the **Kentucky Gazette** in the early 1800s. The newspaper sponsored advertisements of numerous Lexington merchants offering processed commodities and manufactured goods from the Pittsburgh and Philadelphia regions in exchange for locally produced hemp and farm surpluses. Abner Legrand, who was typical of many Lexington merchants of the early 1800s announced in the **Kentucky Gazette** that he has "just received in addition to his excellent assortment" of goods, the following (**Kentucky Gazette and General Advertiser**, September 8, 1807):

---

5   The phrase "general market"--as utilized in this paper--refers to those commodities for domestic use produced either in core centers or by independent manufactories in local towns rather than products that are produced on the homestead or acquired by localized homestead trade at the neighborhood level.

10 boxes 8 by 10 Window Glass from Pittsburgh
1 ton best Pennsylvania craftings
A complete assortment of hammered and cut nails
made of best Pennsylvania Iron
12 reams of best writing paper, from Chambersburg
Pennsylvania
etc, etc.

As much of the Ohio Valley settled in the early 1800s, its primarily agricultural nature aided the development of city-based infant industries in iron making, glass, and other sectors through this particular type of trade. Undoubtedly, the river system set the stage for Pittsburgh's prime access to merchants and settlers both on the Ohio River and within the hinterlands via the Ohio's tributaries.

Localized Economic Development in Central Appalachia

Jane Jacobs has emphasized the city building process as one of **import substitution** where a region begins to substitute the commodities it receives from producing centers with commodities it produces itself (Jacobs, 1984). A hinterland or catchment zone -- the region immediately surrounding the newly emerging town -- usually becomes the principal market for the town's commodities, which in turn generates a continued demand for greater locally produced products. Ultimately, the newly emerging town becomes a central market center and reaches a stage of full development when its own commodities are exported to other distant regions. Such was the case with Pittsburgh as we have already seen.

In the case of Central Appalachia, import substitution as the central process of economic development was limited to the iron related manufactories as indicated in Table 4.3. The development of the iron related manufactories was also localized in the northeastern-most counties of Kentucky bordering the Ohio River. While the census data on the number of manufactories and amount of capital invested are for the year 1860, the process of import substitution began as early as 1811 when iron works emerged in northeast Kentucky and were soon competing for the Ohio Valley market against iron manufactories in the Pittsburgh region. In the **Kentucky Gazette** for instance, Thomas Owings advertised a number of his agricultural landholdings for sale in an effort to raise capital to subsidize the expansion of his iron foundry. The advertisement was worded as follows (**Kentucky Gazette**, May 8, 1811):

BAR IRON

Of a superior quality to any made on this side of the mountains, and equal to Dorsey's celebrated Iron, forged to suit customers. Have but lately found this choice IRON ORE will, on application of any of my customers guarantee to CASTINGS to be of a superior quality--and the BAR IRON much superior to iron generally made in the Pittsburgh country, not inferior to Dorsey Iron.

Being desirous of increasing the Iron and Casting business in the county of Bath, I propose selling all my property in the state of Kentucky except my establishment and future residence in Bath county...

Iron and iron-related manufactories fared rather well in northeast Kentucky and although industry maturity, capital availability, and the river network gave the edge to the Pittsburgh region, in 1860 close to one million dollars was invested in 13 large iron foundries in the Kentucky region.

Forces Hindering Development in Central Appalachia

Despite the development of the northeastern Kentucky counties bordering the Ohio, along with the access to interregional trade flows in the Central Appalachian Ohio River tributary counties, comprehensive import substitution and overall regional development was largely negated in Central Appalachia due to the failure of key river towns to facilitate a transition from subsistence to agricultural surplus trade in the region and their inability to generate a stable market and catchment zone in the highland counties of Central Appalachia. In turn, the minimized development of independent and locally based manufactories structured a dependent trade relationship between Central Appalachia and key Ohio Valley producing centers where agricultural products in the periphery continued to be traded with city produced manufactured goods throughout the 1800s. If we refer again to Table 4.2, we find that as late as 1860 Central Appalachia, and eastern Kentucky in particular, lacked any significant degree of import substitution even in terms of the most basic of manufactories in agricultural implements, blacksmitheries, and leather goods.

Two crucial factors -- intraregional isolation and minimal population flow-through traffic -- operated in conjunction with the rugged topographic terrain and interacted in such way as to reinforce the predominant pattern of subsistence farming and home production in the highlands and negated the comprehensive expansion of import substitution in the river towns of Central Appalachia.

Intraregional Isolation

If a Robinson Crusoe stereotype of the subsistence homesteader engaged in all of the processes of domestic production has any redeeming merit it is to be found in the application of this model to the Central Appalachian highland region during the eighteenth and nineteenth centuries. A major factor structuring and perpetuating a farm mode characterized by a high degree of family and extended kin-oriented self- sufficiency relates directly to the topographical conditions of Central Appalachia. Eastern Kentucky, eastern Tennessee and western Virginia are all rugged terrained areas of steep mountainous slopes, which rise abruptly from the earth and have formed mazes of narrow winding valleys or hollows between them. In this type of topographical setting not only was the region separated from the outside world by a mountainous barricade, but also the mountains acted to separate communities from each other (Eller, 1982: 7):

> ...Each community occupied a distinct cove, hollow, or valley and was separated from its neighbors by a rim of mountains and ridges....Economic and social activities were largely self-contained within these geographic bowls, with individual households relying upon themselves or their neighbors for both the necessities and pleasures of life.

As time passed what often occurred was the populating of these coves and hollows by distinct kin networks. Even today we find in eastern Kentucky communities with names such as Brown's Branch, Baker Hollow, and Mills Creek denoting the convergence and binding of an extended kin-unit to a particular geographic setting. Family localism prevailed in light of the topography and the stage was set for the "absence of highly structured communities" and what emerged instead was neighborhood or hollow-based tribalism marked by a minimal division of labor and extended kin-unit cooperation (Eller, 1982: 9).

Some major routes such as the Kanawha Turnpike and Big Sandy Turnpike along with the Kanawha River in western Virginia and Big Sandy River in eastern Kentucky did provide intraregional access in the interior, but in comparison to southwestern Pennsylvania Appalachia much of the transportation in the highlands was merely "a network of trails and dirt roads" and "such roads were usually steep and often muddy and impassable in the winter and spring" (Eller, 1982: 13).

The inadequate transportation system not only oriented isolated settlement patterns in the region but also limited many mountain farmers access to key regional market points where surpluses could be sent toward the Ohio River Valley. This was a crucial mechanism in reinforcing agricultural production primarily for consumption and eliminated the potential for a major agricultural transition from subsistence to a surplus trade economy in the highland counties. To be sure, a full-blown agricultural surplus trade mode would have insured sufficient commodity purchasing power among

Central Appalachian highland farmers to reduce their dependence upon domestic home production, as was the case among Ohio River farmers. However, as long as this transition was minimized, due to intraregional isolation, the incentive for the continued reliance on homemade manufacture production remained high and acted to limit the degree of regional manufactory development in the Ohio River tributary towns in Central Appalachia. Many of the necessities continued to be produced within the confines of the family farm and the farm communities, and thus when enough surpluses were secured by the highlander to make the rugged trek into the river towns, what he often approached was not an Ohio River tributary town filled with local manufactories but an undeveloped merchant depot site containing a variety of manufactured commodities from Pittsburgh, Cincinnati, Philadelphia, and Baltimore.

Minimal Population Flow-through Traffic

The effect of intraregional isolation impacted in a general disconnectedness between the highland region of Central Appalachia and the Ohio River market network. Flowing from this factor was the negation of any significant population flow-through patterns of traffic.

In his analysis of pre-industrial Appalachia, Eugene Conti has suggested that "in the sense that a frontier means a limit, or boundary, of settlement, east Kentucky even at that early time was not a true frontier but an encapsulated region lying between the town and plantation cultures of the Atlantic Coast and the expanding West" (Conti, 1980: 53). The terrain thus structured primarily a stagnant settlement pattern whereby families and individuals "dispersed themselves over the rugged landscape" (Conti, 1980: 53) while migration flows moved predominately along the Ohio River Valley completely bypassing the harsh interior of Central Appalachia.

Thus, the crucial demand for surplus goods generated by population flow-through patterns which aided tremendously in developing the agricultural and manufactory sectors of the economy in southwestern Pennsylvania Appalachia was completely lacking in Central Appalachia and therefore little incentive existed among the highland farmers to move toward surplus agricultural production as farmers in southwestern Pennsylvania Appalachia had done. Furthermore, the lack of any substantial demand for manufactured goods in the absence of population flow-through patterns placed yet another limitation and restriction on the degree of manufactory development in the river towns which did emerge in Central Appalachia. Aside from import substitution in the iron-related manufactories in northeast Kentucky in counties that directly bordered the Ohio River, region-wide economic change was largely absent in central Appalachia.

The Absence of Import Substitution in the Tributary Towns

A key impact of these geo-economic forces at work in Central Appalachia was the maintenance of subsistence in the region. Ronald Eller's (1980: 16) work on the Appalachian region suggests that as late as 1860-80, the self sufficing family farm, where as many of the products of livelihood as possible were produced, remained of prime importance to the Central and Southern Appalachian highland economy and differentiated it from other agricultural zones in the U.S. during this period:

> The backbone of the preindustrial Appalachian economy was the family farm... Unlike agrarian sections of the Midwest and non-mountain south that had moved steadily toward dependence on a single cash crop, mountain family farms remained essentially diversified and independent, producing primarily for their own use.

Eller further adds that even by 1880, Central and Southern "Appalachia contained a greater concentration of non-commercial family farms than any other area of the nation," and that these farms "offered full support and sustenance for mountain families" (1980: 16). While not all of the Central Appalachian region can be characterized in this way, it was a predominant pattern in the more mountainous highland sections of the region, and it was in these very mountainous sections that we find a complete absence of any significant manufacturing centers and high rates of domestic home production.

We must now turn our attention to mountain counties in order to gain a more complete picture of the necessity of domestic homemade manufactured production in Central Appalachia in 1860. Compiled from the database of 156 counties, a case study of mountain counties in the eastern Kentucky and southwestern Virginia portions of Appalachia was devised to compare the reliance on homemade manufactured production in the mountain counties with other selected areas. The boxplots in Table 4.5 reveal home manufactured production reliance by county populations in comparing the mountain case study category with counties bordering the Ohio River in Kentucky and Virginia, and as expected the significance of homemade production reliance was greater in the highland region of Central Appalachia thus indicating a lessened reliance on the **general market** for these goods.

TABLE 4.5
HOME MANUFACTURED PRODUCTION
OHIO RIVER AND MOUNTAIN COUNTIES
1860

HOME MANUFACTURED PRODUCTION RELIANCE

(A) MOUNTAIN COUNTIES
(B) OHIO RIVER COUNTIES

TABLE 4.6
HOME MANUFACTURED PRODUCTION
RIVER NETWORK COUNTIES AND APPALACHIAN COUNTIES
1860

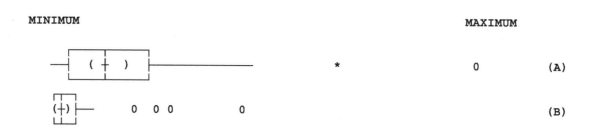

(A) ALL APPALACHIAN COUNTIES
(B) RIVER NETWORK COUNTIES

Even in a number of Ohio River tributary towns, the development of market based manufactories confronted barricades in transforming the subsistence patterns of domestic production in their own counties. In Table 4.6, domestic production reliance is compared between the Ohio River Network counties[6] and all other Appalachian counties. While the findings reveal convergence with the results of Table 4.4 in terms of the population medians of the Ohio River and river network counties, the difference between these two tables rests with the significant number of far outlying cases in the river network population. These far outliers represent river counties that experienced much higher rates of home production reliance than other river counties. Surprisingly enough, a majority of the far outliers were counties located along the Big Sandy and Kanawha tributaries of the Ohio River in Central Appalachia. In eastern Kentucky, for instance, the Ohio River tributary counties Lawrence and Pike had exceedingly higher values of domestic production than counties bordering the Ohio River, thus indicating a substantial number of local farmers with a higher degree of independence from the local market system. Ultimately, the continued reliance on domestic production in counties bordering the Kanawha and Big Sandy limited the expansion of import substitution capacity in Central Appalachia and kept development at a minimal and localized level.

From the standpoint of economic development that was proceeding rapidly along the Ohio Valley region by 1880, Central Appalachia lacked both the capital formation and the economic infrastructure conducive to development. The region, however, would not continue in an undeveloped subsistence status indefinitely. The emergence of the industrial era would bring with it the incorporation of the Central Appalachian region within the industrial world division of labor as a mineral export economy. The penetration of the rail system usurped the barricade of intraregional isolation, and the penetration of metropolitan based capital would organize a massive single industry mineral export economy. The very character of this incorporation process, however, would not signal a transition from undevelopment to development in the region, but a transition from undevelopment to underdevelopment. We will now explore the processes of this transition.

6   Ohio River Network population includes both Kentucky and western Virginia counties which bordered the Ohio River as well as counties which bordered the following river tributaries of the Ohio: Monongahela River in western Virginia, Kanawaha River in western Virginia, and Big Sandy River between Virginia and Kentucky.

Earthman

-for Byron Walker

And now here in an urban compartment
ten months and a thousand miles removed
from the reticence of Appalachia
I am still searching for the ultimate truths.
Turning up rocks, stones and theories:
in relentless pursuit of those dimensions
where seemingly unrelated and random phenomena
(in the formlessness of this complex social amoeba)
interweave and mesh at higher levels

and lost somewhere between presupposition and paradigm
I saw you wondering about
'along the edge' of Coolsville and wilderness
in scruffy hair with a blues tune for earthman.
So obvious in your unobviousness
with Hendrix blaring "Purple Haze" in one mind
and giant black pines in their own music in another.

Perhaps one day we will collectively begin to reconnect
the increasingly disconnected nature of this human landscape:
body, soul and earth.

What can I say my friend?
From the MOB reunion during Homecoming '81
when we vowed to stay sober but did not
and yet somehow managed to make it through Cabaret;
to wondering along old forgotten trailways
through the back hills of southeastern Kentucky;
to atop a rocky mountain
where we sat and watched civilization
as if it were some organic 'being' existing 'out there';
and finally to the graduation line...
Truly the best of times.

How has it changed us?
Was it merely a four-year ritual of sorts,
or did the experiences hit deeper at the foundation
of our beings?
What was it about 'being there' that made a difference
in who we are now becoming?

And still there are deeper primordial questions
on a more human level:
What pattern are we forming in this social quilt?
What design is being carved
and for whom?

70

Perhaps these questions take a lifetime to answer
or perhaps answers can be realized in a hour's conversation
over a bootlegged case of Budweiser
What is our destiny--
to be sure,
it is the 'destiny of identity' to ask such questions.

and thoughts could run onto reams and reams
of endless pages, my friend
but I want to 'save the trees' on the hillsides
so my children won't have to learn what they are
from history books
or see them waxed in some ecosystem museum for
post-modern earthman--
they will still be able to experience the wilderness of wood:
body, soul and earth.
So fewer words can say so much more:

Live long and prosper, fellow earthman;
the journey is just beginning.

CHAPTER FIVE

Subsistence Culture, Central Appalachia And Globalization

Introduction: Appalachia and a Sociology of Subsistence?

Driving along the winding mountain roads of Central Appalachia, a contemporary suburbanite might be rather surprised by the subsistence-oriented homestead pattern dominating the landscape. Also termed "domestic production," subsistence culture encompasses everything from extensive gardening, canning, keeping livestock, and crafting along with home-manufacture of tools and household goods to cultural keepsakes. The comprehensive pervasiveness of these subsistence practices woven within the structures of Appalachian life inspired the popular and ongoing twelve (plus) volume *The Foxfire Series*, a layman's encyclopedia of subsistence and folklore of the Southern Appalachians.

The phenomenon of subsistence in contemporary U.S. society, however, has been largely overlooked in sociological literature. Perhaps a major explanation for the lack of significant attention is rooted in conceptual models born from the classical period of the sociological discipline. Those at the fore of the discipline, especially those aligned with the Parsonian synthesis of the classicists, naturally became more intellectually infatuated with the progressive universalization of the market, the wage-labor/ capital relation, and the onward march of societal differentiation. The transition from Gemeinschaft to Gesellschaft, from mechanical to organic, and from traditional to rational-legal essentially involved the emergence of nations of the West into an historically-evolving Great Divide. Hence, the subsistence economy and trade-by-barter perpetuated in Appalachia were socioeconomic processes embedded in the "older" and now defunct cultural fabric of the western world, and were overlooked in the new enthusiasm of developing sociological hypotheses in the progressive societal differentiation of the West. Eastern societies and the underdeveloped Third World, however, remained critical exceptions, and it is precisely in theoretical accounts of these societal formations that a Sociology of Subsistence flourished.

Central Appalachia: Theories of Poverty and Underdevelopment

Enter Central Appalachia. While a Sociology of Subsistence was lacking, or embryonic at best, there were a plethora of theories of poverty and underdevelopment. The glaring warp of inequality and poverty in a region rich in resources and embedded in one of the most advanced capitalist social formations provided an anomaly for a substantial amount of theoretical work in the sociological discipline. Social theorists were interested primarily in offering an explanation for the condition of Appalachia -- to offer an analysis for concentrated poverty, high unemployment rates, a lagging economic region, as well as a one-industry economy. Further compounding the problem for the scholarly community was the fact that the inhabitants of Appalachia were not of an ethnic or racial origin that had been subject to a historical plight of legal, political, or civil discrimination.

Theoretical accounts emerged in the late 1950s and early 1960s centering Appalachia's problematic in particular deficiencies *internal* to the region. This Modernizationist paradigm generated both a cultural and structural orientation. The structural vein included those theorists who concentrated on topographical variables as the key cause to a region's underdevelopment. The cultural tradition, on the other hand, was composed of theorists who give priority to the meanings, values, ethos, and attitudes of a given people and how these variables influenced development or underdevelopment in a given region.[7]

From the 1950s through the 1970s, Modernizationism dominated the theoretical models with regard to Appalachia. In fact, both the cultural and structural orientations of Modernization became the foundational starting points for political strategies and government policies implemented in the region during these decades. On the one hand, the structural tradition was in fact largely fueled and given credibility by regional development strategists placing primacy on topographical and infrastructural conditions while working in coordination with the Appalachian Regional Commission during the War on Poverty years. On the other hand, the cultural wing, through focusing on the difficulties of Appalachia in the mentality or ethos of the native inhabitants, legitimized a host of social casework policies and programs implemented in the region.

The Modernization Problem

The problem with the explanations proposed by Cultural Modernizationists is that these theorists located the causes of region-wide poverty and the lack of economic diversification in what they termed the "backward" or anti-modern work-ethic values, while at the same time failing to see the actualization of modern work-ethic values in the coal industry. The crucial question these theorists should have posed was not *why the lack of a capitalist work ethic in Appalachia* but rather *why the work ethic only found its expression in the confines of the coal industry and never deviated from the mineral export sector in the formation and perpetuation of other industrial sectors?*

Development emerged in Central Appalachia, but the development was restricted to the confines of the coal industry. The failure of Structural Modernization theorists to confront the tremendous development and expansion in the coal industry led them into locating the prime cause of a lagging infrastructure, underdevelopment, and a lack in capital investment in the region in the sole factor of topography. The key question the Structural Modernizationist should have posed was not *why capital is lacking in the region for investment* but *why capital in its abundant form never deviated from the coal industry to spur diversified economic growth?* Central Appalachia's crucial problem in the present era is not non-development or undevelopment due to geography, but **underdevelopment** in that there has been tremendous growth in the coal industry without development spilling over into other economic sectors.

---

7   It is not so much that the structural and cultural orientations are comprehensively opposed to each other as it is that **strategic priority** in explaining the causes of underdevelopment is located in differing variables or components of a social formation. What has happened in many cases, though, is that strategic priority is so overweighed in either structural or cultural variables, that theorists have often seen their particular structural or cultural variables as the causal mechanism determining all else. In other words, for a cultural internalist, because there are sufficient cultural deficiencies in a given group of people, the technology, educational level, and economic structure of a society reflect these cultural deficiencies. For a structural internalist, however, the explanation is reversed, with the backward economic structure giving rise to any cultural deficiencies that might exist.

Blows Against the Empire:
Cracks in the Modernization Model

From the 1970s on through the present day, new models emerged in direct opposition to the Modernizationists. Lewis (1978), Gaventa (1980), Banks (1980), Arnett (1982), Eller (1982), Billings and Blee (2000), Matvey (1987, 2005) and others all posited the Appalachian problem in the relations between Appalachia and the wider society. The region was viewed as an internal colony, drained of profit from outside or absentee colonizers. Later works dropped the *colonization* baggage and concentrated primarily on exploitative economic relations between central Appalachia and the US economic system. Casting Central Appalachia as an *internal periphery* in the larger U.S. economic system had its roots in Lewis' (1978) *Colonialism in Modern America: The Appalachian Case*, in David S. Walls' essay entitled "Internal Colony or Internal Periphery."

Toward a Core/Peripheral Analysis of the Central Appalachian Mineral Export Economy

Primarily, the processes maintaining and regenerating underdevelopment in the modern era flow from the central Appalachian region's roles at the bottom of particular production-, exchange-, corporate organizational-, division of labor-, and ownership-hierarchies in the larger world economic system. There is, in other words, a spatial expression of capitalism with bottom layered roles and their corresponding employment constituting a "peripheral status" in the wider economic system, while regions housing the top level economic roles and their corresponding employment qualify as core zones or centers. In the following section we briefly examine core/peripheral analysis with regards to poverty and underdevelopment in the Central Appalachian region.

Throughout the history of Central Appalachia the character of relations operating to initiate and reinforce underdevelopment has changed. The initial process setting the stage for underdevelopment was primarily the result of an interface between exchange relations and topographical constraints during the 1750-1880 era. This particular interface consequently patterned the region into a trading hinterland of expanding city-producing zones along the Ohio River and also maintained a predominant subsistence farm system in the region until the close of the nineteenth century. Thus the 1750-1880 era may be considered an era of *uneven development* with respect to Central Appalachia and the larger economy surrounding the region. Principally, production was carried out within the confines of the homestead, and the trade that did emerge was one where local agricultural surplus was exchanged for manufactured goods from Ohio River city zones.

In the advent of the industrial expansion, interregional exchange relations became less significant and property and class relations the key social relationships gearing the region toward *underdevelopment*. Property relations were essentially expressed through the penetration of metropolitan capital in the region and the subsequent transfer of ownership over the land and mineral resources to metropolitan forces. As a mineral export economy formed and steadily replaced the farm subsistence system, a combination of techno-economic forces structured essentially repressive class relations between mine operators and the mine work force and led to the socioeconomic deprivation of the labor force.

Socioeconomic deprivation of the work force, however, was only one dimension to underdevelopment during the 1880-1950 era. On a broader level, the emergence of a single industry enclave in the region and the underutilization of the potential regional labor force in the capitalist division of labor set the initial stage for a culture of subsistence to persist during the industrial era as pockets of subsistence farmers were left untouched by the industrial expansion. This process will be examined through documenting census patterns of the rural farm population in the region and rates of subsistence farming among this segment of the population.

In the modern era, Central Appalachia's underdevelopment despite federal attempts to initiate diversification and development projects in the region is viewed as the combined result of the following factors: 1) the accumulation of uneven development and underdevelopment experienced in the first two eras; 2) profit draining parent/subsidiary relations at the level of economic institutional relationships; 3) dependent political relationships; and, 4) the instability of the mineral export industry with regard to the utilization of the regional labor force. These factors reveal Central Appalachia occupying roles in the modern era at the bottom of production, division of labor, corporate organizational, and ownership hierarchies.

A core/peripheral approach thus allows us to view undevelopment, uneven development, underdevelopment and the development of underdevelopment at particular times in a region's history. As these social relations are mapped out we can then take any variable or socioeconomic indicator and offer analysis based on the crucial social relations uncovered in the core/peripheral analysis.

Revisiting a Culture of Subsistence

The history of Central Appalachia is a history of peripheralization with respect to the larger world economy surrounding it. The question at this point relates to how we integrate a Sociology of Subsistence under the broader core-to-periphery theoretical umbrella. As we have talked about poverty and underdevelopment, we now turn to "subsistence culture" in Central Appalachia. Modernization models lend themselves to conceptualizing "subsistence" as a manifestation of "backward" collective mindsets or stalled culture. From a core-to-periphery model, however, subsistence culture, and the persistence of it in the modern era, is not viewed from the standpoint of cultural backwardness, but rather a dynamic adaptive mechanism of a people in relation to the structural landscape of economic underdevelopment they confront generation after generation. In the following sections we will explore: a) the historical roots of subsistence culture grounded in the pre-industrial period; b) continued pockets of subsistence flourishing due to the incomplete transition of the region to capitalism as well as distortions in the industrial transformation; and, finally, c) the reaffirmation of subsistence culture during the Great Depression era.

1) The Material Roots of a Culture of Subsistence

A virtual storehouse of research exists on the impacts of the industrial transformation of Central Appalachia (Banks 1980a, 1980b, 1983; Caudill, 1963, 1983; Corbin, 1981; Eller, 1982; Gaventa, 1980; Lewis, 1978). Documented in these works are the penetration of metropolitan capital in the region, the emergence of the coal industry in southern West Virginia, southwestern Virginia, eastern Tennessee and eastern Kentucky, and the reorganization of community life in the structuring of coal towns and coal camps. The subsistence farm formation of Central Appalachia was hit hard in those counties where coal production was rapidly organized. The loss of farmland, as documented in Table 5.1, was most pronounced among major coal producing counties during 1900-1930. Harlan County, for instance, had yet to experience significant amounts of coal production as late as 1910 and correlative to this fact was only 9.8% loss of farmland between 1900-1910. By 1929, however, Harlan County had become the leading coal producing county in Kentucky and the impact upon farming was clearly evident with the loss of 67.6% of the county's farmland between 1900-1930. Overall, the major coal producing region of eastern Kentucky lost 36.7% of its farmland between 1900-1930, while the minor coal zone only witnessed a 14.4% loss in farmland. High rates of land loss were not limited to eastern Kentucky, but a general process that impacted upon the entirety of Central Appalachia. Table 5.2 highlights farmland lost for the states of West Virginia, Virginia, Tennessee, Kentucky as well as the major and minor or non-coal counties within these states. The consistencies in land loss in the major coal region strengthen the contentions and research historians have already made on the transformation of the region.

TABLE 5.1
FARMLOSS IN EASTERN KENTUCKY, 1900-1930

County	% Land Loss in Farms 1900-1910	1910 Coal Production	% Land Loss in Farms 1900-1930	1929 Coal Production
Major Coal			36.7	
Bell	31.6	2.068 mt	58.4	2.8 mt
Floyd	3.8	.053 mt	32.4	4.88 mt
Harlan	9.8	----	67.6	14.1 mt
Johnson	1.2	.154 mt	14.0	1.24 mt
Letcher	5.2	----	32.5	6.58 mt
Perry	+1.7	----	21.1	5.80 mt
Pike	+1.7	.551	35.5	7.2 mt
Minor or Non Coal			14.4	
Breathitt	0.0	.024	9.9	.204 mt
Knott	+8.7	----	17.2	.425 mt
Laurel	8.1	.212	20.7	.530 mt
Leslie	2.1	----	23.9	NA
Magoffin	+17.1	----	+3.1	----
Martin	4.0	————	19.9	.353 mt

Source: U.S. Department of Commerce, U.S. Bureau of the Census, Census of Agriculture,1910, Table 1--Farms and Farm Property, Counties 1910,1900; and Census of Agriculture,1930, Volume III, Part II, Table 1--Farms and Farm Acreage 1930 and 1929 by Type of Farm. Washington: Government Printing Office.

TABLE 5.2
FARM LOSS IN CENTRAL APPALACHIA, 1900-1930
(IN MILLIONS OF ACRES)

STATE/REGION	NO. OF COUNTIES	LAND IN FARMS 1900	LAND IN FARMS 1930	LAND LOSS 1900-1930
TENNESSEE CENTRAL APP:	ALL	20.342	18.003	11.5
MAJOR COAL	6	.940	.623	33.7
MINOR/NON COAL	6	1.158	1.044	9.9
WEST VIRGINIA CENTRAL APP:	ALL	10.655	8.802	17.4
MAJOR COAL	9	1.399	.883	36.9
MINOR/NON COAL	9	2.005	1.714	14.5
VIRGINIA CENTRAL APP:	ALL	NA	NA	NA
MAJOR COAL	5	1.087	.851	21.7
MINOR/NON COAL	5	1.232	1.082	12.2
KENTUCKY CENTRAL APP:	ALL	21.979	19.927	9.4
MAJOR COAL	7	1.574	.996	36.7
MINOR/NON COAL	6	1.082	.927	14.4
CENTRAL APP	53	10.476	8.122	22.5
MAJOR COAL	14	2.627	1.668	36.5
MINOR/NON COAL	39	7.850	6.455	17.8

Source: U.S. Department of Commerce, U.S. Bureau of the Census, Census of Agriculture,1910, Table 1--Farms and Farm Property, Counties 1910,1900; and Census of Agriculture,1930, Volume III, Part II, Table 1--Farms and Farm Acreage 1930 and 1929 by Type of Farm. Washington: Government Printing Office.

Of crucial interest is the minor coal zone where rail penetration and the organization of mineral production had yet to invade the existing structures of everyday life. In Table 5.3, for instance, the percent of the population defined as rural farm in the major coal-producing zone of eastern Kentucky and southern West Virginia mirrored national rates from 1930 through 1950, indicating the impacts of industrialization on the farm mode. In the minor coal zone, however, over 50% of the population still resided in rural farm areas as late as 1950.

One point of emphasis is the fact that a majority of the rural farms did not witness a transition from subsistence to cash crop farming in the incorporation period. They remained subsistence oriented, as had been the case in the pre-industrial era. Data in Table 5.4 indicate this pattern. As late as 1930, over 73% of the farms in Central Appalachia were defined as either self-sufficient or part-time farms.

Another method which can be utilized, as an indicator of the character of farming during the industrial era is to document the percent of total farm income derived from the value of farm products used by the farm household. Table 5.5 reveals a solid family farm pattern with 75% of eastern Kentucky's and southern West Virginia's farm income derived from the value of farm goods produced for home use.

TABLE 5.3
RURAL FARM POPULATION AND LABOUR FORCE IN MINING
1930–1950

REGION	1930 POP.	1930 %RURAL FARM	1940 POP.	1940 %RURAL FARM	1950 POP.	1950 %RURAL FARM
U.S.		23.0		24.6		15.3
S. WEST VA./						
E. KENTUCKY	1.123	29.8	1.293	31.6	1.409	21.9
MAJOR COAL	.901	21.4	1.034	23.0	1.151	15.5
MINOR COAL	.222	64.0	.258	66.0	.258	50.6

REGION	1940 LABOUR FORCE	1940 %IN MINING	1950 LABOUR FORCE	1950 %IN MINING
U.S.	45.166	2.0%	56.239	1.6%
S. WEST VA./				
E. KENTUCKY	.335	37.0	.382	37.3
MAJOR COAL	.256	44.0	.291	41.0
MINOR COAL	.078	14.3	.091	22.6

Source: Compiled from following Sources: U.S. Bureau of Census, Census of the Population, 1930 Volume III, Part I, Table 12; and County Data Book, 1947 and 1952, Tables 1 and 3; Items 21-32. Washington: Government Printing Office.

TABLE 5.4
CHARACTER OF FARMING IN CENTRAL APPALACHIA
AND OTHER SELECTED REGIONS, 1930

REGION	NO. OF FARMS	% FARMS SELF SUFFICIENT	% OF FARMS PART TIME	% FARMS SELF-SUB& PART TIME
US	6.288	8.0	5.0	13.0
MID ATLANTIC	.358	6.8	11.8	18.6
PENNSYLVANIA	.172	9.3	12.3	21.6
SOUTH ATLANTIC	1.058	13.3	7.6	20.9
EAST SOUTH CENTRAL	1.062	13.9	5.0	18.9
CENTRAL APP COAL REGION	.048	53.5	19.5	73.0
TENNESSEE	.246	21.9	6.6	28.6
C.APP COAL	.009	46.5	13.0	59.5
VIRGINIA	.171	25.9	12.9	38.7
C.APP COAL	.010	47.7	16.4	64.1
WEST VIRGINIA	.083	39.5	16.6	56.1
C.APP COAL	.013	49.4	23.4	72.8
KENTUCKY	.246	28.6	7.7	36.3
C.APP COAL	.015	65.4	22.2	87.5

Source: U.S. Department of Commerce, U.S. Bureau of the Census, Census of Agriculture, 1930. Volume III, Part II, Table 1--Farms and Farm Acreage 1930 and 1929 by Type of Farm. Washington: Government Printing Office.

TABLE 5.5
PERCENT OF COUNTY INCOME DERIVED FROM
VALUE OF FARM PRODUCTS USED BY FARM HOUSEHOLD
1940

REGION	VALUE OF FARM PRODUCTS SOLD TRADED OR USED BY FARM HOUSEHOLD (in millions of dollars)	%OF FARM INCOME DERIVED FROM VALUE OF FARM PRODUCTS USED BY FARM HSLD.
U.S	41,254.979	NA
S. WEST VA./ E. KENTUCKY	15.424	74.4%
WEST VIRGINIA (major& minor coal	8.406	70.0%
E. KENTUCKY (major& minor coal	7.018	80.0%

Source: U.S. Bureau of the Census, County Data Book 1940, Tables 1 and 3, Items 54,61,62. Washington: Government Printing Office.

2) The Problem of Embeddedness: Distorted Differentiation

Contending high rates of subsistence farming in the minor coal zone continued due to the lack of intensive mineral production only offers partial explanation for this phenomenon. There were a number of other critical forces enabling small-scale family farming to persist among the majority of the population in the minor coal zone and at recognizable levels in the major coal counties. The first of these factors constituted a depressed demand upon the potential regional labor force in Central Appalachia. Aside from the expansion of mineral industry at strategic geographic points in the highland counties, the enclave character of the mineral economy generated a relatively minimal region-wide multiplier effect.

The character of authority relations in the emerging coal towns essentially acted to control and regulate consumption between both the mine work force and the coal subsidiary units operating in the region. With reference to the mine work force, in a region, which was dominated primarily by small-scale subsistence agriculture before the penetration of capital, the emergence of a wage labor force represented the most crucial purchasing power in the Central Appalachian economy. This purchasing power acts as key incentive to spur the development of potential producers of needed commodity goods which were once produced within the confines of the family farm, which in turn leads to an intensified differentiation in the regional division of labor.

In Central Appalachia, however, purchasing power was not turned loose upon the regional economy, but locked within the self-contained enclave of the company town. In fact, in many coal towns nationally coined currency was completely irrelevant as the miners were paid in scrip (Caudill, 1983; Gaventa, 1980; Hevener, 1978; Simon, 1981). The scrip system, or company coined currency, operated to lock the miner into a feudal-like relationship with the company overlord. As services and charges were deducted from his wages, the remainder was often issued in scrip and only "redeemable at the company-owned store, service station, restaurant, and recreation clubs" (Caudill, 1983). Many commodity goods purchased by mine laborers were produced in metropolitan centers in the U.S. and shipped to the company-owned retail outlets in the region. This is not to indicate that if purchasing power was completely freed that all domestic commodity goods would have been produced within the regional economy. Sectional and national chains would have operated in a similar core-to-periphery fashion. The essence of this point, though, is authority relations of the company town system forced fusion between the mine workforce and metropolitan produced commodity goods, thus lowering the potential and incentive for significant development of regionally based commodity producers, as well as lowering the region's ability to attract commodity producers to locate in Central Appalachia.

Above and beyond this factor, the exploitative character of pay relations and pricing (Simon, 1981) negated opportunities for savings among the labor force; however, this issue is essentially muted by the forced operation of the scrip system.

At higher levels of consumption, which are even more crucial to diversified economic development in a given region, the purchasing power and consumption of the units of industry must be taken into account. The multiplier effect at this level of consumption unfolds in response to the expansion of the coal industry in Central Appalachia. As the industry expands, a number of input goods are needed and thus the potential and incentive for linkage and support industries to the principal industry expands with the expansion of the coal industry.

In Central Appalachia, however, the emergence of the coal industry was not an indigenous development, but a metropolitan-induced and metropolitan-organized process. The metropolis not only supplied the capital for the initial emergence of the mineral industry, but also as manufacturing developed in the metropolitan centers, much of the input requirements for capital goods and capital equipment in the mineral export economy were also supplied by metropolitan producers—often at the discretion of the corporate coal parent. Thus, metropolitan-owned subsidiary units felt little incentive and had little control in promoting the development of a viable linkage support sector in the region. By 1930, Pittsburgh and Chicago had become principal producers of mine equipment and machinery not only for coalfields in Pennsylvania, Ohio, Indiana, and Illinois, but the southern fields as well.

The impact of the regulation of consumption through the enclave-oriented coal camps and towns stifled the potential for other forms of economic development in the region. Couple this with concentrated landownership patterns in the region and we find that Central Appalachia emerged during the incorporation era as a single industry mineral export economy heavily dependent upon the metropolis for manufactured products as well as domestic commodity goods. On a region-wide scale, the enclave development of a single industry economy exerted a depressed demand upon potential labor outside those areas immediately affected by the expansion of the mineral industry. Stimulating little diversified economic development in turn negated the draw upon the small-scale farm population in the minor coal region as few opportunities were born for types of wage labor other than in the mineral industry.

3) The Problem of Embeddedness: Industrial Instability

Problems in development extended beyond the depressed draw on the potential regional labor force. A second critical force maintaining ties with subsistence in the region resulted from distortions in the stability of the existing division of labor. Two central manifestations of these distortions were the instability of employment in the mining sector and the negative impact of the Depression years upon the mineral industry. While large-scale vertically-integrated operations did offer a degree of long-term security, in many instances the cyclical upswings and downswings for the scores of mid-size and small-scale coal operations in Central Appalachia rendered complete dependence upon the mineral industry a futile decision for the mountaineer. Ties to the land, homestead, and kin, as Melvin Profitt explains in an autobiographical sketch, offered an alternative solution:

> In this year of 1922 we bought a wagon and a pair of mules; after crops was over I did a lot of hauling for other people that didn't have teams...by 1922, almost all saleable timber had already been cut out, and there wasn't much of a market for ties anyway. The few belly mines near Helechawa hired a few men, but they couldn't sell their coal at all times and they only paid a dollar a day for labor at that. About all that was left for the laborer was to raise his own hogs and hominy (Jackson, 1975).

While the lifestyle of one individual would hardly seem representative, the exceedingly high rates of part-time farms documented earlier in Table 5.4 underscores the fact that alternating between wage labor and subsistence or utilizing subsistence to compensate for low wages paid by the mineral industry was indeed a common pattern rather than an exception to the rule.

Regional histories can be likened to a stage for the unfolding of social relations and the transmission of cultural and material orientations from one generation to the next. The long haul of subsistence in Central Appalachia's history offered both a cultural and material orientation of endurance, survival, and regeneration. Industrialization, however, did not. Instead, it proved unreliable, especially during the Depression years when the market collapse generated a return to the land among a sizable number of mining families. Salstrom (1984) documents the fact that "between 1930 and 1935 the number of farms rose from 82,640 to 104,747" in West Virginia and the "number of people living on farms increased by about 114,000." Furthermore, he notes, by "1939 when 32.6% of the country's census reporting farms said that home-consumption by humans and animals utilized over half of their total production, the figure for West Virginia was 82.4%."

Among many mining families who returned to the land, the Depression signaled a reconnection with origins; a reunification of the present generation with the wisdom embedded in the longstanding historical orientation of subsistence in the region. For those who had alternated between the wage and subsistence mode during the incorporation period, the Depression years merely constituted an intensification of subsistence practices and intracommunity trade as Melvin Profitt explains:

I had very little money by this time, so I got to work and planted a garden; I cleaned up three or four acres of land and planted it in corn...1931 was a good season and most everybody that [put] out stuff had good luck with it...The year of 1932 found folks doing the same thing that they had done for so many years, plowing and planting and trying to make enough food to take them through another year...

Now it was coming winter of 1932. I had a pretty good bunch of hens, a big dommer rooster, a cow...I'd managed around and traded for an old horse; I gave two loads of coal, four 'possum hides, a steel trap, two pumpkins and a bushel of walnuts... (Jackson, 1975).

The Depression years, in a nutshell, acted as a conditioning force re-emphasizing the importance of subsistence to inhabitants in the region. The greatly lowered living standards not only stabilized the subsistence population but also enticed a segment of the mine work force to return to the land and kinfolks still involved in farming. It was this fundamental historical juncture where orientations such as the sense of place, land and kin established during the 1750-1880 era would be reaffirmed rather than eliminated. While the Depression represented the failure of industrialization to sustain the continued expansion of the commodity market, the land and homestead, traits of self-sufficiency and intracommunity trade, and the cooperation required among extended-kin became Appalachia's saving grace.

Probably the most extensive elimination of subsistence as an alternative lifestyle pursued in conjunction with the cyclical upswings and downswing of the coal industry occurred in the latter part of the 1950s and early 1960s. Renewed national attention at the levels of the polity, academia, and media stressed the concept of regional modernity in the highway network, industrial, community, housing, and educational sectors. A flood of welfare transfer payments, food commodity goods, and social caseworkers were channeled into the region. One latent function of the War on Poverty in Appalachia was the destruction of the subsistence lifestyle as the primary adaptive mechanism to underdevelopment in the region. Adaptation was transformed into a collective dependency upon the State for income and commodity goods, and in turn, the region moved more firmly within the mainstream universal market orientation. An end result of the welfare state in Appalachia has been the erosion of subsistence and intensified collective dependence upon the universal commodity market.

Appalachian Subsistence as Culture

In the cultural-symbolic system of Appalachia, there are at least three currents lending themselves to the continuation of subsistence practices in the region. The first consists of the extended cultural heritage of subsistence evident in the Central Appalachian highlands. As previously discussed, the pre-industrial condition of undevelopment, the incomplete transformation of the region to wage labor capitalism, and the Depression Years all had a tremendous impact on preserving a subsistence mode. The embeddedness of these orientations and traditional practices over the long haul of the region's history has shaped and molded the symbolic significance of domestic production among the generations of the modern era.

A second cultural current flows from the first and can be identified as a struggle to preserve particular practices and traditions as a means of reaffirming and asserting one's identity and heritage in the modern era. For Plaut (1979: 268), due to relations that have evolved between rural Appalachia and the industrial world over time, principally the development of the coal industry, there are "two sociocultural systems at work in the rural areas of Appalachia." The first system, Plaut contends, is the traditional system approximating "the **gemeinschaft** of Tonnies typology" and marked by "the relatively small human group bound in kinship and tradition to a rather well-defined piece of geographic territory in which the cycle of life repeats itself in a relatively conservative fashion" (1979: 268). The second sociocultural system is, of course, the modern world characterized by "large, complex, specialized, and hierarchical forms of social organizations found in urbanized, industrialized areas today" (Plaut, 1979: 269).

Plaut recognizes that "to suggest" the gemeinschaft system "still exists as a **social system** in Appalachia is distorting if not romantic." He notes that "there have been too many changes in patterns of ownership, marketing, production and media contact, and migration to suggest that isolated, self-sufficient human communities still operate in remote mountain coves," but Plaut goes on to contend:

> ...the **cultural value preferences** born of such social systems still do exist in contradistinction to the preferences of the cultural systems of the "modern" urban world that surrounds the region (1979:268-69).

Plaut, however, fails to give us comprehensive reasons why these value preferences continue other than the fact that a traditional pattern tends to "repeat itself in a relatively conservative fashion."

Precourt (1983) and Batteau (1983) move a step further by contending that self-sufficiency and domestic production are the manifestation of a social relationship struggling to survive. Batteau (1983: 24-29) notes that "the craftsman, carefully making baskets and chairs out of oak and walnut and hickory bark" represents "those social relationships which have endured, which form the mountain community, and which provide the most important meanings in life for those who were born, raised, and still reside in rural Appalachia." Precourt (1983: 93) urges us to understand that for the Appalachian farmer, domestic production is much more than an economic activity in that such practices were born from an era when subsistence was submerged in a "total system of social relationships and values." Thus the presence of domestic production is a material action orientation constituting part of a much broader struggle on the part of the Appalachians to preserve their identity, meanings, and values that have endured from the distant past. It is not that we have to conceptualize Central Appalachia as a landscape of two distinct sociocultural systems as Plaut suggests, but as **part of** the broader American cultural context which has always placed a high premium on the preservation of traditional heritage despite the fact that the market often usurps and tends to destroy older practices, traits, and meanings through its dynamic of expansion and change. In this view, domestic production is but one material dimension of the process of preservation. Other traits, habits, and traditions, which have endured, constitute the broader spectrum of dimensions of this same process.

Finally, a third cultural current reinforcing domestic production represents the ongoing functions of sociality, moral solidarity, and a common social bonding these practices manifest in the modern era. As a case in point, Wigginton's (1972) insights on the culturally comprehensive nature of "quilting-bees" -- where female kinsfolk and neighbors gathered to produce quilts -- offer us a view of the sociality acting to reinforce this particular material practice:

> ...The simple fact is that quilts were handmade by people for people. Every phase of their production was permeated by giving and sharing. From the trading of scraps and patterns and the actual production in "bees" to the giving away of the final finished work, quilting was an essentially human activity...

> ...Grandmothers made at least one for each of their grandchildren to keep, and then pass on. A belief grew up that, "If a young girl slept under a new quilt, she would dream of th'boy she was going to marry" (Wigginton, 1972; 143-144).

On a broader level, annual crafts festivals are a part of mainstream Appalachian social life. Festivals such as the Daniel Boone Festival in Barbourville, Kentucky, the Dogwood Festival in Knoxville, and the Berea Arts and Crafts Festivals are week-long events in which mountain residents, independent retailers, schools and other organizations all come together in a social setting built upon the selling and trading of garden production and arts and crafts artifacts. Festivals are a crucial expression of sociality and social reinforcement--a reinforcement that centers itself in domestic production.

Subsistence Culture in Central Appalachia

In this chapter we have looked at subsistence practices as cultural responses to underdevelopment. At their heart, they free up the scarcity of income for the household by substituting anything from extensive gardening to home manufacture, thus allowing cash income to be directed toward the market for other commodity goods.

While subsistence practices are still evident at recognizable levels in the region as was noted at the outset of this chapter, in the era of globalization, there have been several additional cultural responses by Appalachia in relation to the larger global economic system surrounding it. At one time subsistence culture in the manifest form of various crafts and home manufacture were produced in the confines of the family homestead. These goods in the global era, however, are now marketed as commodities across the U.S. and to the world at various craft expos and shows, the World Wide Web, and regional tourist spots-- all as authentic representations of Appalachian culture.

Several of the core tourist zones of subsistence culture such as Berea, Kentucky, and Gatlinburg, Tennessee, have grown in popularity where craft and home manufactured goods are marketed to the population at large. For instance, state political elites, most effectively in Tennessee, recognized and capitalized on this phenomenon. In conjunction with national parks and state development projects, the communities of Gatlinburg and Pigeon Forge were rather successfully, in the past half-century, integrated in the mainstream market system as major tourist centers of Appalachian culture. Crafters, quilters, wood workers, keepsake producers, cabinet and cabin builders found a high demand market among flow-through tourists, and have become successful entrepreneurs, and in some cases, capitalists, in the region. The development and success of *Dollywood* echoes the continuing efforts to market the mountain way of life to America and the world at large.

In marketing *economic culture*, or more specifically, *subsistence culture* to the world at large, we confront a gray area that I would phrase the "crafter-capitalist" or "heritage-salesman" syndrome. Does the practice of producing craft goods qualify as *subsistence culture* once domestic production is transformed into mainstream economic activity and the goods are rendered commodities on the market? Home manufacture, once the *antithesis* of the market economy is, in the global era, transformed into ready-made commodities for sale on the market. What appears to be most certain is the individual's ability to capitalize on the very process that separated one from the mainstream market in previous historical eras.

Another avenue of the heritage-salesman syndrome as globalization marches on, we find "subsistence culture" is marketed to the world at large via the WWW by regional entrepreneurs. Again we find capitalist entrepreneurs readily marketing craft goods gathered, in part, from the regional population.

Ultimately, whether craft and subsistence culture is consumed by the household, traded in the local community, or geared toward the universal commodity market, I would suggest such practices be viewed as something active, dynamic, adaptive, culturally reflexive, and value generating. It is not, as some have suggested, a stalled, backward, or *Yesterday's People* phenomenon, but rather a continued unfolding of the Appalachian cultural reserve employed and engaged by the inhabitants of the Appalachian region.

Subsistence culture in other words, and what little of it is left in the present era, can accurately be viewed as the manifested outcome of the confluence of both structural and cultural currents that, in turn, impact upon Appalachia's sociocultural landscape (Matvey 1987). It is not merely the structural forces of core/peripheral systems that shape Appalachia, but it is rather a material and symbolic cultural response of a given population confronting and interacting with those underdeveloped regional structures. It is simply an adaptive and dynamic cultural strategy—in this case a strategy of cultural subsistence. Over time, this vibrant cultural strategy has become the region's cultural heritage, and in some cases, its saving grace.

Sketches of Memory

Here in the coastal flatlands of Carolina
some years later
are only traces of you, Appalachia--
anecdotes, incidents, and episodes embedded
in the sketches of memory

and now I perceive
how you were more than region, place
or even state of mind--
but rather a constellation of human relations
meshed in a rich context of
homestead, coal train, mountain dialect
and the hollow's morning mist

here in the flatlands of the pee dee region
some 8 years later
the context remains a fact in present perception
but the relation is diluted

between then and now i migrated
among the towering superstructures
of inner city;
through the affluent conversational blur
of suburbia;
among the tiny rural markers of American civilization;
and waded in the shipwreck of theoretical logic and jargon;
seeking attachment and commitment in the
concerns of common folk;
wondering through the wisdom of ancient eastern cultural
traditions...

always, however
returning to your finest backdrop,
the acclivity of eastern Kentucky--
how deep
these habits from the heart.

and yet, now returning only to discover
i've spent much of my personal consciousness
trying to recapture a set of interrelationships
which no longer exist--
played out only once on the stage of reality

here now, in the solitude of backdrop
what can you teach me,
Appalachia
here in the wooded hills
here in the silence of your character—
it has taken 8 years to learn your first lesson

CHAPTER SIX

Globalization and Contemporary Collective Spiritualities:
The Development of Buddhism and The Growing Appeal of Eastern Spiritualities in U.S. Society

> "…Buddhism is a path of supreme optimism, for one of its basic tenets is that no human life or experience is to be wasted, abandoned, or forgotten, but all should be transformed into a source of vibrant life, deep wisdom, and compassionate living. This is the connotation of the classical statement that sums up the goal of Buddhist life: "Transform delusion into enlightenment." On the everyday level of experience, Shin Buddhists speak of this transformation as "bits of rubble turn to gold…." (Unno: 2002, Shin Buddhism: Bits of Rubble Turn to Gold).""

Part One: Globalization and Buddhism in America: A Three-Pronged Approach

One peaceful effect of the globalization process appears to be the penetration and subsequent growth of Buddhism in U.S. culture. Throughout much of the modern period a First World Nation like the U.S. exported its religions to a variety of Second and Third World nations, but since the second half of the twentieth century, Buddhism has arrived from the East and set up shop. We will now explore the development of Buddhism in the West.

In 2000 there were a little over one million Buddhists in the U.S. It sounds like a small number compared to the hundreds of millions of Catholics and Protestants, but it represents a growth rate of 170% over 1990 in terms of the number of adherents in the U.S. Buddhism is generally very sectarian, but when we examine its integration in U.S. society, we find both a rich historical and multidimensional process. We will explore these forms of integration now, but let us open by noting that globalization has played a major role in Buddhism's development and expansion, especially over the last 40 years.

Buddhism has taken root in U.S. society through a three-pronged process. These are not necessarily sequential or historical prongs, although they may give the appearance as such. What we can say, to be sure, is that the globalization process affects all three prongs. The first we will term Traditional-

Sectarian Buddhism, predating the WWI period, followed by Globalizational-Sectarian Buddhism beginning in the 1960s-70s, and finally through Post Modern-Syncretism which involves a blending of Buddhism with other religious traditions.

Traditional-Sectarianism (1900s-1970s)

In this first wave of Buddhism we find Shin and Nichiren Shu Buddhist churches and temples mobilizing to support the spiritual needs of the Japanese and Japanese-American Buddhist communities in the U.S. These two forms of Buddhism represent the largest of Buddhist sects in Japan and followed the emigration of Japanese to Hawaii and then the West Coast of the U.S. throughout the early era.

U.S. Buddhism since the pre-WWI period up until the 1970s primarily served and mirrored the Japanese American community. In the post WWII era, after internment of the Japanese-American ended, the bulk of Japanese communities returned to the West Coast, but several scores of communities sprang up in the Midwest and Eastern U.S. zones.

The history of the Cleveland Buddhist Temple reveals one example how the opening of the Temple met the needs of a post-WWII Japanese Buddhist community in Cleveland:

> "During the period of 1943-1944, Japanese-American Buddhists who resettled in this area after being discharged from internment camps strongly desired to gather and practice the Buddha-Dharma in their own temple.
>
> "On January 7, 1945, the Cleveland Young Buddhist Association was dedicated. At this time services were being held at a Unitarian church and in the homes of members.
>
> "In 1955 a building was purchased on East 81st Street in Cleveland, but it was heavily damaged in the Hough riots of August 1966.
>
> "With financial assistance from Buddhist temples and individuals throughout the United States, the present temple on East 214 Street and Euclid Avenue was acquired in 1968. The main building and the minister's residence were extensively remodeled by temple members.
>
> "In May of 1970 a grand dedication service was held. The gate of the temple is now open to anyone wishing to seek refuge in the Buddha's teachings." (http://samsara.law.cwru.edu/~cbt/ Cleveland Buddhist Temple: History of the Temple)

Today, in Shin Buddhism, the BCA (Buddhist Churches of America) oversee some 100 temples, groups and/or organizations in the U.S. The bulk of temples are located on the West Coast, and the following is a statement on its beginnings made by the BCA headquarters:

> "Shin Buddhism first reached the Kingdom of Hawaii in 1889 with the arrival of the Rev. Soryu Kagai of the Honpa Hongwanji Temple, Kyoto, Japan, who was sent to serve the needs of the Japanese immigrating to the Hawaiian Islands.
>
> "Some ten years later, in 1899, Reverends Shuei Sonoda and Kakuryo Nishijima were dispatched from the Honpa Hongwanji to San Francisco, California, to minister to the growing Japanese population on the mainland United States.
>
> "Within a short time thereafter, Shin Buddhist temples and groups were established throughout the West Coast.
>
> "During World War II, the Japanese American population on the West Coast was moved to United States government-established relocation centers or relocated to non-security areas of the Midwest and Eastern parts of the country. This led to the establishment of Shin Buddhist temples in the major population centers east of the Mississippi River.

"Today, there are more than 100 Shin Buddhist temples, branch temples, fellowships and groups which comprise the Buddhist Churches of America." (BCA Web Page: The Beginnings at http://www.buddhistchurchesofamerica.com/aboutus/beginnings.shtml)

The BCA maintains a directory of Shin temples in the U.S. and of these, 22 have websites that define the individual history of their respective temples. An examination of the 22 Shin temples reveals a rich history of Buddhism in America as it related to the pre-war, war and post-war periods. Some temples trace their history to the late 1800s, with many more mobilizing in the early 1900s. In terms of Traditional-Sectarianism, temples sprang up throughout the pre-war period, and many of those relocated to internment camps during the war era, returned to California and the West Coast and reestablished their temples after the war. Of the 22 temple websites sampled, the average year of the birth of a Shin temple or mobilization for a Shin temple was 1921. (For a list of Shin temples please see: http://samsara.law.cwru.edu/~cbt/bcadir.html)

Globalizational Sectarianism (1960s-Present)

One major difference between the Traditional and Globalizational Sectarianism is embedded in the organization framework of the religious entity. In Traditional-Sectarianism we find the scope of the entity was national with a small overseas bureau tending to immigrants in other nations. As a group settles and evolves, the overseas bureau sets up temples to serve the community's needs. In Globalization Sectarianism, however, the religious entity takes on a global scope, headquartered in a home nation but vertically and horizontally integrated across the globe in a number of host societies.

A second crucial distinction between Traditional and Globalizational Sectarianism is target group for propagation. Whereas Traditional Shin and Nichiren Shu arose in service to developing Japanese American communities on the West Coast, other forms of Buddhism like Zen, and the Nichiren Shoshu Soka Gakkai primarily looked to a growing population of Americans as adherents.

Globalizational Sectarianism penetrated the U.S. in the 1960s-70s through either the establishment of strict sects imported from Japan, including several Zen schools on the one hand, while on the other we find American or European individuals being trained in Japan and then returning as priests to propagate to curious Americans.

Early Zen spread through the development of monasteries and Zen centers. Shunryu Suzuki's experience is one such example.

"Already a deeply respected Zen master in Japan, Suzuki-roshi came to America in 1959, intending only a short visit. But he was so impressed by the quality of "beginner's mind" and the seriousness he found among Americans interested in Zen that he finally became a permanent resident, making his home in San Francisco. Through people wanting to join him in his practice, the meditation group called Zen Center came into being and, under his abbotship, grew to three major locations, including Zen Mountain Center, the first Zen training monastery outside Asia...." (Back Cover: Zen Mind/Beginner's Mind)

Another example of the early penetration of Zen: In 1970, Shasta Abbey, a Soto Zen Seminary and Monastery opened its doors in Northern California. Its history details one route Globalizational Sectarianism took in the early 1970s:

"The Order of Buddhist Contemplatives is dedicated to the practice of the Serene Reflection Meditation tradition, known as Ts'ao-Tung Ch'an in China and S t Zen in Japan. The Order was incorporated in 1983 by Rev. Master Jiyu-Kennett to serve as

87

the international umbrella organization for the monasteries, priories (local temples), and meditation groups led by priests of our lineage in Britain, Canada, Germany, the Netherlands, and the United States.

"A British-born Buddhist master trained in Malaysia and Japan, Rev. Master Kennett came to the United States in 1969. A year later, Shasta Abbey, a Buddhist seminary and training monastery, was founded in northern California. In 1972 she founded Throssel Hole Priory, now Throssel Hole Buddhist Abbey, in the U.K. Rev. Master Kennett served as the first Abbess of Shasta Abbey and Head of the Order until her death in 1996." (http://www.obcon.org/)

From Shasta Abbey's opening in the early 1970s, we can now find Zen temples, monasteries, and centers from a variety of schools and sects all over the American religious landscape.

Around the time Zen took off in U.S. society, the Nichiren Shoshu Soka Gakkai was taking root in major metropolitan centers throughout the U.S. and brought the teachings of the Nichiren Shoshu priesthood to the country. It experienced periods of rapid growth. One of its major goals was propagation primarily targeted upon Americans as well as Japanese-Americans. The group was not limited to the West Coast like Shin or Nichiren Shu Buddhism, but was an organizational development spanning throughout the U.S.

Globalizational Sectarianism here includes those forms of Buddhism that became international religions, associations, and groups -- far more than a religion with an adjunct overseas bureau. Internationally, the Soka Gakkai grew in leaps and bounds, with 11 million adherents worldwide, a number comparable to the worldwide membership of the United Methodist Church. We find that Zen flourished as well.

We should also point out that the growth and success of Zen and the Nichiren Shoshu Soka Gakkai had a tremendous impact upon the Traditional Sectarian Buddhism of Japanese Americans. Shin and forms of Nichirenism such as Nichiren Shu are now increasingly developing and expanding their mission movements, temples, and churches throughout U.S. society. Americans are now being ordained as priests in Nichiren Shu and returning to propagate in their home regions. One of those newly ordained American priests has developed a Sangha, or congregation, in Lexington, KY -- far from the more Traditional Sectarian West Coast. In a globalizing world, in order to survive, there is pressure to take the steps toward mobilizing as a global religious institution.

Post Modern-Syncretism (1970s to Present)

Of all the Buddhist traditions that have been the most successful in the U.S. since the 1970s, Zen is by far miles ahead. Irrespective of whether it was incorporated by Americans or Japanese priests, Zen not only came to the U.S. in its sectarian form but the nature of its practice, comprising breathing meditation, allowed one to add this meditative form to one's original religion, in much the same way as one would add yoga to one's daily life. This is the first dimension of syncretism. One did not throw away their original religion such as Judaism and Christianity, but added the meditative techniques upon the foundation and, hence, formed a kind of personal hybridization of the religions. It became increasingly possible to speak in terms of being or becoming a "Christian Buddhist" or "Judaic Buddhist." In the book Beside Still Waters, Jews, Christians, and the Way of the Buddha, Christians and Jews describe how they implemented techniques of Buddhism on top of their existing religions. Living Zen/Loving God is another example of how Zen was incorporated into one's existing religion. Finally, Boykin's Zen For Christians: A Beginner's Guide offers several chapters on adding and applying Zazen breathing meditation to one's own religion.

We also find syncretism in the works of Thich Nant Hanh, a Vietnamese Zen Buddhist priest. His books, Going Home: Jesus and Buddha and Living Buddha/Living Christ are a spiritual blending of the two central deities: The Buddha and The Christ. This is another form of blending or adding that does not require one give up on one's original religion such as Christianity while learning a reverence and respect for the Buddha. In <u>The Good Heart: A Buddhist Perspective on the Teachings of Jesus</u>, by the Dalai Lama, we find a manuscript offering an "historic interfaith encounter" between Christians and Tibetan Buddhists as the Dalai Lama delivers his perspective on the Gospels.

A point I wish to make here before concluding, is that these first two forms of hybridization are created with only two religious practices--the original religion and the adding of Zen, Tibetan or other Buddhist faiths. In addition, these forms of syncretic Zen are more liberalized and open than Zen schools with a strong sectarian blend. They differ from the more traditional Zen sects and monasteries that require the adherent to denounce former religious commitments in joining a more orthodox path of sectarian Zen.

There is yet a third way, regarding post-modern syncretism, and probably the most watered-down path, but a valid spiritual path, nonetheless. This third way includes the New Age Movement borrowing elements, deities, and doctrine from Zen and then mixing them along with a hodgepodge of dozens of other religions and spiritualities.

Part Two: Buddhism: Practices, Deities and Scripture

The major traditions or sects in the U.S. for Buddhism include Zen, Shin, Nichiren Shu, Soka Gakkai, Nichiren Shoshu, Tibetan, and "devotees" of the Bodhisattva Kuan Yin. Let us examine a number of these traditions and sects.

Shin Buddhism

In Shin Buddhism the Buddha Amida is the supreme Object of Worship. Amida while still a Bodhisattva made 48 vows with regard to helping others attain Buddhahood. One vow in particular revealed that he would not attain Buddhahood himself until he had saved every being that called upon his name. This became known as the Primal Vow. (see Dr. Alfred Bloom's Shin Dharma Net for an introduction to Shin Buddhism: http://www.shindharmanet.com/)

There are three central sutras in Shin Buddhism: Larger Pure Land Sutra, Smaller Pure Land Sutra and The Contemplative Sutra. Sutras are like gospels in the Christian definition, clusters of teachings, parables and stories of the Buddha. These sutras deal specifically with the vows Amida made when a Bodhisattva and also a description of the Western Paradise, similar to the Western notion of Heaven.

In the Larger Pure Land Sutra, the 18th vow is regarded as the key Primal Vow made by Amida.

> (Primal Vow) (18) If, when I attain Buddhahood, sentient beings in the lands of the ten directions who sincerely and joyfully entrust themselves to me, desire to be born in my land, and call my Name even ten times, should not be born there, may I not attain perfect Enlightenment. Excluded, however, are those who commit the five gravest offences and abuse the right Dharma. (Dr. Bloom's Shin Dharma Net: The Forty Eight Vows).

Shin Buddhists generally chant various prayers along with the mantra "Namu Amida Butsu" or "Na Man Da Bu." One major poem chanted is the Shoshiinge, while three others are Sanbutsuge, Juseige, and Jinirai.

As noted earlier Amida Buddha is the Object of Worship. In terms of the Butsudan (Buddha's House) is an altar with either a scroll image or a Standing Amida Buddha with 48 rays of light emanating from him, which symbolize the 48 vows.

Perhaps two of the most down to earth accounts of the essence of Shin Buddhism are the works by Taitetsu Unno. In <u>Shin Buddhism: Bits of Rubble Turn to Gold</u> and <u>River of Fire/River of Water</u>,

Unno examines the depths of Shin Practice, most notably the distinction between "Self Power" and "Other Power," akin to the Christian notion of Good Works and Grace. Finally, in <u>Zen Shin Talks</u>, by Sensei Ogui we also gain a flavor of the distinctiveness of Zen and Shin on the one hand, and the blending of spiritual ideas across these two sects on the other hand.

Nichiren Shu

Unlike Shin Buddhism where Amida Buddha of the Western Paradise is the central object of worship, Nichiren Shu venerates the original Shakyamuni Buddha – the historical Buddha from India who is said to have attained enlightenment sitting under a Bohdi tree. Under the Nichiren Shu umbrella, the central object of worship is a scroll known as the Gohonzon, which is a blend of Chinese, Japanese, and Sanskrit calligraphy describing the Lotus Sutra's famous Ceremony in the Air. This Ceremony, described in the Lotus Sutra, gathers tens of thousands of Bodhisattvas and Buddhas in mid-air above the earth, reveals the Buddha's eternal enlightenment, and entrusts Bodhisattvas of the Earth to carry out propagation in the future era of Mappo.

In the 13th century, the child who would become the man Nichiren was born in a fishing village in Awa province in Japan. From his humble beginnings, Nichiren became a Buddhist priest and a prolific writer, eventually expounding strict adherence to the Lotus Sutra as the truest form of Buddhism. Nichiren was the first to inscribe the Gohonzon and many Nichiren Shu members utilize a copy of a Nichiren-inscribed Gohonzon in their home practice, setting up home altars where the Gohonzon is enshrined.

In Nichiren Shu, Buddhists chant texts/stories from the Lotus Sutra. Generally the 2nd and 16th chapters of the Lotus Sutra are recited along with "Namu Myoho Renge Kyo" -- the central mantra of the Nichiren sects. Namu here, means "devotion to" while "Myo Ho Renge Kyo" is the title of the Lotus Sutra, which will be examined shortly.

Soka Gakkai, Nichiren Shoshu

From 1960 to 1990 in the U.S., the Nichiren Shoshu priesthood and Soka Gakkai lay organizations were vertically integrated as a global religious entity. The Gakkai sent hundreds of devotees to a variety of metropolitan areas in the U.S. to propagate the organization. As adherents joined in leaps and bounds, not only were Gakkai community centers constructed, but also temples of the Nichiren Shoshu priesthood took root in several core metropolitan areas.

Unlike Nichiren Shu, in the Fuji school encompassing both the Soka Gakkai and the Nichiren Shoshu, Nichiren is elevated to the status of **true original Buddha**. Here, Shakyamuni is looked at or is perceived as merely an historical figure. Like Nichiren Shu, the central object of worship is the Gohonzon. In Nichiren Shoshu, housed at the head temple in Japan, is what is termed the Dai Gohonzon inscribed by Nichiren himself, while temples and individual members practice with copies of the Gohonzon inscribed by successive High Priests of the Nichiren Shoshu. The Dai Gohonzon, like the Gohonzon worshipped by the Nichiren Shu, contains the description of the Ceremony in the Air; however, the main emphasis is upon the Gohonzon embodying the Enlightened Life of the Buddha Nichiren. Centrally, practitioners chant to fuse with this enlightened life of Nichiren to attain their own personal enlightenment. Since the 13th Century Japanese Priest Nichiren is elevated to status of original Buddha, unlike Nichiren Shu and its affiliates, there are no statues of Shakyamuni integrated with the Gohonzon in temples or on believers' home altars.

The believers of the Fuji school see fusion of the calligraphy Nam Myoho Renge Kyo down the center of the Gohonzon representing the "Law" of the universe, while on the other hand is the signature of "Nichiren" at the bottom center of the Gohonzon, representing the "True Original Buddha." According to Fuji tradition this represents a fusion of the Person (Nichiren) and the Law

(Nam Myoho Renge Kyo). As adherents chant to the Gohonzon, they learn to tap into this Law of the Universe through summoning their own Buddhahood from the depths of their lives.

In the Fuji school, the Lotus Sutra and writings of Nichiren are viewed as central doctrine, and here, as with Nichiren Shu, the main sutras that are chanted are the 2nd and 16th chapters of the Lotus Sutra. The chant is Nam-Myoho-Renge-Kyo differing from the utilization of "Namu" in Nichiren Shu.

The Soka Gakkai and the Nichiren Shoshu split in the early 1990s, a comprehensive and complete split, though both groups continue to accept the validity of the Dai Gohonzon. As a result of that split, the Soka Gakkai utilizes a Gohonzon for its members transcribed by the 26th High Priest, Nichikan Shonin – an historical High Priest with whom they have no political-religious differences. Nichiren Shoshu views this as heresy and utilizes Gohonzons transcribed by the 67th High Priest, who is the current High Priest of Nichiren Shoshu.

Another point of emphasis, the Nichiren Shoshu consider themselves as the only orthodox version of the teachings of Nichiren. The sect has a long-standing dispute with Nichiren Shu that dates from the passing of Nichiren in the 13th century. The relatively recent split with the Soka Gakkai in 1990s, whereby the organization of the Gakkai was excommunicated from the Shoshu, reinforced notions of orthodoxy in the Nichiren Shoshu group.

Zen Buddhism

There are literally hundreds of variants to the Zen tradition. The wide variety of Zen not only makes it a thorny issue for analysis, but it differs radically from the other forms of Buddhism we have discussed thus far.

First, there really is no central object of worship in Zen Buddhism. Upon visiting temples and Zen centers, one may find an elaborate altar area with a statue of Shakyamuni Buddha. However, not all Zen temples and centers display statues of Buddhist deities. Some temples and centers are bare rooms with mats for sitting and meditating. This is usually termed "bare bones Buddhism" where the focus is strictly on meditative practice.

Practice here widely differs from Shin, Nichiren Shu, and the Fuji School. While the focus of Shin and Nichiren is sutra and mantra chanting, and while some Zen sects do recite and chant sutras, the primarily practice is upon breathing and silent meditation. Meditation focuses the mind by learning to sit silently and detach or dispel unwanted thought patterns. The goal is mindfulness of every moment irrespective of the activity involved. In some Zen sects there is not only sitting silent meditation, but also "Walking Meditation" and "Work Meditation." An excellent guide to the Zen path and practice can be found in Rev. Daizui MacPhillamy's Buddhism from Within: An Intuitive Introduction to Buddhism, and also the famous Zen Mind Beginner's Mind: Informal Talks on Zen Mediation and Practice by Shunryu Suzuki.

Kuan Yin in Buddhism

We have, up until this point spoken only of sectarian Buddhism. As we have seen, various sects have differing objects of worship, such as Amida with Shin, Shakyamuni with Nichiren Shu, and Nichiren with the Soka Gakkai and Nichiren Shoshu. There is, however, more to the Buddhism that penetrated U.S. culture and developed and that is to be found in the female Buddhist deity, Kuan Yin.

For a religion so sectarian, with vast differences in doctrine and practice, Kuan Yin is a deity who touches many forms of Buddhism. In Zen we find monasteries and temples with her statue or portrait displayed. In China's Pure Land sects she is one of three deities to be venerated and an integral part of the central object of worship.

Kuan Yin's appeal, though, has more to do with how the masses receive her into their homes rather than whether the local temple displays her icon. She is, essentially, the hearer of the cries of the world.

Kuan Yin occupies the concern of the 25th chapter of the Lotus Sutra. There, as a Bodhisattva, she is ready to rescue people from all disaster and distress. She is given a powerful role in the healing and eliminating of suffering. As a deity in the Lotus Sutra, she is endeared to all those sects who venerate the Lotus Sutra, with the exception of the Fuji school, where she is barely even mentioned. In Shin, she is endeared due to the fact that Amida was her teacher, and the central object of focus in Shin is Amida.

In one sense Kuan Yin does not have a home in Buddhist Japan. She is more the folk heroine accessible to all adherents of all sects, but rarely the central figure of a Buddhist sect. It is more common to find a statue or portrait in Asian homes along with the offering of incense to her image. She makes an appearance in Buddhism and tells people, "I'm listening," and when the adherents try to reward her through offerings she defers and asks them to be given to Shakyamuni and other Buddhas.

Only if we look at China do we find a more sectarian resemblance of the Bodhisattva, Kuan Yin. In China, high in the mountains on the island of Pu Tao Shan are temples erected which venerate her as the central figure of worship. Pu Tao Shan Island is a Mecca for millions who follow and worship the Bodhisattva. Before the Cultural Revolution there were hundreds of temples built to Kuan Yin, where she alone was the object of worship. Today some have been rebuilt, and these temples attract adherents/tourists from across the globe to worship. (see Kuan Yin, Palmar and Ramsay p. 30-36 and Kuan Yin, Chun Fang Yu, Chapter 9)

Kuan Yin has been introduced into U.S. culture in a number of ways. First is through the folk religion of Japanese, Chinese and Asian Buddhist communities. In the same way many American homes have garden or indoor statues of Mary, some Asian homes have altars and statues of Kuan Yin. A Vietnamese friend once stated that when Kuan Yin's icon is displayed it must occupy the highest space in the house when other icons are present. Kuan Yin adherents do not actively recruit followers -- the way Kuan Yin is diffused is through interpersonal contact between those of Asian communities and mainstream American society. If communities are closed and there is little social contact, the probability of Kuan Yin diffusion is very low.

Another method through which Kuan Yin has spread is through society's contact with Buddhist monasteries, seminaries, Buddhist retreats, and temples that may have the Bodhisattva on display.

Still, further diffusion has been through New Age Movement. Essentially the New Age Movement stripped Kuan Yin from all her Buddhist baggage and recast her as a "Goddess." There she becomes part of the vast array of deities, gods and goddesses of the New Age Tradition. For those who actively seek her, there is the possibility they may find the rich Buddhist backdrop to which she is intimately related.

Although propagation may be minimal, especially in comparison to the headway made by the Zen and Nichiren Shoshu Soka Gakkai from the 1970s on, word of the Bodhisattva will eventually spread.

The Lotus Sutra

The Lotus Sutra is the central scriptural text for all Nichiren-based sects, including Nichiren Shoshu and the Soka Gakkai. The Lotus Sutra contains not only the story of Kuan Yin's saving powers from suffering (Chapter 25), but also several parables revealing how Shakyamuni Buddha helps sentient beings attain enlightenment.

There is, though, at the heart of the Sutra, in Chapter 16, a radical idea of enlightenment that appears to place this teaching at odds with all the other teachings and sutras of the Buddha's lifetime. In the very beginning of Chapter 16, the Buddha reveals the essence of his enlightenment:

At that time the World-Honored One, seeing that the bodhisattvas repeated their request three times and more, spoke to them, saying: "You must listen carefully and hear of the Thus Come One's secret and his transcendental powers. In all the worlds the heavenly and human beings and asuras all believe that the present Shakyamuni Buddha, after leaving the palace of the Shakyas, seated himself in the place of practice not far from the city of Gaya and there attained annuttara-samyak-sambodhi. But good men, it has been immeasurable, boundless hundreds, thousands, ten thousands, millions of nayutas of kalpas since I in fact attained Buddha hood.

Suppose a person were to take five hundred, a thousand, ten thousand, a million nayuta asamkhya thousand-million-fold worlds and grind them to dust. Then, moving eastward, each time he passes five hundred, a thousand, ten thousand, a million nayuta asamkhya worlds he drops a particle of dust. He continues eastward in this way until he has finished dropping all the particles. Good men, what is your opinion? Can the total number of all these worlds be imagined or calculated?"

The bodhisattva Maitreya and the others said to the Buddha: "World-Honored One, these worlds are immeasurable, boundless--one cannot calculate their number, nor does the mind have the power to encompass them. Even all the voice-hearers and pratyekabuddhas with their wisdom free of outflows could not imagine or understand how many there are. Although we abide in the stage of avivartika, we cannot comprehend such a matter. World-Honored One, these worlds are immeasurable and boundless." (http://www.sgi-usa.org/buddhism/library/Buddhism/LotusSutra/text/Chap16.htm)

What is the crucial point? Clearly that the enlightenment of the Buddha is boundless and eternal. The Buddha who once taught that he achieved enlightenment sitting under the Bohdi tree, now tells us that the time passing since he in fact attained enlightenment is incomprehensible. The figures he gives are as googles of numbers so vast as to overwhelm and bewilder the mind to the conclusion that the Buddha's enlightenment occurred in the infinite past.

This "time" of the Buddha's enlightenment is beyond the appearance of humans on the earth, beyond the creation of the waters, beyond the creation of the earth, beyond the creation of the heavens, beyond the creation of the cosmos, and the Big Bang. Before all this was the enlightened wisdom of the Buddha.

Many Buddhists will say that "Buddhism is atheistic," but the fact of the matter is the Lotus Sutras suggests if not a God-like being, then a cosmic being of some sort whose wisdom (enlightenment) is infinite and everlasting. Buddhists will not call this a soul as much as they will point to the eternal life force of the Buddha's being, but this is all semantics due to the fact that we find an "intelligence" in the infinite past.

Buddhists also believe in an underlying law, laws or cause of the universe. Some sects see this as the unchanging eternal essence of reality. The Soka Gakkai, for instance, believes that chanting the mantra Nam Myoho Renge Kyo, will bring one in rhythm with this law or these laws. Nam Myoho Renge Kyo is defined as the ultimate life force in the universe.

This is not so far off from some of the more radical versions of Theistic Metaphysics that see an "intelligent" power in the laws of the universe before, during and after the Big Bang. They claim in experiments with light and photons, both as a particle and a wave, reveal a wisdom in its workings. In Lee Buaman's <u>God at the Speed of Light</u>, are several descriptions of "light" experiments that back up the notion of intelligent design.

It may be true that Buddhists do not believe in "God" or a Creator of the Cosmos, but nevertheless, as followers of the Lotus Sutra, they must recognize the cosmic nature of the Buddha's eternal enlightenment. Was he a cosmic being or a merely cosmic force? Was he an incomprehensible wisdom that has guided the development of cosmos and life on earth, or is he part of the pantheistic notion that "God" is everything? In this case the Buddha is everything, including all laws of the cosmos, all enlightened beings.

Part Three: The Attraction of Eastern Religious Organizations

Introduction

When we examine the Judaic-Christian backdrop most Americans are born into, socialized within, and reach their adult stage in, we find a significant minority of our young exploring and examining eastern religions, schools of thought, or spiritual organizations. Clearly before the global age, about the only contact Americans had with the East was through either karate schools grounded in Japanese culture, and yoga classes emerging from India. The cultural floodgates, however, opened, perhaps most notably, in the late '60s and early '70s as eastern philosophy and thought began to take root in the States.

As we have seen, these entities range from Zen Buddhism to organizations that utilize mantra-chants such as the Japanese-based Soka Gakkai, Nichiren Shoshu, Nichiren Shu, Shin, or Indian-grounded meditative religions. Along with these is the recent surge of Tibetan-oriented spiritual organizations. In addition, author and Vietnamese Zen Monk Thich Nhant Hanh, who wrote the bestseller ***Living Buddha/Living Christ***, has attracted thousands of Americans at speaking engagements, as has the Dalai Lama from Tibet, who has also done whirlwind tours of the U.S. in the last several years. While all of these avenues have widened, particularly in an era of Globalization and in our growing love affair with the East, cultural contact has gone far beyond the taste for foreign food, evolving toward contact with the wisdom and spirituality of the East among America's youth.

What is the attraction of the East? There are, in my estimation, at least seven central reasons for the appeal eastern organizations and religions have upon our youth. These include the attraction of the cultural sales pitch, the attraction of the social and cultural "new," the attraction of the ritual, the attraction of a daily practice, the attraction of the life-learning experience and mentorship, and finally, the attraction of an honest sense of social belonging.

First, of course, is the sales pitch. Essentially this is the packaging and giftwrap of the eastern philosophy. The fact of the matter is that this philosophy or organization comes as a gift, freely offered, and, like the Biblical apple, filled with knowledge and wisdom. Primarily, this gift wrap, so to speak unfolds during an introductory meeting where other Americans stand up and give honest experiences of their lives before they entered the organization, the benefits of the practice, and how their lives have changed since they became part of the new philosophy. I call it a "cultural" sales pitch because at its heart it deals with a cultural gift, and is often quite attractively packaged. Coupled with the sales pitch is often a celebrity icon such as Richard Gere in Tibetan Buddhism, who acts to legitimize the organization to youth who subsequently make the connection between the particular religious organization and the celebrity. In the Soka Gakkai for instance, group leaders are always reinforcing the notion that "Tina Turner and Herbie Hancock" chant and are members.

The first attraction flows into the second and deals with the attraction of the "new." What I am referring to here is the opportunity of a brand new beginning. In the particular organization are a new group of friendly faces ready to attend to every question, every need, and every request of the inquisitive minds showing an interest in the organization. The attractiveness of a group of new friends is also coupled with a new philosophy or worldview. The organization not only has friendly faces but all of the answers to life's most difficult questions. "Why am I here," "Why was I born to the family

I was born to," "What is the meaning of life," and among a litany of others, "what is the secret of happiness?"

Buddhist or Eastern organizations that excel here have in their packages, the answers to all of these questions, and youth who have struggled with these questions against the backdrop of American culture, often take refuge in schools of thought or organizations who provide these answers.

The third and fourth appeals deal with the ritual and repetitive nature of the daily practice at the core of the group. A significant number of Americans have always been drawn to ritual. Consider the 50 million plus Catholics in the country—the mass, with the exception of the weekly homily—is grounded in a hour long ritual that is repeated weekly. For more intensive Catholics is the Rosary, a ritualistic mantra-based 25 minute daily ritual that a number of Catholics practice. Many eastern oriented organizations offer a mantra. In Buddhist organizations in particular is the reading of the Buddha's sutras, often in melodic chants and repeated on a daily basis. The Soka Gakkai and other Nichiren-based Japanese religious bodies chant the mantric phrase "Nam-Myoho-Renge-Kyo" in addition to the sutra chanting of the 2nd and 16th chapters of the Lotus Sutra. In fact, the phrase "Nam-Myoho-Renge-Kyo" is so much at the core of their practice the entire organizational configuration is constructed upon and around the chanting of that phrase. Chanting the phrase promises to bring good health, material benefits, and good fortune to anyone who practices. The fact that these practices are not only rituals, but rituals embedded in a daily practice, work to intensify the spiritual experience in young Americans. The ritual is viewed as something essential and good, leading to a positive life experience, and often repeating this practice twice-daily works to reinforce the joy of the Spiritual in the life of the practitioner.

The fifth and sixth central reasons for the growth of eastern-oriented religious organizations are the offerings of an ongoing learning experience and the reinforcing role of mentorship. The long and the short of the fifth reason rests with the fact that unlike Judaic-Christian religions, eastern organizations, particularly Buddhist organizations are often, in addition to being religions, full-blown educational schools of thought. These schools offer a not just set of beliefs and answers on life's questions, but a life-long learning experience. There is, in other words, a progression toward enlightenment or "Buddhahood" as one enters and then progresses on the Buddhist path. There are, then, rewards for sticking with and developing one's practice. It is an ongoing growing experience. And finally, coupled with the learning experience comes the opportunity to take over the process of socializing and teaching new members. This is a point where members are now fully socialized into the worldview and philosophy of the organization and now take over as leaders and managers of the organization. We say this process is reinforcing due to the fact that leadership and teaching in the organization forces a fusion between the individual and school of thought.

Finally, a latent effect and also the seventh reason for the attraction of eastern schools or religious organizations, is the sense of social belonging offered to members who make the group their life choice. "Belonging" in the sense that not only has the organization provided answers, friends, fellowship, reinforcing ritual and daily practice, but belonging in the sense of one's finding one's way in the world. In many of these organizations the outside world is taught to be and viewed as "dreadful and dangerous," and this world often exists in an "evil" state. Hence, the organization buffers the individual/global relationship from the evil, offering a comfort zone in identity and culture that provides at its heart, a sense of belonging.

The Changing Nature of Membership in Eastern Religions

Who joins organizations from the East? At one time, sociologists as well as Christian Apologists felt only distressed youth became part of eastern religions or cults. They theorized that these individuals must be unstable, lack values, have a weak core or hold little belief in traditional American religions and organizations, that they were, in fact, odd or at odds with American Society and "drifted" into dangerous cults. This particular view has now become defunct due to several emergent social facts in the culture at large.

First, the globalization process is now well underway and works to bring, particularly through the Internet, a diverse array of ideas, values, worldviews, philosophies, beliefs, and schools of thought in contact with American society. Especially in a free democracy competing ideals and ideas can take root and develop without restriction.

A second reason rests with the migratory evolution of Buddhism in particular, and eastern thought in general. For a long time, it was considered that Buddhism began in the country of India, and migrated from west to east where it finally took root and became the central religion of Japan. From India, to China, to Korea to Japan, was part of the evolution of Mahayana Buddhism that took a northern route east. What is happening today, though, is the spread of Zen and Nichiren and Shin Buddhist sects from Japan in the east to the west including Europe and the US. Christian missionary movements to Africa and Asia are only one migratory movement, and from West to East, while the sheer number of Japanese, Tibetan and Vietnamese Buddhist movements from east to west have become quite popular in the globalized age.

Third, closely related to the globalization process is "cultural federationalism." Cultural federationalism deals with the growing legitimacy of other cultural forms, religions and schools as these entities come into contact with each other through the globalization process. Federationalism refers to the population of entities -- in this case, religions. A global gathering of world religions, which has occurred several times, requires a federationalism of religions—in other words, all the various religions of the world. A gathering of only Christian religions may qualify as a gathering of Christianity but not a "gathering of global religions." The equation must read "all" religions in the "global" gathering and what also occurs in this global gathering is the "legitimation" of all religions. For our purposes here, we can see as globalization unfolds, international religions and religious organizations are achieving legitimacy on the American stage due to cultural federationalism of these entities.

Fourth, and another reason eastern religions and schools of thought have become commonplace in the American experience, is the growing stress on international or global education. Global education reverberates back and legitimizes other cultural entities such as eastern religious forms. Common today are the student exchange programs, semesters at sea, increases in the number of international students studying at U.S. educational institutions, international-oriented majors and fields of study, and study abroad programs. Hence, part of the educational experience for Americans is to make the connection with another culture or the global. The equation is increasingly international and global. No longer can one isolate one's educational experience in the confines of a single society; one must actively and dynamically fuse with a second or group of cultures as part of the higher educational experience.

Finally, what makes youth from the mainstream turn to eastern ideas and ideals is the growing cultural premium of a "seeking" experience that has moved progressively away from the "societal-suburban" model of the 1950s. In the 1960s many youth rejected the suburban model grounded in the materialist "American Dream" experience. The Beatnik, Hippie and Youth movements challenged the idealized suburban lifestyle offered to youth. The anti-war movement further brought voices from the east calling for peace, particularly the fusion of West and East in the marriage of John Lennon to Yoko Ono. In the 60s Americans were increasingly brought into contact with globally based icons and ideals. This international contact has expanded since the 60s and become commonplace since the new Millennium and *where* youth "seek" for teachings, answers, and beliefs is no longer within an American "ethic" or cultural storehouse. What has replaced the societal ethic or the "suburban" model is increasingly a globally situated ethic, comprised of dozens upon dozens of models. Consider, for instance, one of these models, the Green movement. "Living Green," and "going Green" are not merely American ideals but global ones, based upon and legitimized through the global community of societies and cultural entities. Where one retrieves information regarding these movements is no longer confined to American borders.

So in a large sense, what was once viewed as groups of youth with atypical and even anti-American values who went into eastern oriented religions, today the scope has broadened to include mainstream American youth and students seeking answers from the global cultural storehouse.

Concluding Remarks

Buddhism has witnessed an explosive growth rate from 1990 where the religion consisted of slightly over 400,000 adults, to 2001 (Ibid: See Tables) at slightly over 1,000,000 adult adherents (www.adherents.com). That is over a 170% increase in one decade. The estimated *total* population of Buddhists are provided for 2004 at slightly over 1,500,000, and this too represents an increase over 2001, albeit a smaller increase. Buddhists, of course, are only one dimension of the eastern spiritual expansion. If we include Sikhists heavily grounded in India's state of Punjab, we find that in the U.S. a 300% growth rate from 1990 to 2001. Hinduism is not far behind, with a growth rate over 200% from 227,000 to 766,000 adherents, respectively. Taoists too, have witnessed growth, though not as explosive as Sikhism or Hinduism. Finally, Bahai' increased 240%, while New Age, which draws heavily on eastern spiritual concepts, witnessed a 200% growth rate from 1990 to 2001.

These increasing incremental shifts upward, the legitimation of eastern religious bodies in the U.S., and the ways we interact and come to know the East have necessarily expanded, particularly in the Globalized and Post Modern eras. As Part One of this chapter represented changes in organizational structure from the Traditional Sectarianism period to both the Globalized and Post Modern periods, this essentially signifies a "push" and reaching out from the particular religion or organization to the American audience. However, in Part Three we find a growing "pull" on the part of that same American audience toward eastern religions and organizations as shifts in ethic orientations from the societal to global levels increasingly are made manifest.

Entrepreneur's Dream.

He wobbles with Charliechaplin stability
on an economic tightwire of few winners.
Perhaps the Pirates will take one Today--
drowns out the safetynetlessness.
Thoughts churn like gears: the huge
brainpiece of survival oiled in workethic.

His son manages the computer he was talked into
buying three years ago and spews out graphs
formulas and long-term outlooks. But his is
the mathematics of pad and pencil: carrying threes
fives and eights like second nature and doodling
figures through the long afternoons of few words.
"Happen to have any seventy-five watters?"
"Third shelf over." And

the overkill of "that damn mall they put up"
eats deeper in the back of his head like a
continuous miner digging out the last stretch of
seam in a West Virginia coal bed: the listless
caverns of three a.m.

Here another America appears: Studebakers
and the guys talking parts, politics and war days
as the background music of the old National Register
continually rang into the alarm of seven a.m.

CHAPTER SEVEN

Globalization and The Globe as System
Theoretical and Empirical Considerations

I. Models of Globalization: The Formative Years

Both the heightened theoretical state of awareness and intellectual infatuation with global-oriented phenomena, or what Robertson (1987a, 1989) has more accurately coined as the emerging "perception and fact" of the "world as a single place," opens new directions for the future of the sociological discipline. Those truly committed to uncovering the potential conceptual depths and implications of the modern global system find the infatuation is intermixed with toil. Oddly enough, theorists at the fore of the field find themselves standing in a relationship with the global situation strikingly similar to the position in which the classicists stood a century earlier in relation to the Great Shift. Despite their divergences, in one way or another, Weber, Marx, Durkheim, and Tonnies strived throughout most of their careers to approximate an absolute conceptual apparatus that in turn would explain the substantive entirety of the Great Shift. In the modern era, I contend that not only is there the similarity of the position we stand within with respect to the classicists, but our conceptual frameworks of global interdependence appear more as echoes of the classicists. Consider, for instance, two theoretical strands within the field of global sociology: World Systems Analysis and the Global Integration Perspective.

Although the first theoretical strand is quite divided on a number of levels—among Dependency Theorists, Wallersteinians, Bergesen's Globologists and neo-Marxians loosely associated with World System analysis—convergence is evident with acceptance that global interdependence pivots upon a core/periphery relationship (Bergesen, 1980; Wallerstein, 1979). Essentially, there is little problem with a conceptual scheme offering a view to both the economic rank/status of societies and the economic interrelationships between these societies. The major objection emerges with the presupposition that the core/periphery relation is the axis upon which the global social system is formed and revolves (Wallerstein, 1979).

The essential foundation of the core/periphery relation is economic, but the conceptual content of the economic essence is varied and the source of considerable debate within this theoretical strand. Wallerstein and Frank hinge the relationship upon world exchange relations between core and peripheral nations (Wallerstein, 1979), while Bergesen (1980: 9-12) reformulates a Brennerian notion of class and asserts global property and ownership relations as the foundational cornerstone of the core/periphery interrelationship.

The economic essence of this line of reasoning was strong enough to induce theorists like Boli-Bennett (1980) and Meyer (1980) --representing the second theoretical strand -- to take a stance toward Wallerstein in an analogous manner to that which Weber stood in relation to Marx. Boli-Bennett and Meyer, to be sure, viewed increased interdependence as critical concern of the modern global system, yet sought to broaden the central properties inherent in the global system complex. In a similar respect that Weber reformulated the Marxian conceptualization of social class through adding the dimensions of power and status as vital components of the grid, Boli-Bennett (1980: 87-95) redefined the central axis of the complex as an arena of "integration" for nation states. In doing so, he added the dimensions of (a) the degree of nation state integration and (b) the degree of structural pluralization of center countries to the concept of (c) core and periphery in building an analysis of state dominance of individual societies and their overall connectivity to the global system. Boli-Bennett's central line of analysis, complemented and elaborated by Meyer (1980), suggested that the "nation state" — as a property of world-system in its own right — could act independent of the economic factor in defining both intra- and inter- societal programs of action, namely in the drive toward modernity. The fact that "technocratic" and bureaucratic elites (Boli-Bennett, 1980: 84) flourished not only in core states but peripheral ones as well suggested state dominance and modernity derived from a level beyond the economic. Primarily, the degree of value commitments of societal polities to a "fairly coherent and uniform set" of normative value orientations played a crucial role in determining the degree of integration a society held with the larger system (Boli-Bennett, 1980: 87). Thus, the conceptual spectrum of properties inherent in a definition of the global system widened.

It should be stressed that the Global Integrationist reaction to World System Analysis was necessary, and although its central concentration is on the role of the polity as a primary steering mechanism in modernity and societal/global change, an important presupposition within this theoretical perspective is an apriori normative set of values, standards and orientations operating at the global level, which, in turn, have a tremendous impact upon an individual society's relationship with the overall system.

In yet a third theoretical strand, Robertson (1987a; 1989) speaks of these value orientations and normative set of standards in terms of a "range of definitions" from which societal polities draw upon (and to a certain degree are constrained by) in confronting their own societalization and in constructing courses of societal modernity. For Robertson, both the global economic system of stratification and the integration and collective commitment of societal polities to a broader "range of definitions" constitute one major component of a four component analytical scheme in understanding what he terms the modern global circumstance (Robertson, 1985: 233-38; 1989). In a straightforward criticism leveled against the economic axis of the World System Perspective, Robertson (1987b: 3) contends that "the economic factor is only one of the facets of the making of the modern international system, which itself is, in turn, but one of a number of dimensions of globalization." For Robertson (1985; 1987b; 1989: 15), the modern global condition involves a socio-evolutionary interplay between "four processual components," which include a "system of societies, societies, individuals, and mankind," which in turn, "crystallize" in the "thematization of humanity" and the modern global circumstance. Accordingly, economic and political connectivity are only two aspects of one dimension of the globalizing process. A tightening-up of the world also involves the subjective perceptions of individuals and mankind in general in relation to the global condition.

The wide variety of theories of globalization, first during the formative years and now well into the new millennium, suggest a multidimensional expression of globalization involving not merely a select group, but rather, the entirety of societies. Despite the diversity of manifestations of globalization, there are analytical denominators common to a majority, if not all, of the processes of globalization. In this chapter we will explore five basic properties of Globalization: Global Moral Density, Global Connectivity, Global Federationalism, the Global Cultural Realm, and finally, the move toward a model of the "Globe as System."

II. The Infrastructure and Structure of Globalization

A) Global Moral Density

The infrastructure of globalization consists of a steady build-up of what will be termed global moral density. Global moral density (Matvey, 1988) refers to a heightened density of interaction, dialogue, contact across societal lines. Global moral density is refined from Durkheim's concept of moral/dynamic density. Keep in mind that for Durkheim, macrostructural change was brought on primarily by an intrasocietal increase in dynamic social contact, or what he termed moral dynamic density, whereby the intensified social density created new social facts, collective frames of reference, and subsequently fostered the conditions for societal differentiation (Harms, 1981: 403-04). Also important to note is the fact that Durkheim's concept of moral density did not merely refer to an increase in volume or population density. More to the point was an interaction of consciousnesses with density representing "the amount of interaction or the rate at which particular consciousnesses come into contact with each other" and reacted upon one another (Harms, 1981: 403). In refining the concept, global moral density suggests a growing density of interaction, but at the distinctly global level, which, in turn, has implications for the development of social change and new collective frames of reference at this level.

One should also take note that direct face-to-face interaction is not a necessary prerequisite for the build up of global moral density. In today's world, computerization can be utilized across national boundaries facilitating the build up of density at the global level. Computerization functions to facilitate the build up of global moral density through the creation of numerous "indirect social relationships" (Calhoun, 1987). But it additionally provides a format for a fairly comprehensive degree of interactivity (Rogers, 1986) between connected parties. Calhoun (1987) has demonstrated that one of the hallmark features in both the shift toward and unfolding of progressive modernity rests with an increase in the number and volume of indirect relationships upon which social and institutional life rely. Computerization's power rests with the capacity to create extremely comprehensive indirect relationships through providing a particular technological format for the multidimensional interaction of consciousnesses. It permits, in other words, not only the rapid transfer of large volumes of information over great geographic distances, but interactive on-line communication, dialogue, conferencing, tasking and "telework" (Rogers, 1986: 188). Only relatively recently removed from an era of dependence upon postal and telephone networks, "what" we can do and the "ways" we interact in the absence of face-to-face relationships have necessarily expanded through computerization. Due to this fact, computer-assisted global density provides the potential for not only interconnectedness, but an alternative dimension for the development of new forms of solidarities, communal ties and collective frames of reference.

An Illustration: Global Moral Density in the Educational Sphere

Increases in raw international contact in the past half century have undoubtedly, though not exclusively, played a significant role in fostering the proliferation of perceptual awareness of the "global" which Robertson (1987a) has emphasized. An additional dimension of global moral density, then, aside from the rising rates of raw international contact, are the growing perceptions and commitments to the "global" in various spheres of social life. One example of the build-up in perceptual global moral density is revealed in the educational sphere where the sharpening escalation of international education creates intensified commitments among administrations and university bureaucrats to the reality of "global" education. There are, in other words, stronger and bolder commitments in the university system to all of the various dimensions of internationalized education. Global moral density here is revealed in not only raw contact, but the awareness and subsequent institutionalization of international education in many post-secondary schools.

There are at least three central realms of international education at the modern university. These realms include 1) programs encouraging direct international contact through students traveling abroad; 2) a strong international focus through internationally oriented programs, departments and majors along with a strong international orientation of traditional majors; and, 3) international student migrations outside of structured programs, particularly with the First World acting as a magnet force attracting these diverse migrations.

1) Programs with Direct Student Contact Abroad

At the most basic level are the traditionally oriented student exchange and study abroad programs where students journey to different nations and live with host families for an academic semester or more. In general, these programs have been made much more accessible to students in recent years. Another form of direct international contact is international-oriented field trips designed to increase the student's awareness of another culture and the international community.

Both of these orientations are based upon an underlying principle of a "transcultural" experience as essential to the learning process. The notion is that in an increasingly globalized world, higher learning cannot be totally complete or intellectually self-actualized without experiencing a second culture — a variation in the overall continuum of humanity. The Study Abroad Program at the University of Maryland reveals this principle in one of its orientation brochures:

> ...much more diversity exists around the globe. Understanding this diversity, appreciating what is universal and what is unique to culture, learning how to ask questions and answer them in ways natively unfamiliar, and appreciating what at first may be strange and then perhaps beautiful: these tasks are basic to a college education. Study Abroad offers you the possibility to experience a particular culture or area which may have nothing to do with your major but is important for its own sake.

There is also a view that individuals have relationships transcending beyond the individual/ society relationship. It is the transcultural experience, which allows the individual to jump above his or her own cultural perspective and examine several cultural perspectives at one and the same moment. Relativizing culture in this way develops another viable relationship -- the individual/global relationship. The Maryland Study Abroad Program asserts: "By studying abroad, you will be forced to examine your assumptions about yourself, America and the culture in which you are living. In the process you will gain a unique awareness of yourself and the world."

Yet another rationale for the educational transcultural experience, is the notion that transcultural experiences bring us closer to our commonalities—the humanity in all of us. Kansai Gaidai of Japan, a university exchanging exceptionally large numbers of its student body each year with students at sister universities internationally offers this insight:

> ...we believe that a knowledge of traditions and cultures different than our own draws us closer to the human family of which we are all a part, while making us more aware of both the possibilities and limitations of our own heritage.

2) International Focus

Universities have also increasingly developed an international focus through internationally oriented majors, field and area studies programs. While these do not necessarily take the student out of the home society, these programs focus specifically on international studies or some specialized field of focus in international studies. They also tend to foster international contact, dialogue, research and interaction through a heavy recruitment of international faculty.

Latin American Studies, Russian Studies, Asian Studies, along with growing study programs and majors in International Affairs are major departments within central academic universities. The core underlying rationale behind many of these programs is not merely an investigative knowledge of the outside world, but a growing "international focus" to deal with the complexities of a globalizing world and to prepare students for roles in a more globalized world. These principles are reflected in many administrators' descriptions and rationales of their International Studies Programs. At the University of Pittsburgh International Program, for instance, we find the following descriptions and rationale:

> International relations are no longer primarily relations between governments. All of the actors on the global scene, including corporations, associations, societies, and significantly, universities, confront common international challenges....The bonds between countries are becoming more critical and we should be prepared to nurture these relationships. An International education is a vital step in developing the necessary awareness of an increasingly interdependent world.

Similarly the University of North Carolina's International Program states:

> The office of International Programs of the University of North Carolina at Chapel Hill recognized that the worldwide situation is one of changing relations, institutions, and values...the future of society is international in scope, not national, regional, or local...
>
> ...We need to be prepared for global citizenry and for contributing to international decisions and issues in a world of growing interdependence of nations.

Wesley Posvar, former President of the University of Pittsburgh noted the following regarding the international focus of a modern university:

> As we approach the 21st century, no educational institution in this country can claim to serve American students, American Science, and American policy if it fails to incorporate internationalism at the core of its educational mission.

3) Student Migrations

Direct international contacts and the growing internationalization of universities through international programs and a global focus are not the only expressions of global moral density within the university. Major universities, particularly in core centers, act as magnets for large migrations of students from a variety of societies, particularly peripheral ones. The university, as a kind of global institution, then, draws and brings together international diversity.

In the U.S. for instance, there have been steady increases in the number of foreign students studying in the U.S. In 1989 some 366,354 foreign students attended U.S. colleges. This represented an increase of 10,167 students from 1988. Asian students constitute about 50% of the total foreign student enrollment in the U.S., but there are also sizable contingents from India, Iran, Pakistan, and Nigeria in the U.S. Shift ahead almost 15 years and we find in 2002-03, the total number of international students studying at American Universities jumped dramatically to 586,000 students. By 2007 this level had dropped slightly to 582,000 foreign students in the US (IIE). IIE Network (Institute of International Education) reports for 2002-03 that

> several major sending countries saw strong increases, including India, Korea and Kenya. Numbers from China also increased, but at a reduced rate. For the second consecutive year, India, which increased by 12% to 74,603 students, was the leading country of origin for international students in the United States, followed by China

(64,757, up 2%) and Korea (up 5% to 51,519). Mexico, at #7, increased by 2% to 12,801 students, Hong Kong, at #15, increased by 4% to 8,076, and Kenya, at #16, increased by 11% to 7,862. Canada, #6 with 26,513, was unchanged (IIE)

Many of these students are clustered at major US universities and provide a considerable source of dialogue, exchange, contact and interaction with American students. The neighborhoods surrounding the major university are often the most internationally diverse settings in the U.S. Student migrations and the communities springing up as a result of this diversity must be regarded as a major source for international or global social density in the U.S.

Bureaucratic Mechanisms

The international orientation of many major universities has propelled the specialization of an administrative and bureaucratic apparatus to deal with the variety and complexity of "international aspects" within a university. At the University of Pittsburgh, for instance, the University Center for International Studies is the bureaucratic mechanism that manages this international complexity. Holzner remarks on the bureaucratic mechanism:

> UCIS, is the focal point for the University international research, teaching, and public service activities. It is a University wide center, not a school or department. USCI has no faculty of its own but works with hundreds of members of the faculty. It awards no degrees but reaches more than 10,000 of the University's students each year...
>
> ...UCIS supports international work of all of the University's schools and departments, providing horizontal links across the vertical structures of the institution. It offers assistance to students wishing to study abroad and to foreign students studying at Pitt. It helps faculty obtain grants and identify resources. It develops and manages international programs and projects across disciplinary boundaries...In all its activities UCIS seeks to promote linkages across national boundaries for the purpose of strengthening the University's International Dimension.

While Pitt is one case, there are similar bureaucratic mechanisms at other major universities. Some universities have developed extensive structural linkages with sister universities in a variety of countries and have generated stable flows of faculty, students, research, and other academic materials across societal lines.

B) Global Connectivity

The structures of globalization through which the complexities of global moral density are ordered, integrated and managed consist of a dual-dimensional configuration of global ritualization and global connectivity. While the ritualization of global life is fairly self-evident, involving the ceremonial rites and formalities of patterned, ongoing, and structured interactions at the transsocietal level, Global Connectivity (Matvey, 1988) represents a quasi-evolutionary pattern toward the formation of global spheres of social life. The increasing international- orientedness and internationalization of societal sectors represent this dynamic at lower levels, while the rapid proliferation of global institutional and organizational forms represents a more developed form of connectivity.

The internationalization of societal sectors has steadily expanded over the past century, and is characterized by heightened interconnectivity and flows of information, communication, and commitments across societal lines, specifically through sectoral channels. There is, of course, a wide variation in the format of these networks ranging from open and voluteristic flows between specialists within, let us say, the academic or medical sectors, two highly integrated flows within financially oriented networks.

Global institutionalization represents a substantially elevated structure of global integration and embodies not only the development of global institutions and organizations at the distinctly global level, but the increasingly legitimate—and in some cases, quasi-sacred—salience of these institutions in the global context precisely because they are perceived to hold a fundamental relationship to individual societies, the system of modern societies, the individual and mankind — what Robertson (1987a) defines as four central components of the "modern global circumstance." In other words, the telic-concerns, objectives and prime-directives of particular institutions play some functional role in relation to the whole of humankind and its systems.

Global Connectivity is guided by an underlying working logic meriting further theoretical attention at this point. First, Global Connectivity is a multifaceted process, which is to say, that a variety of social sectors witness some degree of internationalization and global institutionalization. Second, this multifaceted character of connectivity is guided by the pre-existing degree of differentiation in societies in general. Central to the concept of progressive societal differentiation is not merely the splitting up and compartmentalizing of the spheres of social life, but chiefly it is the institutionalization and legitimation of these spheres as specialized stages of authority in orchestrating particular sphere-specific affairs of social life. What occurs on an intersocietal level involves the coming together, hence, the term connectivity of "like" spheres.

Third, for global connectivity to proceed in the truest sense of the term, there must be a relatively standard level of intrasocietal differentiation of social spheres across societies. As a case in point, Wuthnow (1980: 27, 43-46) notes that while there was internationalization in science and an international scientific community as early as the 17th century, internationalization primarily was limited to European boundaries. This limitation can be primarily explained by an era of uneven intrasocietal differentiation across the globe at this time. As Wuthnow (1980: 27) correctly points out to us, China surely held scientific achievements in her history but no autonomous "institutionalized" scientific sphere approximating what was occurring throughout the European continent. Thus, the result was not a global scientific community, but rather a European-bound community where a fairly standard level of differentiation across these societies had begun to unfold.

The past century and a half can be most accurately viewed as an era of standardization or universalization of intrasocietal differentiation across the globe. More recently, trends in modernity point toward an increase in the level of differentiation within what are primarily considered Eastern, Gemeinschaft, agrarian, and Third World societal systems. As Department of Education, Department of Environmental Resources, and a Department of Cultural Development, etc., become commonplace collective household terms in these societies, the commitment to the overall normative structure of modernity equips societies with a host of sphere-specific realms and representatives.

Finally, it is becoming increasing problematic in the modern world to locate central spheres of social life, which have not undergone some degree of internationalization. In environment, education, health, economy, culture and other domains, intersocietal contact, ritual, and in many cases institutionalized organization is highly evident. This is not to suggest that global-oriented spheres operate with the same degree of power, status and force as the nation-state. It is clear that any discussion of the global must recognize the nation-state as the most vital and oftentimes absolute mechanism of steering action over its society. Nevertheless, the salience of an increasingly diverse number of actors at the global level must also be taken into account, and not merely as mechanisms which legitimate the state system (Meyer, 1980: 122) --although, this is indeed one of the functions of such entities -- but as global oriented spheres which have a degree of influence upon societal and global life.

An Illustration of Connectivity: Growth and Legitimacy of the United Nations

In the discussing the global connectivity dynamic, one must make a distinction between international governmental organizations (IGOs) and international non-governmental organizations (INGOs). The epicenter of governmental organization is the UN, an association of dozens of specialized agencies, programs, sub-organizational forms and autonomous but affiliated global organizations. The most common global organizations affiliated with the UN are (1) UN programs, organizational forms which are highly specialized, but directly responsible to the authority and budget allotments of the UN; and (2) UN specialized agencies, which are more autonomous global institutions affiliated with the UN. Some of the UN specialized agencies were in existence long before the creation of the UN. The Universal Postal Union, the International Labor Organization, the World Meteorological Organization represent global institutions existing prior to the UN but becoming UN affiliates in the late 1940s. This, in itself, indicates the UN as a centralized quasi-governmental body attempting to coordinate the complexities of social organization at the global level.

It should again be emphasized that while the scope of global organization is much larger, UN affiliated global organizations do not operate with the same power and authority as the nation-state. The UN, for instance, holds a peacekeeping force, but it has no global military machinery to speak of. It can pass resolutions, but has no real way to enforce these resolutions if individual member or non-member states do not act upon these agreements. Similarly, world environmental organizations hold no power to enact world environmental standards that individual nations must then impose upon their peoples and business units. They usually disseminate information and recommend changes in industrial pollution policies in various nation-states, but again it is the individual nation-state bureaucracy that must give its seal of approval before such recommendations become established. Nevertheless, governmental global organizations do play a key role at attempts in disseminating information, diplomacy, and in attempts to plan and coordinate social action.

Non-governmental global organizations are simply independent, non-UN affiliated global organizations and institutions. The World Council of Churches, International Olympic Organizing Committee, the International Council of Scientific Unions are examples of these.

A look at the governmental global organizations can prove quite useful for our purposes here. In the following sections we consider two central dynamics of the globalization process with respect to global institutionalization: The first includes the growth in global governmental and non governmental organizations, while the second centers on notions of legitimacy regarding global governmental organizations—particularly the UN.

1) Growth: A Three Pronged Illustration

There has been tremendous growth in the UN from 1945 through the latter half of the Twentieth Century and on into the first decade of the new millennium, revealed in three dimensions. The first dimension or prong is simply the raw numbers of nation states joining the overarching IGO in the manifest form of the United Nations. Table 7.1 gives growth through 1990 of the Twentieth Century, and one will note the dramatic increase after 1960s following the decolonization of African States. By 1990 there were over 160 UN member nations. Shift ahead twenty years to 2010 and we now find 191 nation states holding membership in the UN.

A second prong deals with the growth of IGOs or International Governmental Organizations. In Table 7.1 we also find growth in the global governmental organization itself, as in specifically UN affiliated organizations. Here we see modest increases in a small number of international organizations. Some of these organizations are listed in Table 7.2. However, this figure does not include the total population of IGOs, either loosely connected to or independent of the UN's umbrella organizational structure. By 2010 there were some 355 core IGOs. A listing of such can be found at the following URL:

http://www.library.northwestern.edu/govinfo/resource/internat/igo.html

Furthermore, keep in mind that these organizations are only major UN-affiliated and non-UN IGOs. They do not include non-UN global organizations or international non-governmental organizations—in short, INGOs. What happens if we combine IGOs and INGOs? The UIA (Union of International Associations) produces a Who's Who in International organizations. They note

> Volume 6, or the *Who's Who in International Organizations*, lists over 25,601 presidents, general secretaries, executive directors, chairmen and other officers active in every field of human endeavor. Some 15,354 international organizations are represented... (UIA)

15,354 combined NGOs and INGOs sounds impressive, but a Who's Who does not exhaust the total global organizations population. The third prong of our empirical illustration centers upon the *total* number of global organizations, governmental and non-governmental. Hence, if we calculated all NGOs and INGOs on a global scale we can identify over 60,000 global organizations as of 2010! The UIA's *Yearbook of International Organization* further breaks this down into active and inactive NGOs and INGOs, but the sheer numbers are still impressive at 35,000 active international organizations as of 2010. (UIA)

Differentiation in society is a process through which a single institution begins to split into two or more institutions, or sub organizations, specializes in a particular need and is thereafter regarded as a legitimate stage of authority to coordinate actives, interaction and organization upon this specialized stage. The development of global organizations clearly reflects a process of differentiation and specialization at the global level. The UN, of course, is viewed as the central force for governmental global organization, and there has been extensive differentiation and specialization of this global institutional form since its creation. At the global level, however, the process of global organizational differentiation and specialization extends far beyond global governmental organization and into the much broader realm of global organization itself.

Table 7.1
Growth in UN Affiliated Global Organizational Structures
Number of Member States and
Principal UN Affiliated Global Organizational Forms

Years	# Nations Joined	Total # UN Nations	Cumulative %	UN Related Global Organizations	Total # UN Related Global Organizations
Pre-1945				6	6
1945	50	50	0.31	3	9
1946-1950	10	60	0.38	4	13
1951-1955	16	76	0.48	0	13
1956-1960	24	100	0.63	4	17
1961-1965	18	118	0.74	4	21
1966-1970	9	127	0.79	3	24
1971-1975	17	144	0.90	5	29
1975-1980	9	153	0.96	3	32
1981-1990	7	160	1.00	0	32

Source: Compiled from Universal Almanac, 1991. Pages 462.

Table 7.2
Major UN Related Organizational Forms

Established	Organization	Member Nations	Sphere	Headquarters	Status
1865	ITU	160	Communications	Geneva	UNSA
1873	WMO	158	Environment	Geneva	UNSA
1875	UPU	168	Communication	Berne	UNSA
1883	WIPO	112	Academic	Geneva	UNSA
1919	ILO	150	Labour	Geneva	UNSA
1923	INTERPOL	146	Criminal Justice	Saint-Cloud, Fr	IND
1945	FAO	158	Food Strategy	Rome	UNSA
	IBRD	151	Finance	DC	UNSA
	IMF	151	Finance	DC	UNSA
1946	UNESCO	158	Cultural Relations	Paris	UNSA
	UNICEF	159	Children	NY,NY	UNP
1947	ICAO	156	Airspace	Montreal	UNSA
1948	GATT	125	Economy	Geneva	UNSA
	WHO	166	Health	Geneva	UNSA
1950	UNHCR	159	Refugees	Geneva	UNP
1956	IFC	131	Finance	DC	UNSA
1957	IAEA	113	Environment	Vienna	UNSA
1958	IMO	127	Environment/Econ	London	UNSA
1960	IDA	135	Finance	DC	UNSA
1963	WFP	159	Food Strategy	Rome	UNP
1964	UNCTAD	159	Economy	Geneva	UNP
1965	UNDP	159	Modernity	NY,NY	UNP
	UNITAR	159	Modernity	NY, NY	UNP
1966	UNIDO	118	Modernity	Vienna	UNSA
1967	G-77	127	Economy	NY, NY	IND
1969	UNFPA	159	Population	NY, NY	UNP
1972	UNDRO	159	Disasters	Geneva	UNP
	UNEP	159	Environment	Nairobi, Kenya	UNP
1973	INTELSAT	144	Communications	DC	IND
	UNU	159	Academic	Tokyo	UNP
1974	WFC	159	Food Strategy	Rome	UNP
1977	IFAD	139	Food Strategy	Rome	UNSA
1978	HABITAT	159	Housing	Nairobi, Kenya	UNSA
1979	INSTRAW	159	Women	Santo Domingo, DR	UNP

Source: Universal Almanac, 1991. Pages 461-69.

2) Issues of Legitimacy

A key point of interest is the "perception" of the concept of "global organization." Do elites, organizations and institutions within society view global organization as a legitimate and appropriate stage for aiding in managing the complexities of the modern world? One way to examine this phenomenon is to examine how social units describe an organization. A person who views a global organization as a "satanic force or the Beast of the Revelation" obviously neither perceives the organization as legitimate or appropriate. An organization, however, that is described as a "moral hope for mankind" is fusing a great deal of moral legitimacy into the organization.

One indicator of the descriptive imagery surrounding the UN can be gauged in the way heads of state describe the organization. This of course does not take into account other sociocultural entities like social groups, religions, social movements, or even individuals, but heads of state do represent the pinnacle of societal authority.

How do top societal elites describe a global organization like the UN? In 1985, the UN held a special 30th anniversary commemorative session. Heads of state were asked to give addresses regarding the UN. Table 7.3 represents a content analysis of those speeches. Searched for in this content analysis were specific descriptions of the UN as a global organizational format. In other words, specific references were sought which embodied some form of descriptive imagery of the organizational body itself.

Many heads of state utilized no descriptive imagery. Rather than making specific reference to the organizational body itself, they gave historical accounts of the UN's successes, pitfalls and future potentials. In a majority of the addresses the UN was given high rates of praise. There were a significant minority of heads of state who took a moment or two to make specific descriptive references to the UN as an organizational format. These organizational descriptions were distinguished on the basis of "mechanistic" imagery and "humanitic" imagery. Mechanistic imagery describes the UN as some type of forum or organization that is necessary or indispensable in the growing complexity of the modern world. Humanitic descriptions, on the other, tend to fuse certain moral or quasi-sacred qualities into descriptions of the UN.

The content analysis reveals both mechanistic and humanitic descriptions present across every geographic sphere. Tables 7.3 and 7.4 reveal a gauge and sampling of both types of these descriptions. Findings in Table 7.3 reveal roughly equalized levels of mechanistic and humanitic imagery. Also broken down on the basis of regional blocks, the analysis reveals a fairly even distribution of mechanistic/humanitic imagery across continents with the exception of a significant clustering of mechanistic imagery in the old Eastern Europe/Soviet zone. Important to emphasize is both forms of descriptive imagery, mechanistic and humanitic, afford legitimacy, but it is the latter which tends to fuse the organizational form within a higher moral dimension, hence elevating its legitimacy to a quasi-sacred level.

Table 7.3
Content Analysis of Addresses by Heads of State
UN Special Commemorative Session, 1985

Region	Total # of Addresses	Mechan	Humam	NR
Africa	27	4	5	18
Asia	30	4	6	20
L.A. & Carr.	25	4	3	18
E. Europe	10	5	1	4
W. Europe & other	21	2	3	16
Others	7	1	1	5
Totals	120	20	19	81

Source: UN Chronicle. 1985. 22:4 : 1-72.

Table 7.4
Samples of Mechanistic/Humanitic Catch Terms
UN Special Commemorative Session, October 1985
(page # in parentheses)

Mechanistic Descriptions:

"...international forum..." (24)

"...indispensable instrument..."(24)

"...international body will remain an essential instrument..." (31)

"...irreplaceable framework..."(39)

"...most efficient instrument created by mankind to meet the challenge confronting it during this stage of its evolution..."(27)

"...international instrument..."(53)

"...forum of multilateral diplomacy..."(53)

"...universal framework..." (54)

Humanitic Descriptions:

"It embodies the conscience of the world...last moral threshold..." (65)

"...moral force..." (27)

"...moral authority of the collective voice of mankind..." (27)

"...international embodiment of the ideals of peace and the liberty of peoples..." (27)

"...ultimate hope..." (35)

"...conscience for peace and ray of hope in the midst of the dark forces of evil...(38)

"...the authentic voice of humanity's conscience..." (40)

"...the basis of hope in the material and intellectual progress of peoples and countries..." (56)

"...humanity's only hope..."(26)

Source: UN Chronicle. 1985. 22:4 : 1-72.

III. Global Federationalism:
The Integrative Feature of the Global System

Globalization, as revealed through connectivity, does not involve the dissolving of national society within a larger global one. The structures of globalization, particularly in global institutions, have often ordered social density through an integrative process of Global Federationalism — that is, a drive toward the full representation and participation of national representatives and specialists in formally structured transsocietal institutional environments. While these environments tend to center around supranational goals and global-humanistic themes, they also verify the present state system through orchestrating, integrating and ordering national societal identities within a larger organizational context.

Global Federationalism, to elaborate, can be defined as the interwovenism and ordering of societal specialists and/or participants within global organizational frameworks in conjunction with a supranational prime directive or objective. In transcending the societal context, rather than producing stressing tensions pointing toward the deterioration of the state system, global-oriented frameworks generally reconfirm the fundamental value of national societies. Reconfirmation and, in some cases, veneration of the state system, is evidenced with the fact that representatives of the various states are viewed as necessary stitches in the overall fabric of an international organization or ritual. The core theme underpinning such institutions often appears as a supranational prime directive or objective, primarily sphere-specific as in the case of one of the World Health Organization's directives to approximate "heath for all" by the year 2000 (UN Chronicle, 1986). Revolving around particular prime directives are representatives and specialists of the state system, integrated and given legitimacy in the interwovenism, degree of connectivity and commitment of the set of states participating in these institutions. Thus many of these organizations institutions take on the appearance of the "federation of planets" in the Star Trek scenario —cultural and nationalistic divergences are not merely expected, they are embedded within the very grid of the sociocultural entity. In other words, it is the divergence and differences, which must gather and participate upon this common stage to legitimate the very essence of "global" in a global-oriented organization.

A structured example in the institutional sense is the opening and closing ceremonies of the Olympic Games. The Games reflect particular aspects of humanity and the human circumstance; on one hand competition both inter- and intrasocietally, and on the other the social and individual dimension of sport and sportsmanship in the context of community, society, and globe. As one of the more longstanding global institutions, a number of symbols (e.g., the torch, the flag of rings, the releasing of the doves, etc.) are interwoven within the Games and can be analyzed as symbolic properties deriving specifically from the substantive content of the transsocietal sphere rather than properties, which emerge from the sum of the parts involved. Nationalities and national sentiments are not diminished within this transsocietal context, but on the contrary, enhanced. Fueling the enhancement process are precisely the sphere-specific supra-ordinate sentiments and symbols through which patriotic and nationalistic sentiments are ordered and given meaning on an international level.

In terms of the federationalism embedded in the Games, the expected norm is full participation of the diversity of nation-states, which also acts to legitimize this event. Failure of legitimization was witnessed in two sessions of summer Olympic Games (1980, 1984) with absent majority players due to political atmosphere and the Games therefore failed to be filled with its proper combinations of federated diversity and such diversity is central to this equation.

This norm reverberates through other global organizational forms and events as well. Although not representing nations, but rather religions, the very success of the gathering of religious elites in Assisi in 1986 (Time, 1986) directly depended on the degree of diversity present. If the gathering only included Christians, Muslims and Hindus, a large chunk of world religious picture would be missing, and hence the event viewed incomplete. The invitation for inclusion of all religious beliefs justifies the terming of this gathering as a global event.

Federationalism is also heavily embedded within the organizational format of the World Health Organization. Legitimation of the "Health for All by the Year 2000" strategy was granted by the World Health Executive Board and the World Health Assembly only after the initial strategic report compiled and synthesized "data supplied to WHO by 140 countries" (UN Chronicle, 1986). Moreover, a calling for a truly global response to a "global epidemic" requires a diversity of scientism from a plurality of national contexts -- not merely an American or British response. It was thus a significant media event that China, even though only reporting two cases of AIDS in 1988, sent for the first time, a representative to the World Conference on AIDS in that year — the stage is made more complete.

Another illustration includes the World Conference of Cities. The Conference centers upon the directive of making cities more livable, and again, important and vital is the congregation of representative elites from the major and minor world cities for dialogue and comparison.

The federationalism embedded in the grid of global organizational form also fosters an internal pull from the given organization to the external world further inducing increases in the number of participants in the organization. On the reverse end, societies continuing to differentiate, looking outward toward the world, produces an active societal push to link with the world on a multidimensional basis. In the Olympic Games of 1984, despite the Communist absence, giving the needed diversity as discussed above, the number of nation participants increased from previous games. Again, decolonialization of much of the Third World also acts as a mechanism of increase, but the crucial question is why the societal system desires linkage. Reasons for individual linkage may vary, however the crucial point is we now witness the rapid creation of sphere-specific global environments opening space for the participation of a plurality of societies.

Federationalism can be most accurately defined as an ideal global-organizational format derived from the interface of the heightened value placed upon humanity and the system of societal polities on the one hand, and the increasingly standardized level of intersocietal differentiation across societies on the other. "Ideal" should be emphasized. Throughout the history of the Olympic Games, the UN, scientific intergovernmental organizations and other organizational forms, numerous objections have emerged regarding matters of politicalization and bias, unfavorable balance of power, exclusionary practices, and First World dominance. Nevertheless, inherent in the core of such objections is, in fact, an underlying appeal for the empirical real to approximate the ideal.

IV. Global Culture

In speaking of the "global" as system, one must consider not only structural features such as global moral density and global connectivity, but cultural features as well. One must consider theoretical conceptualizations such as the Global Normative or Global Cultural as the overarching body of standards, norms, value orientations and expectations, and sets of meanings and ends influencing and governing the processes of societal and institutional life in the global system. These include not only orientations governing decentralized international interaction or highly structured global institutions, but significant systems of meaning through which particular entities and aspects of global condition are interpreted, including societalization, modernity, globality, technology and change, population, cultural integration and revitalization, and the vast array of issues, problems, and potentials confronting the whole of modern societies. In short, the Global Cultural represents "patterns of meaning" which "give the action system (in this case, the global system) its primary sense of direction" (Parsons, 1977: p. 178).

It is possible at this point to examine a small portion of this "system of meaning" for our purposes here. In this section we will situate notions like societalization, modernity, globality, and humanity within a working "systems" context. At the most general of levels, these notions are held as ideals by the system of societies, ideals brought into being by individual societies and governing very large portions of the social realities of nation-states. In Parsonian imagery, terms like "modernity" and "globality" are the cultural reserve feeding information into the entire system of societies. Simply put, they are pattern-maintaining ideals and ethics for individual societal systems. This is an interesting twist, for terms like modernity and globalization have often been referred to as agents of "social change" for the individual society. Yet, at the global level, and if we are to speak of the globe as a system, societalization, modernity, and globality all work to stabilize order and structure at the world level. In short, societalization adds more legitimate actors to the family of nations, modernity standardizes social infrastructures and structures across societies, and globality provides a sort of rush hour of connectedness between societies.

Societalization, for instance, generally refers to the process of becoming a legitimate societal unit in the modern world. At the level of global culture, societalization is defined as achieving the status of the "nation-state." It is the nation-state, which is now the most widely accepted form for complete societalization. Ethnic and religious forces may be constantly at work in the heart of many societal systems, but they are not viewed as appropriate global actors unless these forces are tied to a legitimate state system. Individual cultures are to be backed by the structural apparatus of the "nation-state" if these cultures are to have legitimate voice in the modern global system.

A large part of global history for individual societies has been the breaking away from colonial baggage and the subsequent joining of the world as legitimate "nation-state" actors. Thus becoming a society has not meant "change" for the global system as much as it has solidified a global order of legitimate state units.

The volatility of ethnic conflict in the world today only magnifies the importance and value social actors place on "societalization." Each actor, whether through violent (the conflict in Yugoslavia) or peaceful (Ghandi and India) means, is striving for a legitimate voice in the world system. But to achieve that voice means "nation-state" status. It is the "state" system, which is recognized as the means to achieve accepted identity in the modern world. This propels societalization as not merely a process, but an ideal in the modern world.

Becoming a society, however, involves more than achieving "nation-state" status. Once a "state" is initiated into the modern world, then an array of other processes become imperative. For an individual society these include the kind of values expressed, heritage put forward, and the kind of "societal identity" presented to the larger world order. These are all cultural questions, questions from which societal systems draw upon their own unique histories for answers. Societalization is ongoing, and the problems of structure (attaining nation-state status) give way to the problems of culture (attaining unity and presenting the societal self).

Modernity, most interestingly, can be conceptualized not just as a program of action, process, or state of being, but rather, an ideal and ethic operating in the global system. In one of his earlier essays Wallerstein asks the question of why poor nations do not rise up and smite the rich (1979). The answer, I suggest, is that a ripe global culture exists which situates "modernity" as a societal work ethic bought into by rich and poor societies alike. For the First World, it may very well be a work ethic of "post-modernity" or postindustrial society, but the ideal is held with all the vigor of a cultural ethic. Less developed societal systems also buy into the ethic, for it is something strived for no matter the economic and social condition of the particular peripheral society.

At the broadest of levels, "modernity" simply means success in the world system; how that "success" is defined is open to interpretation based on the interpenetration of the individual societal system's cultural store with global notions of modernity. There are, however, some accepted guidelines. Notions of societal modernity are guided by what Boli-Bennett terms "a fairly uniform set of standards" defining "external success" in the wider system of societies, internal prosperity for one's own society, and the "mechanisms to be used to achieve internal and external success" (Boli-Bennett, 1980: 87). This is not to equate "modernity" with "westernization," although a plethora of notions of modernity are fueled by the success of the western world in what might be termed societal modernization. There is, however, a store of cultural energy in each individual societal system, which will work in combination with more standardized conceptualizations at the global level for enacting programs and plans of actions toward modernity.

Along with modernity, globality itself can be conceptualized as a cultural ideal. Globality simply put refers to a society's integration within the global order, the connectedness of the individual society, and its respective sectors, to the larger global whole. Connectedness, it should be stressed again, does not indicate a withering away or melting of the "state" system in the face of some larger global village or community. Connectedness, to be sure, refers to the connectivity of the nation-state system and its sub-sectors to the larger global order. Federationalism, as previously discussed, more accurately defines this condition. National societies are not stripped of their flags when they join the larger global system, but rather the flags are celebrated. There is, in other words, individual identity (the societal system) in the larger group context (the family of nations).

While modernity on the one hand, equips states and their sectors with a daily work ethic for societal upgrading, globality creates a sort of rush hour of connectivity. Nation-states buy into federationalism and connectedness as much as they buy into notions of modernity. Globality defines one's proper place in the world, or the larger scheme of things. Connectedness, in the face of a plethora of nation-states, expands the potential of the individual nation-state.

Connectedness unites states with something much larger than themselves in terms of participation in global events, rituals, organizations, and institutions. These are all part and parcel of the larger global order, an order that has become more distinct and real in the past few centuries than at any time previous in civilizational history.

In addition to notions of societalization, modernity, and globality, are other global cultural ideals such as the notion of "humanity." In extending this line of reasoning with specific reference to the creation of global institutions and organizations, humanity can be categorized as a sort of pre-contractual solidarity at the global level, acting as a common frame of reference, permitting and encouraging a dialogue of diversity at the global level. The greater intensity through which sociocultural entities and collectivities respond to the symbolic significance of humanity as a crucial reference point, it is increasingly likely emergent "humanity" solidifies as the social solidarity underpinning a heterogeneous cultural mosaic at the global level. Humanity further provides the symbolic substance of higher appeal upon which global organizational forms and events draw. Consider, for instance, John Paul II's remarks at the spiritual summit of 160 religious elites in Assisi in late 1986:

> ...Our meeting attests only—and this is its real significance for the people of our time—that in the great battle for peace, humanity, in its very diversity, must draw from its deepest and most vivifying sources, where its conscience is formed and upon which is founded the moral action of all people (Time, Nov. 10, 1986)

Diversity here is recognized, if not applauded, but the concept of humanity and the fact the "religious" is viewed the "deepest and most vivifying" part of humanity is more fundamental. On this basis, particular "ways of prayer" are relativized in relation to humanity, and prayer as part of the human condition and circumstance becomes more paramount, in turn permitting and encouraging a gathering of styles of prayer. Humanity, as a force being appealed to as the common frame of reference, allows us to jump above fences previously separating social units. While it can certainly be questioned whether such an event is even quasi- organizational, similar appeals to humanity can be found in highly structured institutional forms such as the UN. At the closing of the UN Assembly's 40th anniversary session in October of 1985, Secretary-General Javier Perez de Cuellar, speaking to what was coined the "largest gathering of world leaders" since the UN's creation, noted in his address:

> Leaders of nations are assembled here and behind them all is the single collective constituency of the human race. Every such gathering at a historic point involves a report to that constituency—to its vast, silent majority which wants peace with justice and dignity, with freedom from fear and the hope of a better tomorrow (UN Chronicle, 1985).

Similarly, President Ershad of Bangladesh, commented, "we may have gathered here as separate nations, but we should not forget that we are all members of a family...we are all here representing mankind (UN Chronicle, 1985).

In the World Health Organization's mobilization against AIDS, terms such as "global epidemic" and "global attack" are stressed in reference to the protection of humanity and the global community (UN Chronicle, 1987). Ultimately, the evolutionary commitment of individuals and sociocultural entities to an intercultural concept of humanity encourages particular goals (AIDS prevention, health, peace, etc.) to be constructed not merely as societal goals, but as transsocietal goals for the whole of humanity, which in turn allows for an active integration of social diversity on a common stage.

V. The Globe as System: Theoretical Considerations

Diagram 7.1

A

ECONOMY

Economic Development

Resource Ownership

World Trade Networks

Core/Peripheral Status

G

POLITY

The Nation State

Globalizing Sectors

Global Institutions

L

GLOBAL CULTURAL

Societalization Ideals

Modernity Ideals

Globality Ideals

Humanity Ideals

I

GLOBAL INTEGRATION

Federationalism

Global Institutionalization

Global Ritualism

In many respects, throughout this paper, the notion of "systems" has been present in speaking about the modern global condition. Globalization is a process, simply put, systematizing the globe. Loose knit interaction on the global level in recent years has witnessed institutionalization. Problems in the modern world are not merely societal problems but global problems and increasingly addressed by global institutions and organizations. Even the nation-state increasingly employs a federation scenario to tackle particular issues. The Gulf War was one such issue.

But how do we speak of "systems" when we are dealing with the globe? If a "systems" approach is to be utilized, we can follow the Parsonian lead by suggesting that there must be adaptive, goal attainment, integrative, and pattern maintaining features of this system. An AGIL schema, Diagram 7.1, can be useful in pinpointing various aspects of globalization we have been discussing in previous sections.

Simply put, the thrust of this paper has suggested that globalization represents a tightened world, but one which retains features such as the nation state, while adding dimensions such as the global institution and a heightened amount of contact and interaction at the global level. In "systems" terms, federationalism by and large is a fundamental integrative feature of the system. It is a working logic for ordering and structuring the coming together of nation states and their sectors in global organizational formats. Federationalism is integrative precisely because it provides the format for fitting the parts into the larger whole. Whether this is the UN where formal nation states are represented or a longstanding organization like the World Health Organization, federationalism provides a schema for ordered integration and interaction. Consequently, Federationalism is situated in the integrative sector of the AGIL model.

As we discussed at a previous point, notions of societalization, modernity, globality, and humanity occupy part of an emergent global culture. As societies strive toward modernity (post-modernity) a global system solidifies. We can begin to speak of customary socio-structural features like common structures of intrasocietal differentiation across the system of societies. Many of these features, non-existent a hundred years ago in many peripheral societies, are now common properties of core and peripheral societal systems alike. The commitment of a large number of societies to an ideal we have come to call "modernity" undoubtedly has been one of the central forces at work in creating standardized levels of intrasocietal differentiation.

We can further speak of pattern maintenance in terms of the degree of the societal system's connectedness with the larger whole. Structures of intersocietal connectivity can be discerned and distinguished as patterned forums and frameworks for the gatherings of global diversity, while a highly held ideal such as "globality" is the significant aspect of global culture ordaining this very process of connectivity.

In the goal attainment sphere, we find a distinct set of actors at the global level. First and foremost, the nation-state, or the political state operating with the most fundamental force of societal power and authority. In addition, globalizing societal sectors are also included. Sectors are not merely joined to the nation-state vertically, but linked with like sectors horizontally. They represent embryos for future global ritualization and institutionalization (another integrative feature of the system).

There are also the plethora of global organizations and institutions already on the playing field in the modern global system. These cannot be dismissed, especially the UN as a coordinating institution, for they represent goal-attaining action units at the global level. They may not act with the same authority of the nation-state, but they nevertheless exist in the modern global circumstance.

Finally, in this scheme, the economy, or rather, world economic system is put forward as the adaptive sphere. Societies in a larger system are viewed not only in terms of their level of economic development and impacts upon the distributive system, but in terms of their core or peripheral status in the world system. A peripheral status coupled with a base of low economic development and poor resource allocation or ownership is most likely situated in the Fourth or Fifth Worlds. As a system, its adaptive capacity is generally weak or poor, and this in turn adds tensions to the society's relationship with the larger global system. Central problems in this society converge with basic needs and adaptation.

The purpose of this section is to begin thinking in at least "systems terms" when discussing globalization or aspects of the global condition. From Durkheim to Parsons, there is a strong "systems" imagery in sociological literature. The problem has been that the term "system" has been rather restricted to use in conjunction with the "national society" or nation state. How we get beyond that point is to map out the very features and properties of the modern global system. Is a global institution merely an organizational format in the human circumstance or does it, in addition, serve some broader and wider purpose? In other words, how does it function in the larger scheme?

Global connectivity as expressed through global institutionalization is merely in its infancy. In the past half-century we have seen the birth of new goal-attaining formats and forums in the modern human condition. We cannot say, at this period, that we are at the "end of history" with the development of the constitutional nation state. The nation-state is but one development in the overall processes of globalization. Future societies, for instance, may place a very high premium on global institutional formats (i.e., social control, global problems, etc.) rather than the volunteerism of a small set of national societies (i.e., nation-states participating in the Gulf War).

Global organization and global connectivity at the level of the globe are evident processes at work. They have systems generating potential and can be viewed to function in that light. Time will eventually tell how much more common they will actually become and with what scope of authority they will essentially act.

new york and other things.

well
how else was grand central station
supposed to be
in this late october
in this seasonal change to new york's gush of cold

not winter yet
yet this ever pulsing monument to the golden
age of transportation gives refuge
to the outcast
the ostracized cowboys of urbanity with their own visions
perhaps mutated, but nevertheless a
coherent storyline
of how life unfolds in the city.

Ferlinghetti, Kerouac, Ginsberg
came closest
the attempt to mainstream this scatter of visionaries
within a dominant literary poetic theme...

But now as an autumn leaf falls
even these voices recede.

Now here on a leafless twig
The ongoing rush hour of destiny unfolds.

CHAPTER EIGHT

Global and Societal Computerization Authored and Presented by Joseph J. Matvey, III, Ph.D. and Tsze Chan, Ph.D.

This chapter, perhaps more than any others in this volume represents a loose-knit federation of concepts, structural parameters and cultural ideal orientations. The ideas presented here developed from an all night dialogue session between myself and my colleague, Tsze Chan. They took place in an empty classroom building at Francis Marion College in Florence, South Carolina. We owned the blackboard that evening and made good use of it in modeling, mapping and charting our theoretical and empirical direction. Several months later, the dialogue continued on Chan's home turf in Washington DC at University of Maryland. We pored through our pages of notes, again in dialogue, but this time grasping for an overview, integration, and ordering of those notes.

The following chapter, then, heavily drawing upon societal and global determinants as well as cultural ideal orientations, represents more of what might be termed "a conference draft" or more so, a basic working outline we presented at Penn State University in the winter of 1988. Unlike the other essays, this federation of structural and cultural conditions is offered more as a typology for the growing phenomenon of Global and Societal Computerization.

Introduction

At first sight, societal and global computerization as sociological themes appears most appropriate in discussions and inquiries of so-called post-modern societal systems. Computerization, in fact, achieved central relevance in sociological thought during the initial thematization of Post-Industrialism. Although debate continues on the relevance of particular notions regarding transformative and epochal shifts at the theoretical core of Post-Industrialism, there are clearly technological and techno-occupational characteristics common to this particular societal type. One technological characteristic is revealed in the comprehensive manifestation of computerization throughout the structural and cultural fabric of the social system. While heightened computer use by individuals and the emergence of computers as household items are two indicators of this phenomenon, more fundamental is the proliferation of institutional and sectoral utilization along with the linkages within and across these sectors. There appears to be, in other words, a growing density of inter- and intra-sectoral computer-assisted networks of communication and information. These networks are partially a response to the expanding functional adaptability of the computer over the past half-century on the one hand, and the growing complexity of management and information coordination needs fostered by higher rates of societal and intra-sectoral differentiation on the other.

Computerization and the System of Societies

Despite the pervasiveness of computerization in information- based post-industrial society, there are logical justifications in applying themes of societal and global computerization across the entire system of societies. First, there is, in fact, evidence of numerous drives and active initiatives — whether directed by a central political bureaucracy or particular institutional sectors within a system — toward computerization in less developed countries (LDCs). Although these may be limited in terms of nationwide span and scope due to numerous structural constraints, they nevertheless embed the computerization process within larger drives and orientations on the part of state toward modernity.

A second central reason for considering computerization as a process with global implications is while access and utilization of computers by the general population is essentially irrelevant in vast numbers of underdeveloped countries, computerization in terms of its significance to specific central sectors is visibly evident. Sectors are essentially more fundamental to the theme of societal computerization, primarily due to the fact that it is the institutional sector, in the sociological sense of the word, which is a pivotal organizing force and steering mechanism over communication and information flows and production and exchange. Institutional and sectoral elites, particularly in the less developed world, occupy the command positions for decisions regarding social change and modernity in these societies. Although computerization may be out of reach for the masses, it may also increasingly be viewed as a necessary technology by elites of specific sectors; hence the sectoral focus, in most cases, is a starting point for inquiry and analysis of the emergence and development of computerization in the less developed world.

A third point of consideration, constituting the central focus of this chapter, rests with the globalization process and its subsequent impacts upon societal drives toward computerization. Globalization can be defined as the tightening of the world into a more "compressed" and interdependent landscape. In a rapidly globalizing world, the information and communication networks of sectors discussed above do not neatly end at the borders of a societal system. While there tends to be a general vertical-integrative pattern among institutional and organizational sectors within a social system, there are also numerous horizontal links between "like" sectors and organizational forms at the distinctly global level. This tends to bond societal elites and sectoral specialists within globally-oriented networks of communication and productivity flows. This dynamic not only affects societies with a post-industrial base or on the verge of modernization, but underdeveloped Fourth and Fifth World societies alike.

Toward a Model of Societal/Global Computerization

At the level of the system of modern societies, we present a typology of determinants through which the general phenomenon of "societal computerization" is examined. The reasons as to why a society undertakes computerization, the format of computerization and its subsequent diffusion through various social sectors, and the variety of problems confronted in computerization are best illuminated in a schema illustrating the structural parameters and ideal orientations of computerization at both the global and societal levels.

The general model of societal computerization combines theoretical insights from the world stratification perspective, Boli-Bennett's and Meyer's stress on "global integration," Robertsonian ideas of globalization and globality, Calhoun's focus on tertiary and indirect social relationships, Parsonian notions of societal and sectoral differentiation, and Bell's emphasis on technological infrastructure and societal type. We draw from multiple perspectives in the move toward a general model of societal computerization for a number of reasons. First, while a world stratification perspective (distinguishing societies on the basis of economic rank) may tell us a great deal about the actual degree of computerization existing in a society, the very same perspective may tell us little or nothing in the way of the degree of value commitment a societal polity holds toward computerization. China is a classic case.

A similar line of reasoning can be employed if one adheres strictly to a "post-industrial" perspective, which, in placing heavy emphasis on the technological base of a society as criteria for computerization, confines sociological inquiry to a small set of technologically advanced societies. We agree that questions concerning the degree of computerization, "how computerization affects us as a society," "by what format should we develop computerization," and also the specific individual societal problems of computerization will differ and be highly particularized based upon techno-societal type. Nevertheless, the fact that such "questions" are raised at all illuminates the fundamental "significance" of computerization. Hence the phenomenon of computerization has achieved a level of global significance as noted earlier, and thus must be situated in a theoretical context well beyond the limited scope of economic rank-status or techno-societal type.

Drawing on Robertsonian insights, we contend the thematization of societal computerization must be understood in terms of the emerging universal significance of computerization in the modern system of societies on the one hand, and also in relation to the particularized context of the individual societal system on the other. Hence, the model not only includes categories defining global and societal value commitments toward computerization, but also categories situating societies with regard to the structural constraint and possibility. We present a preliminary typology schematizing four crucial realms for addressing the concerns and determinants of societal computerization.

In referring to the four-box scheme, emphasized are the structural parameters for computerization at the global and societal levels on the one hand, and the ideal orientations of computerization at those same levels on the other. These realms are relatively autonomous, but are also dynamically interpenetrating. That is to say, the model is non-recursive with any given realm providing influencing, constraining, and stimulus inputs to other realms.

Table 8.1

A Preliminary Typology of Determinant Realms
of Societal Computerization

	Structural Parameters	Ideal Orientations
Global	Ranking and Relations: Politico-Economic and Techno-Informational Centrality and Integration	World Informational Environment: Culture of Modernity Connectivity
	Function: Relative Positioning Subjective Perception	Function: Global Field of Definitions
Societal	Environmental Systemic Relational	Politico-Cultural Framework
	Function: Specific Constraints Format	Function: Goal Mobilization Directedness

>>>>>Particularizing Constraints>>>>>>
<<<<<Transformative Stimului<<<<<<<<<<

Global Structural Parameters: Ranking and Relations

A set of structural parameters at the global level is primarily based upon the positioning of individual societies in regard to both the degree of and potential for the development of societal computerization. In the course of ranking societal systems we are obviously invoking a type of international stratification system for societal computerization. How can such a scheme be appropriately visualized and upon what criteria should it be constructed? Will, in fact, an international stratification system of societal computerization be a mirror image of global economic stratification, or is the relative positioning of a societal system based upon a wider set of dimensions?

In an analogous manner to that in which Weber reconceptualized the Marxian notion of social class through broadening its economistic foundation to include dimensions of power and prestige, we contend both political and techno-informational dimensions must compliment the economic dimension as criteria for a stratification system of societal computerization. Ranking on the basis of Economic, Political and Techno-informational considerations includes not merely the internal strengths and capabilities of individual societies, but the network of transsocietal interrelationships in these dimensions that bind societal systems to each other within the context of the wider global system. The character and quality of these relationships themselves are a determinant force in the stratifying of modern societies, and corresponding changes in the nature of these relationships signal potential upward or downward mobility within the overall system.

1) The World Economic System: Centrality and Ranking

First, economic ranking requires one to examine computerization in relation to the world economic hierarchy and its corresponding interrelationships. At the most basic of levels, one presupposes that societies in core positions hold greater economic resources and potential to computerize, while peripheral systems lack and are dependent upon the core for such resources. A more interesting question however, concerns the degree to which computerization is effected by core-to-periphery relations. In other words, to what extent is the rapid proliferation of computerization in lead societies based upon the multiplicity of economic ties these societies hold with each other and with peripheral systems?

An additional issue concerns the degree to which global economic relationships stimulate the potential for non-computerized societal systems to computerize. In other words, to what extent do dependent relationships deter or promote computer-use in the periphery. We speak of this factor not only in terms of the emerging multinational corporate push to create a global market for computer-related technology, but also in relation to computerization needs fostered by a number of subsidiary organizational environments created in peripheral settings. The use of computer-related technologies generally requires a scientific-technical class capable of initiating and maintaining computerization, but in peripheral settings, as Calhoun (1987) documented in the case of the Sudan, such a class is virtually non-existent.

While scientific-technical labor may be initially imported from core zones of computerization, to what extent will this stimulate the later development of an indigenous scientific technical class? Peripheral settings often face the dual problem of the lack of educational resources to develop a scientific-technical class and the corresponding "brain drain" of the class that does exist.

2) Politico-Centrality and Integration

In addition to the economic dimension, we contend two other spheres are crucial in terms of societal potential for computerization. Political centrality represents a second dimension as it is primarily based upon internal properties such "state dominance," and "political centralization" and "bureaucratization," on the one hand, and external relations which include geo-political influence, linkage with global or intersocietal political structures, and the network of political ties a particular society is embedded within on the other. As William Aspray documented in "International Diffusion of Computer Technology, 1945-1955," both Canada's and Australia's access to computer technologies was achieved in part due to the binding political relationship these societies held with Britain. Similarly, as Maier (1988) pointed out, China, quite economically and infrastructurally unsuited for computerization, benefited in the pre-1960 period due to political ties with the Soviet Union. From a historical perspective, we must toil with the question of how political dependency in the broadest sense of the word opens avenues for access to computerization. A corollary issue pivots upon the notion of political tensions existing between a non-computerized society and core zones of computerization.

To what extent will such tensions restrict both scientific and private sector transfer of computer technologies?

3) Techno-Informational Centrality in the Global System

Finally, a third dimension following the positioning in economic and political spheres is the techno-informational centrality in the global system. While the relative status in this hierarchy is based predominately upon the level of technological infrastructure and the significance of the scientific sector within a society, it is also achieved through increases in the multiplicity of external ties of the society with a global network of techno-informational flows and exchange. These ties include scientific technology transfers and exchange, access to global computerized environments, international scientific dependency or expansionism, participation in international scientific community and conferences, and the proliferation of intersocietal technical and scientific linkages. In other words, an increase in external ties generally acts as a positive current upon the level of societal techno-informational development. While political-economic relations often determine the character of such ties, scientific ties are also determined by the volunteristic commitment toward and mobilization of the scientific sector toward connectivity with the global tech-informational network.

Empirically, what must be addressed is the degree to which the extent of techno-scientific ties and relations improves a society's potential to computerize. At the same time we must also address the issue of the control of technological transfer from lead to secondary societies of computerization.

This tri-dimensional structure designates the contextual boundaries individual societal systems operate within relative to other societal systems. This relational structure, in other words, specifies the constraints and potentials for the individual society in terms of the potential for societal computerization. Furthermore, this relational structure forms the basis for the "subjective perception" a societal system holds of itself in relation to other societal systems.

Another point for consideration is the distinctly "global" in determining the potential for computerization. We can begin to entertain the social fact of the computerization of the globe in the sense that such a phenomenon itself becomes a source of social change for individual societal systems. We will now explore in further detail the universal significance of computerization from the standpoint of the global value dimension.

Global Ideal Orientations: A General Field of Definitions

At the global level computerization is essentially perceived as one of the more significant instruments facilitating the technological "compression" and "interdependence" of the globe. This of course does not suggest technological primacy in the globalization process, rather a dynamic socio-cultural formation evolving in the direction of intensified intersocietal interaction and utilizing computerization as a kind of social highway to assist this process. Computerization is valued for its power of linkage — in other words, it represents accessing the wider global system for individual societal systems. Globalization ordains and demands a sort of rush hour of association and participation of societal and sectoral entities within larger global contexts and formats. As this dynamic intensifies, computerization's significance continues to expand. "Plugging into the world" and "accessing the system" may be catch phrases, but they also accurately describe a dynamic process lending itself to the creation of a "single world." In fact, as computerization is more comprehensively embedded in the technological aspects of globalization, it now becomes possible to speak of global computerization or the objective computerization of the globe. Global Computerization refers to the proliferation and degree of intersocietal computerized or computer-assisted linkages binding societal systems, social sectors and various institutional entities at the distinctly global level. The important point, however, is that access is both critical and paramount for all societal systems and other societal/

global institutions, and computerization is increasingly valued for is its perceived and very real ability to assist in access and connectivity.

1) Computerization and The Global Field of Definitions

In presupposing computerization's universal significance, we pose the question regarding the extent to which a set of standards, orientations and field of definitions toward computerization emerge at the distinctly global level and act as a positive current not so much upon the degree of but the commitments of societies to computerize. We contend such orientations are existent and derived in part from the objective existence of global computerization itself. Objective global computerization is not an isolated technological phenomenon in and of itself, but it is encroached within an overarching trajectory of global change confronting the whole of individual societies. This global trajectory, simply put, involves the crystallization of what Robertson (1989) terms the "world as single place."

In following Robertsonian insights, the image of a single world does not necessary represent "a global village" or the melting of societal forms within a global societal form. Rather than viewing the globe as a universal, homogenous, all-subsuming system, we conceptualize the globe as an increasingly held informational environment. As an informational stage, the globe increasingly becomes a referent point, holding normative "fields of definitions" societies draw upon and, to a certain degree, are constrained by in confronting and constructing societal identity and societal courses of action in relation to the globe. We can begin to speak of "the presentation of the societal self in global life" or "a proper place in the world" as increasingly salient sociological categories.

2) Computerization: Modernity and Connectivity

A major role of computerization at the global ideal level is its now- established embeddedness in the process and ideal of Modernity, or the upgrading of the internal societal system. Modernity is guided by what Boli-Bennett (1980) has coined as "a fairly uniform set of standards" defining "external success" in the wider system of societies, "internal success" of one's own society, and the "mechanisms" to achieve success. While connectivity is an important part of the diffusion of such standards in the international community, computerization is also increasingly perceived as a mechanism to achieve modernity and manage the complexities brought about by modernity. Computerization in the educational sector, in the political bureaucracy, the financial sector represents a means to achieve and coordinate a globally accepted and mandated end.

Computerization has achieved global-wide significance precisely because it embodies a shared set of value commitments regarding notions of societal "progress," "efficiency," "coordination," "information control and processing," and "accessibility to the world." Computerization, in short, embodies the ethical core of modernity and connectivity. Is it any wonder that the developing world increasingly defines a commitment to computerization as a means to modernity, or why societies desire "satellite" access as a means to connectivity — computerization means "coming up for air" and crossing the threshold toward a proper place in the world.

Societal Structural Parameters: Specification of Problems, Constraint and Possibility

While structural parameters at the global level often set constraints and possibilities upon societal systems with specific reference to the overall degree or rate of computerization in any given society, and global orientations toward computerization suggest standards for emulation, there are internal and internal-to-external structural dynamics operating which will strongly affect the format, style, diffusion, differential application and structural penetration of computerization in a societal system.

1) Environmental Parameters: Infrastructure and Structure

Three internal structural parameters become crucial:

Environmental, Systemic, and Relational. First, *environmental parameters* refers to present physical and infrastructural foundations upon which a societal system is built. The physical dimension includes geographic location, size, density of population, age structure, and reserve and diversity of natural resources. The infrastructure encompasses the level of development of technology with specific reference to basic communication channels in a societal system (i.e., highway networks, telephone systems, urban layouts, urban and rural connectivity, transportation system, etc.).

Undoubtedly, while the restructuring and the revolution of communication networks are outcomes of computerization, the initial configuration of computerization is delimited by the existing infrastructural grid. For example, the diffusion of computer technology and knowledge will be disseminated through the pre-established communication network of a societal system. If recognizable gaps or distortions exist in the network, or if the network is generally weak, the diffusion of this technology and knowledge will be minimal, with a tendency toward a clustered configuration, concentrating in urban centers and university settings. Furthermore, a societal system with weak internal communication linkage does not provide a favorable environment for the type of large scale spatial integration (national area networks) achieved through computerization. A well-structured network on the other hand, as in the case of Japan and the U.S., facilitates the development of computer communications that is national in scope, as found in coast to coast networking, simulcast-conferencing, national bulletin boards, etc. While the clustered concentration of computerization in particular urban zones may permit access and connectivity to the wider global computer communications systems, nation spanning connectivity may be impossible given various environmental constraints.

2) Systemic Parameters: Complexity and Differentiation

Second, *systemic parameters* are closely associated with environmental parameters, but address the internal social structure of a social system. Following the Parsonian (1977) and neo-functionalist paradigmatic orientations, a general concern begins with the internal differentiation between sectors of a social system. We presuppose a greater degree of differentiation existing in a societal system tends to produce a higher state of complexity to be managed and coordinated. Complexity may assume the multidimensional form of integration, communication flows, and information storage and retrieval. A high state of differentiation also specifies, defines and refines operations, procedures, functions and tasks, requiring efficient mechanisms for command, control, and communication. In both instances, computerization functions to solve these basic needs created by a high level of differentiation.

Examining the empirical unfolding of societal computerization, one will observe the differential application of computerization among societal sectors even in the lead societies of computerization. In other words, computerization may be heavily embedded with the medical sector but virtually non-existent with the agricultural or human services sector. Hence, some sectors become lead sectors or assume a state of sectoral primacy with reference to computerization. What accounts for the sectoral lopsidedness in computerization's development? We suggest three interrelated determinant factors.

A first determinant is the degree of differentiation within societal sectors. The same logic in reasoning can be applied to intrasectoral differentiation as was applied to intersectoral differentiation. Greater complexity within a sector will tend to produce a greater need for coordination, and also increase the flexibility of a sector in confronting its own computerization. For instance, a highly internally differentiated social sector will tend to produce technical specified strata capable to accommodate and manage computerization

A second determinant pivots upon the external relations of the societal sector. Here, we are concerned with either the voluntary or externally induced linkage of a intrasocietal sector with international or transsocietal sectors, in other words, how integrated or hybridized is a particular sector in relation to the international system. If for instance, an intrasocietal medical sector has heavy ties with global health organizations, the international medical community and societies with computerized medical sectors, the chances, opportunity, and expectations toward computerization necessarily increase. Also, particularly in the underdeveloped world we often witness highly modernized multinational corporate induced economic production sectors alongside more traditional and indigenous sectors. It is the former that tend to mirror or conform to the computerized techno-organizational style and format of the multinational, not due to any intrinsic characteristics of the sector, but rather due to its dependence, hybridization, and connectivity with an international sector.

Finally, a third determinant centers upon the primacy of a scientific-technical orientation of sector. A sector relying heavily upon a scientific-technical base usually requires a direct application of computers. Indeed, the computer was initially developed for the purpose of calculations and decoding operations in the scientific and military sectors, respectively. The functional compatibility of the computer to the needs of the governmental and financial sectors easily led to the transfer of computer technology to these sectors. The subsequent proliferation of computer functions specifically in areas of communications networking and information management in turn, led to the further diffusion of computerization to a variety of other societal sectors. This suggests, however, a sectoral primacy in scientific-oriented sectors, followed by sectors with high needs for coordinating calculation, followed by sectors with high needs for coordinating communication and information.

3) Relational Parameters: Tertiary and Indirect Social Relationships and Integration

We now examine the third and final societal structural parameter, the *relational parameter*, closely associated to the degree of societal differentiation. The relational parameter focuses upon the orchestrated relationships of the society or the integration of a societal system on the one hand and the stratified occupational structure on the other.

With regards to integration, following Calhoun's (1987) insights, a crucial role of computerization is its integrating function through facilitating numerous "indirect" and "tertiary" relationships. This of course runs hand in hand with the degree of differentiation in a society. The greater the level of differentiation and complexity, the more integration is accomplished through indirect relationships. Therefore, a society dominated by tertiary relationships provides a highly conducive environment for the development of computerization — primarily in the sense that in eliminating the central status of intimate and direct face-to-face relationships the computer emerges as a crucial force to establish societal integration.

With regards to the occupational structure, an occupational group that is primarily concerned with information processing, information management and retrieval will tend to be the lead strata in computerization. At the same time, resistance to computerization may occur in the strata where there exists a high capital-labor substitution rate.

The permutations of these structural parameters present a wide range of constraints and the corresponding format of computerization. It remains an empirical question to categorize a society according to these structural characteristics. Analytically, a societal system with weak spatial communication links, with a low level of societal differentiation and correspondingly low level of differentiation within sectors, weak links to the international sectors or other sectors within the societal system, and with a relatively low scientific-technical orientation would tend to find itself with both high constraints and low needs in facing the task of computerization. Correspondingly, what kind of tensions are produced in the face of global "expectations" and "definitions" obligating a society to modernize and connect in conjunction with an internal system non-conducive to this development? Will this create a tiny but highly prestigious scientific-technical elite generally unconcerned with upgrading the internal social structure and more concerned with the development of a single sector?

Societal Ideal Orientations: Goal Mobilization and Directedness

1) Reflexive Interpretation and the Global Field of Definitions

While a fairly coherent "field of definitions" emerges at the global level for the significance and meaning of computerization, societal-specific goal orientations are primarily generated through a process of reflexive interpretation. Reflexive interpretation is the societal filtering of a more general field of definitions in conjunction with the internal cultural system and the boundaries defined by global and societal structural parameters.

We contend transformative power exists within the goal orientations of the internal societal system precisely because generated in this realm is a mobilized course of action in relation to a society's present circumstances. Global structural parameters often define the "actual perception" a societal system holds of its standing in relation to other societal systems. Societal Structural parameters define a specific set of problems for the format and diffusion of computerization. The global field of definitions exists as a set of expectations in terms of "what a society" should actually do and "why a society" should computerize. In other words, and especially the case for the developing world, politico-cultural goal mobilization represents somewhat of an interbalancing between globally prescribed orientations and the very real material constraints these societal systems confront.

At this point specific goal orientations emerge with regard to societal computerization. For instance, a strong commitment to computerization can yield structural change in infrastructural communications, systemic differentiation, and relational integration and stratification. This in turn may be accompanied by externally oriented moves such as overseas student and scientific exchange, increased technological trade and transfer, greater levels of connectivity. Both internally and externally oriented changes offer the possibility of a change in the relative position of a societal system in the broader global system.

2) Orientational: Primacy and Fluency and The Global Field of Definitions

The first task at hand at this juncture rests with an examination of the internal cultural system, specifically relating to its continuity with the more general and global field of definitions regarding computerization. In coming to grips with both the global and societal ideal orientations of computerization, some societal or sectoral formations will take a commanding lead in the symbolization or valorization of computerization. The term, *orientational primacy* may be utilized when referring to societal systems or societal sectors at the cutting edge of computerization.

While part of the valorization process in the general field of definitions emerges from the objective computerization of the globe, also clear is the fact that a number of lead societies of computerization are strategic value generators and contributors to this field of definitions other societies draw upon. These lead societies can be thought of as "active initiators" of the field of definitions. They are the *showcase* that demonstrates the results of high commitment to the values of speed, efficiency, access and progress of computerization. In this respect, lead societies of computerization can be viewed not merely in a state of cultural continuity with the global, but the active definers and shapers of these orientations. Below societies and their sectors exhibiting orientational primacy other societal systems and sectors can be conceptualized to exist in various states of *orientational fluency* in relation to the general field of definitions. Orientational fluency defines the degree of cultural receptiveness toward universal orientations. Furthermore, orientational fluency can be defined as a continuum of continuity with respect to the internal cultural system's integration or meshing with global orientations.

3) Cultural Syncretism and Reticence and the Global Field of Definitions

A culture can be Syncretic or Reticent. This represents another continuum and is grounded in longstanding religio-cultural orientations regarding man, nature, technology, society, and images of the world. It also casts a societal system's cultural flexibility in fusing external orientations with the internal cultural framework.

Cultural syncretism, broadly defined, refers to a relatively high state of flexibility of the internal cultural system in adopting and incorporating meanings and symbols from other societal systems and at the international level within the internal framework. Cultural syncretism may take the incorporating form as in the case of Japan, which, while remaining culturally independent has the built-in ability to seek elements from the outside world and incorporate these in a uniquely Japanese fashion. Syncretism may also take a more pluralistic form where the guiding cultural ethos essentially expands and is modified in the process of enveloping new meanings and symbols from the external world.

Cultural reticence, on the other hand, implies a cultural condition highly resistant to outside incorporation and influences, tending to view the external as purely "alien" or "evil" and the internal as "sacred." Resistances to not only standardized notions of computerization, but also to the more general standardized definitions of modernity and connectivity may destroy any hoped state of orientational fluency of the existing society.

Cultural syncretism or cultural reticence, in shaping a society's degree of orientational fluency, provides a base for the generation of particular internal commitments toward computerization, which are either heavily congruent or heavily divergent from globally defined orientations.

Globalization and the Diffusion of Computerization

In this final section we turn our attention to the objective Globalization Process, particularly in the last half-century, and examine the growing influence of Globalization upon societal systems to computerize. We suggest five central aspects of Globalization in conditioning and shaping the global field of definitions regarding societal computerization.

1) Socialization through Association

First, often within global institutional and organizational environments, social elites and representatives of the LDCs witness the tremendous dependence of their First World associates upon computerization in terms of research, modeling, on-line communication, the construction of programs of actions, and general day-to-day work tasks and routines. The global institution and global gatherings, conferences, and events often function as arenas for the dissemination of these value orientations toward and modes of dependence upon computerization from First World members to members of LDCs. In other words, through their very association in global institution, societal elites and non-technical representatives are socialized to revere computerization as one of the necessary rhythms and drives in the modern world.

2) Global Area Networks

Second, global connectivity in the form of both internationalized sectors and global institutions tends to encourage computer dependence among associated societal sectors and specialists. A number of global institutions, like the World Health Organization for instance, function at a much more extensive capacity than an annual ritualistic gathering of various national representatives. Some are complex, enduring work environments necessitating continued interaction and inputs from sphere-specialists operating in various national contexts. In this sense, intensified commitments to globally oriented interaction make geographic space problematic. While increases in the frequency of regional and global conferencing partially solves this problem, the development of a global computerized infrastructure in societal systems allows masses of information and interaction to flow quite easily across national boundaries. Global Computerized Infrastructure refers to the technological hardware, and apparatus societal systems and sectors within those societal systems plug into in accessing wider global networks. It essentially provides connectedness and linkage, and the most fundamental expression of a global infrastructure of computerization includes the GAN (global area network).

There is a proliferation in recent years of GANs, primarily in the form of international network systems providing opportunities for communication, dialogue, techno-informational flows, and an increase of social density at a distinctly global level. GANs are utilized by not only highly structured global institutional forms, but also by specialists and individuals who form temporary loose knit global associations through connectivity. GANs take numerous forms including international conferencing by specialists in the academic, scientific, and political spheres. They are also increasingly used to tighten the interdependence of the global financial communities and multinational corporate networks.

What is central for our purposes here with regard to GANs is the ability and degree to which societal sectors and specialists can access the variety of GANs, as access tend to be more difficult and expensive for least developed nations. In the less developed world, increased pressures and expectations to computerize interface with numerous internal structural constraints creating particularized tensions and frustrations not common in more developed societal systems. Tombaugh's (1984) evaluation of an International Scientific Computer Conference provides one example. Although close to one-third of the invited scientists from the developing world and slightly over 20% from the developed world participated in the computer conference, Tombaugh surveyed non-participants from both socio-economic settings to categorize reasons for non-participation. Tombaugh noted that "time constraints were a greater problem for those in the industrialized countries, while difficulties with costs, the telecommunication link, and access to a terminal had higher mean ratings" for the scientific community in the developing world (1984: 138). Moreover, another consideration is the need created in the less developed world for a qualified scientific/technical personnel to maintain computerized infrastructure and systems, once initiated.

3) Global Information Environment

A third dimension of global computerization and its impacts upon societal systems, is the emergence and concentration of a global informational environment and the corresponding rush on the part of societal systems and sectors to link with this media. Societal sectors often utilize the satellite and global media system as a telecommunications GAN. Satellite systems require computer-assisted earth stations whereby global and regional information is gathered and disseminated. In the First World cable networks as well as individual home satellite owners accomplish this task, while in the less developed world, central institutions often act as the nucleus of access for international communication and information. Moreover, as less developed societies and their sectors purchase satellite systems along with its basic infrastructure, their is a corresponding penetration of media networks across individual societal systems to the point one can easily speak of the global media as one sphere in the process of global connectivity. Penetration creates heightened interdependence through adding to the proliferation of national media personnel in contact with more globally centralized and computer-dependent media specialists.

4) Standards and Computerization

A fourth dimension inducing societal and sectoral computerization centers on emergent cultural orientations. Heightened reliance upon the computer as a linking form and a tool for day-to-day operations acts to create a set of standards within global institutions regarding computerization.

Standards and sets of expectations often create pressures upon more underdeveloped systems and sectors to computerize. The Sudan, for instance, offers a case of a societal system where sectoral computerization is beginning to emerge, but nevertheless highly significant to the society's drive toward modernity. Recently, a micro-computer-based information-management system was introduced within the Sudanese Planning Ministry. Although a planning ministry is highly internally focused, the plight of the less developed world has pushed many of these institutional forms within a larger transsocietal network of relationships as Calhoun details:

> ...a contemporary Third World country, especially one which depends heavily on foreign donors and related agencies for its economic well-being, is drawn into a web of record keeping, data provision and paperwork which its domestic economy would not necessitate. This is the result of its external dependency, because the international organizations which provide aid and monitor credit make the provision, manipulation and management of information central (Calhoun, 1987: 362).

In the Sudan, computerization as a means of information management becomes the saving grace, meeting the "standardized" demands of global institutions while maintaining the flows of assistance. The struggle for modernity proceeds.

5) Global Urban Environments

The emergence of Global Urban Environments may be considered yet another crucial development in the globalization process heightening the significance of computerization in less developed societal systems. Although the computer provides an indirect avenue to international interaction across geographic space, global moral density is also spatially expressed in urban environments. In particular, rapid increases in international travel and communication, in global-oriented business ventures and commitments, in global conferencing and organizational gatherings, in access, linkage and interdependence with other urban centers, and even in international commodity flows from one urban zone to the next have increasingly made all societies host to at least one or more urban zones which can be designated as a global urban center. The emergence and subsequent expansion of global urban environments reinforces the drives of societies toward computerization, particularly in the less developed world.

Heightened international density within urban zones has long created pressures for the standardization of urban infrastructure regardless of the societal context. In other words, as international interaction increases — even in the fourth and fifth world urban zones — there is a push toward standardized communications, services, office complexes, and technological infrastructure. Already, much of this is a reality in the less developed world, with the corporate sector of the urban zones a mirror image, to a certain extent, of the First World. What emerges, however, is an intensification of linkages, inputs and outputs across national boundaries in global urban centers, especially in information retrieval and management. Couple this with a growing interdependence between various global urban centers and one finds that as computerization becomes more comprehensive and pervasive within First World urban infrastructure, added pressure is placed upon the less developed world to provide the necessary technological apparatus so both interdependence and international density, perceived in many ways as a development tool, can be maintained and sustained at adequate levels.

Concluding Notes

While the considerations above by no means exhaust the potential number of global social dynamics influencing both the rate and significance of global computerization, they should give some idea of the numerous multifaceted connections, well beyond the scope of the economic and political, existing between a variety of sectors across societies. These links and connections have tended to build rapidly in recent years, whether through highly orchestrated and structured global organizational environments or decentralized communication and productivity flows between institutional specialists from differing national environments. What has been emphasized is simply that computerization is far more than a post-industrial phenomenon. It is increasing perceived as part of equation of modernity for the less developed world and highly embedded in the processes of globalization. These processes affect all societies regardless of economic base or technological type, and it is clear that globalization increases both the incentives and pressures for the less developed world to computerize, although computerization is highly geographically clustered and limited to specific urban-based sectors in many of these societies.

It should also be pointed out that changes or intensifications in the degree and format of computerization as a result of ongoing globalization tend to send reverberations throughout the entire modern global system. Higher rates of computerization in global-oriented environments and institutional settings, for instance, sends inputs to the global cultural where the meaning of computerization in modern global and societal life is continually redefined and upgraded. For instance, a quarter of a century ago computerization was more confined to notions of its role in modernity and internal systems upgrading. Computerization now emerges in the global culture as an increasingly strengthened ideal in linking the world. The broadening and redefining process for the value and meaning of computerization is generated not merely due to technological developments, but through the increasing social density and institutionalized interaction at the global level and the drives on the part of global institutional elites to incorporate computer technology in managing and ordering the density and interaction.

A redefined computerization ethic, in turn, signals numerous inputs to individual societies in terms of commitments to computerization. Part of the package of societal computerization, can no longer be primarily defined in terms of expenditures on mainframes and micros. This package must also include linkage hardware: satellite systems, upgraded telecommunications systems, and corporate offices and advanced educational facilities with the capability for on-line access to global systems of information.

There is also, of course, a wider question regarding global computerization and comprehensive social change in the less developed world, particularly the Fourth and Fifth Worlds. What other kind of tensions are produced in the face of global "expectations" and "definitions" obligating a society to computerize and connect in conjunction with an internal structural system highly non-conducive to this development? Will computerization in this instance continue to reinforce a tiny but highly prestigious urban-based political and scientific-technical elite who may be both highly involved with the modernization of a few central sectors and intricately connected to the larger global system, but generally immobilized in terms of upgrading the entire internal social structure and fabric?

Certainly there can be little doubt of the significance of computerization to all societies. What is unclear at this point in historical time, however, is whether its power will be harnessed, adapted and geared toward large-scale progressive and comprehensive social change in the less developed world.

organic decay

What dark night of the collective soul is this?
where once thriving factories
are shut down cold
and stand and lifeless monuments from another history
--now not even remembered.

And what stony ground is this
where farmers weep broken dreams across the heartland
whose subsidies can no longer hope to heal this pride
eroded like wheat fields in broken earth
which drain and mix with acid rain and shine bright
from stream to shining stream.

What organic decay is this
where those working class hands rest idle
and tap tap tap against the brain in the despair
of human anxiety
and watch television for three thousand hours continuous
and eat mcdonald's cheeseburgers in living rooms across america.

O america, land of the pilgrim's pride
and entrepreneurs with bold ideas for a brave new world
land of opportunity and dreamers...

Well what dreams are these surfacing from an empty liter
of kentucky bourbon
who wobble on barstools for stability and
whose barely open eyes no longer yearn for
the homerun ball in the bottom of the ninth
or the pass on fourth and long

Who lost hope
when men of the high office body politic
caused the common heart to burn with passion
over those mighty words of liberty, democracy, and justice
and who delivered waste, decay, and the welfare state.

O America: behold the great whore of babylon
who sits on your hillsides
with the kings of monopoly capital.
and what men are these who walk in the shadows of such
corporate towers
who are driven to such acts of desperation in hunger's name
who no longer feel or see or hear or know

the words you so gently speak: liberty, democracy, justice.
they have become your end product america:
rational, strategic, calculating and watered-down robotic
instruments of movement.

What dark night of the collective soul is this
where no children dream.

CHAPTER NINE

The Technological Compression of the Globe: Indicators and Indexes

Part 1: Global Computerization and Globalization

Globalization. Globality. Post-Modernity. Transculturalism. Multi-Culturalism. Post-Industrialism. All of these are the jargonistic catchwords of the new millennium, within and beyond the academia, but do these conceptualizations have any meaning outside of the First World or beyond the borders of the most developed societies. What meaning or significance does a computer, let alone a television set or radio mean to the masses living in the underdeveloped and so-called Third- or "bottom" of the world?

The centrality of technological or communications connectedness is quite evident in many of the so-called modern and/or post modern societies. If we take one indicator of connectedness, such as "internet" usage over the past 20 years we can view the growing embeddedness of computerization in the First World. In terms of computerization rates from 1985–2005, we find in 1985 the U.S. held the lead over select European and various First world societies, with 90.1 computers per every 1000 persons. By 2000 however, most first world nations, especially in Europe, equalized the U.S. at levels near or above 500 computers per 1000 persons. We can see that trend quite clearly in a small sampling of first world nation states including Norway, United Kingdom and Netherlands. All lagged behind the US in 1985, but by 2005 these same societies rivaled the US in terms of computer use per 1000 persons.

Table 9.1
Computerization in the First World

Computers per 1000 Persons	1985	2000	2005
Norway	28.4	515	681
United Kingdom	36.4	441	623
Netherlands	22.4	450	655
Ireland	23.8	404	507
Germany	24.0	361	614
Belgium	20.1	405	491
US	90.1	580	687

(Source: See Data Source)

Furthermore, since 1985, Taiwan, Japan, and Canada witnessed equalization in computerization rates when compared to the U.S., and in fact, several societies took the lead over the U.S. These included such societies in the "700 per 1000 Persons" levels such as Australia, Sweden, South Korea, Switzerland and among others, New Zealand.

Table 9.2
Globalization and the Objective Computerization of the Globe

Computers per 1000 persons	1985	1991	1995	2000	2005
United States	90.1	245.4	364.7	580	687
Europe	14.3	60.2	113	248.9	503
World Wide	7.8	25.2	44.9	90.3	156

(Source: See Data Source)

If we take a look at the Globe as the unit of analysis, we find a steady trend upward, even in non-First World nations, toward computerization. Of the 6.1 billion people on earth, there are some 1 billion Internet users connected to global cyberspace. This is not so remarkable when we examine other indicators of connectivity such as land phone use and cell phone use. Here we find 1.2 billion connected through land phone lines, while almost double, at 2.3 billion for mobile phone units. We might be tempted to quit at this point, noting that 1 in 6 are connected globally through computers and land phones, while 1 in 3 are joined through the use of the cell phone. It is not that easy to forge such conclusions.

Theoretical Considerations: Computerization and the Global

Societal and Global Computerization, I contend, can be applied both theoretically and empirically in terms of its relevance to the entire system of societies. Along with computerization as one indicator of globalization, we find several other relevant trends of connectedness including mass media indicators such as television, radio, newspaper, and land and cellular phone use. All of these illuminate the concept of connectedness, and in turn, are regulated and ordered by the globalization process. Hence we will not only analyze Internet Users per 1000 persons at the societal and global levels, but also examine computerization's brother and sister technologies that range from Television, Radio, Newspaper, Cell and Land Phones. All of these are key items in linking not only the national society, but also the global society and culture as well.

In reiterating a fundamental passage from Chapter Eight we find that at the most general of levels, computerization is essentially perceived as one of the more significant instruments facilitating the **technological** "compression" and "interdependence" of the globe. This, of course does not suggest technological primacy in the globalization process, rather, a dynamic **socio-cultural** formation evolving in the direction of intensified intersocietal interaction and utilizing computerization as a kind of social highway to assist this process. Computerization is valued for its **power of linkage**, in other words, it represents accessing the wider global system for individual societal systems. Globalization ordains and demands a sort of rush hour of association and participation of societal and sectoral entities within larger global contexts and formats. As this dynamic intensifies, computerization's significance continues to expand. Plugging into the world and accessing the system may be catch phrases, but they also accurately describe a dynamic process lending itself to the creation of a "single world." In fact, as computerization is more comprehensively embedded in the technological aspects of globalization, it now becomes possible to speak of **global computerization** or the objective computerization of the globe. Global Computerization refers to the proliferation and degree of intersocietal computerized or computer-assisted linkages binding societal systems, social sectors and various institutional entities at

135

the distinctly global level. The important point, however, is that access is both critical and paramount for all societal systems and other societal/global institutions, and computerization is increasingly valued for its perceived and very real ability to assist in access and connectivity.

Part 2: Methodological and Empirical Concerns

The methodology of this work is grounded in, analyzed, and draws conclusions from a 191 UN-defined system of societies or nation states. This "global" database contains roughly 20 variables or indicators of techno-communicational connectedness. A description of the database is provided below, which contains both variable names and their label definitions. While most variables are connectedness indicators, there are also several categorical variables that rank order the global system of societies into several tiers or "worlds" for sociological analysis. Finally, aside from categorical variables and connectedness indicators, there are several more basic "developmental" or "socio-economic" variables ranging from Gross Domestic Product to Urbanization to Literacy and among others, Life Expectancy.

Much of the world today is described and viewed as either a system of Developed and Less Developed Countries (LDCs) or as a categorical ordering of First, Second, and Third Worlds. Another catch phrase that flows or has evolved from the "worlds" methodology is Wallerstein's Core, Semi Periphery and Periphery model. All of these schemes are useful, and while I would not challenge the basic "LDC," "3 Worlds," or "Core to Periphery" thrust of these nation state arrangements, I would develop a more detailed and intricate classification system.

In this work I will propose a 5-tier system centrally grounded in the GDP RANK order of those societies. Hence, Afghanistan, at $800 GDP per Capita, is clearly in the fifth tier of the GDP RANK, while Japan at $31,600 is situated in the first tier. Hence, I propose a 5 tier ranking grounded in Gross Domestic Product per Capita, and will simply term this the "GDP RANK" model.

The Global Database (2005)

The construction of the Global Database utilized in this work is from several sources. Two almanacs, The World Almanac and the Time Almanac provided much of the raw developmental and socioeconomic data, while online statistics were gathered from such sources as The CIA World Fact Book and The World Almanac online. Most, if not all of the raw data--with the exception of time series trends in computerization--among the First World that was presented in the Introduction, reflects data from the year 2005.

In Table 9.3 of the Global Database summary, we find 191 observations (obs), 19 variables/indicators (vars), and the Label Definitions of the Variables off to the right. Variables such as INTPER refer to the indicator of Internet Users per 1000 persons. TVPER follows and represents the number of TVs per 1000 persons. Such is the case with RADIOPER, NEWS, LANDPER, and CELLPER. These variables are summed and assigned Means and other descriptive statistics such as Standard Deviations and Minimum and Maximum Values. Primarily, the variables are summed and categorized by either 1st though 5th Tiers or by a 5th WORLD and All Other Countries classification.

Table 9.3
The Global Database

```
Contains data from glodatup.dta
  Obs:   191 (max= 32766)
  Vars:   19 (max=    99)
 Width:   87 (max=   200)
```

1.	COUNTRY	str15	%15s	Nation State
2.	POP	float	%9.0g	Population
3.	URBAN	float	%9.0g	Urbanization
4.	GDP	float	%9.0g	Gross Domestic Product
5.	LIFE	float	%9.0g	Life Expectancy
6.	UNEM	float	%9.0g	Unemployed
7.	INFL	float	%9.0g	Inflation
8.	TVPER	float	%9.0g	TVs Per 1000 Persons
9.	RADIOPER	float	%9.0g	Radios Per 1000 Persons
10.	NEWS	float	%9.0g	Newspaper Circ. Per 1000
11.	LITERACY	float	%9.0g	Literate
12.	INTPER	float	%9.0g	Internet Use Per1000 Persons
13.	OLCAT	float	%9.0g	On Line Connectivity Rank
14.	TVCAT	float	%9.0g	Television Connectivity
15.	RADCAT	float	%9.0g	Radio Connectivity
16.	GDPRANK	float	%9.0g	GDP Per Capita
17.	FIFTHW	float	%9.0g	The Fifth World
18.	LANDPER	float	%9.0g	Land Phones per 1000 Persons
19.	CELLPER	float	%9.0g	Cell Phones per 1000 Persons

State of the Worlds: GDP RANK

Before examining the indicators of connectedness and their interrelationships, it will prove useful to look at some basic descriptive statistics for several developmental and socioeconomic variables based on the GDP RANK order. This will give us a sort of "State" of the Globe and allow us to quantitatively understand the usefulness of the categorical variables such as GDP RANK in the Five World or Five Tier model.

Referring to Table 9.4, notice the statistical drop from the 1st through 5th Tier of the ranking system. In almost every socioeconomic variable there is significant variance among each grouping. Life Expectancy descends from 78 years to 72 to 68 to 58 to 50 across the tiers, while Urbanization witnesses a substantial drop as well from 77 to 67 to 54 to 35 to 30 percent.

Table 9.4
Developmental and Socio-economic Statistics: Ranked 1ˢᵗ to 5ᵗʰ Tier (GDP Rank)

Descriptive Statistics: URBAN, GDP, LIFE, UNEM, INFL, LITERACY

Variable	GDPRANK	N	N*	Mean	SE Mean	StDev	Median
URBAN	1	29	1	77.53	3.39	18.25	83.40
	2	53	0	67.02	2.17	15.79	66.30
	3	40	0	54.21	3.10	19.58	51.95
	4	49	0	35.61	2.11	14.74	34.90
	5	19	0	30.58	4.06	17.69	26.50
GDP	1	30	0	33557	1588	8698	31050
	2	53	0	13287	728	5299	12000
	3	40	0	4935	178	1128	4700
	4	49	0	1895.9	75.8	530.3	1900.0
	5	19	0	800.0	32.4	141.4	800.0
LIFE	1	30	0	78.14	1.03	5.65	79.26
	2	53	0	72.20	1.07	7.78	73.26
	3	40	0	68.52	1.59	10.03	70.84
	4	49	0	58.12	1.36	9.50	59.25
	5	19	0	50.74	2.26	9.86	48.47
UNEM	1	30	0	6.83	1.07	5.88	5.10
	2	52	1	11.50	1.37	9.86	9.80
	3	37	3	17.04	2.63	16.00	12.30
	4	34	15	17.00	2.99	17.45	12.50
	5	7	12	47.14	7.55	19.97	50.00
INFL	1	30	0	2.440	0.428	2.344	2.050
	2	53	0	4.558	0.471	3.431	3.400
	3	40	0	5.788	0.854	5.402	4.450
	4	48	1	13.35	5.47	37.87	7.00
	5	18	1	9.27	1.49	6.30	10.30
LITERACY	1	30	0	97.00	1.00	5.48	99.00
	2	52	1	91.68	1.53	11.04	96.00
	3	39	1	85.29	2.25	14.06	88.50
	4	49	0	67.32	3.14	21.97	67.50
	5	19	0	54.66	3.95	17.21	55.00

Part 3: Variables of Connectedness

As we have viewed socioeconomic variables often described as indicators of Modernity or Post-Modernity, we now turn to the globalization process that includes a specific set of techno-communicational indicators. These indicators or variables reveal the character of connectedness among nations to the global system of societies. Hence, high rates of Internet Usage, Cell Phones or Televisions per 1000 Persons portray high rates of technological connectedness and compression. In our global database, these include:

Variable Labels of Connectedness Indicators

INTPER	Internet Users per 1000 persons,
TVPER	TVs per 1000 persons,
RADIOPER	Radios per 1000 persons,

NEWS	Newspaper Circulation per 1000 persons,
LANDPER	Land phone use per 1000 persons
CELLPER	Cellular phone use per 1000 persons

In one way or another, these variables indicate both intra- and inter- societal connectivity or connectedness. While it is true that these indicators primarily depict the "technological" aspects of connectedness, they may also be viewed as social highway markers that allow for connectivity not only within but also across societal boundaries.

In addition, as indicators of connectedness we might expect some correlation between and among these variables. In other words, do we find that Internet Use per 1000 persons might be positively related to the number of TVs per 1000 persons or Radios per 1000 persons? In some way, all these variables illuminate the connectedness aspects of "globalization" and as such, we expect to find strong relationships evident. In Table 9.5 are the results of the correlations of these variables.

Table 9.5
Correlations of Connectedness:

Correlations: CELLPER, LANDPER, INTPER, NEWS, RADIOPER, TVPER

	CELLPER	LANDPER	INTPER	NEWS	RADIOPER
LANDPER	0.750				
	0.000				
INTPER	0.831	0.867			
	0.000	0.000			
NEWS	0.610	0.674	0.740		
	0.000	0.000	0.000		
RADIOPER	0.578	0.736	0.734	0.630	
	0.000	0.000	0.000	0.000	
TVPER	0.744	0.819	0.789	0.648	0.748
	0.000	0.000	0.000	0.000	0.000

The relationships are not only significant, but also significantly strong. Examine Internet Use per 1000 persons with every other connectedness indicator. The relationship is quite entwined and does not dip below .734. In fact the weakest correlation appears to be Radio per 1000 persons with Cell Phones per 1000 persons at 0.58. Cell Phones per 1000 persons also experiences a significant relationship with Internet usage at 0.831 as these both represent "newer" technologies under the communications umbrella.

GDP RANK and Connectedness

Here, we now turn our view to Table 9.6 to GDP RANK to examine the variation across the 5 tiers in terms of connectedness indicators. In fact, what we find below is almost a mirror image to the relationship between GDP RANK and the developmental and socio-economic variables. Consider the descent of the "means" of "Internet Use per 1000 persons" across the tiers. We fall from 582 in the 1st Tier to 251 to 100 to 34 and to 9 in the 5th tier. The most developed form of connectivity in the global system of societies appears to be "Radios per 1000 persons" with the 1st Tier at almost 1 radio for every person. This figure drops and dips substantially though from nearly 500 in the 2nd World to lows clustering around 200 Radios per 1000 persons for both the 4th and 5th Tiers.

Table 9.6
Connectedness Indicators: Ranked 1ˢᵗ to 5ᵗʰ Tier (GDP Rank)

Descriptive Statistics: TVPER, RADIOPER, INTPER, NEWS, LANDPER, CELLPER

Variable	GDPRANK	N	N*	Mean	SE Mean	StDev	Median
TVPER	1	30	0	566.3	32.7	179.3	553.0
	2	53	0	331.7	21.3	155.1	312.0
	3	40	0	181.3	18.8	118.8	176.5
	4	49	0	62.3	11.4	79.7	34.0
	5	17	2	39.2	17.4	71.7	15.0
RADIOPER	1	30	0	922.5	72.3	396.1	939.0
	2	53	0	476.5	30.0	218.7	434.0
	3	40	0	369.4	38.8	245.5	287.0
	4	49	0	242.2	31.6	221.3	146.0
	5	18	1	201.2	33.2	140.7	156.0
INTPER	1	30	0	582.2	29.3	160.4	601.3
	2	53	0	251.0	23.8	173.5	227.2
	3	40	0	100.9	13.7	86.7	67.6
	4	49	0	34.06	5.08	35.53	25.13
	5	19	0	8.75	1.91	8.34	4.84
NEWS	1	30	0	273.9	27.8	152.1	291.5
	2	50	3	117.9	14.9	105.2	99.8
	3	34	6	68.2	12.6	73.4	44.5
	4	41	8	22.98	6.18	39.55	8.60
	5	15	4	5.79	1.31	5.09	4.60
LANDPER	1	30	0	534.4	33.3	182.6	507.9
	2	53	0	283.5	19.6	143.0	276.4
	3	40	0	138.5	14.0	88.2	128.7
	4	49	0	34.86	6.22	43.53	16.25
	5	18	1	9.51	2.26	9.61	7.61
CELLPER	1	30	0	916.3	55.7	305.0	960.5
	2	53	0	632.0	40.1	292.1	619.3
	3	40	0	325.1	29.4	186.1	306.2
	4	48	1	89.89	9.93	68.78	75.36
	5	18	1	39.23	5.96	25.29	35.81

Part 4: The Significance of Computerization across One-Third of the Globe: A Look at China and India

China and India not only represent interesting cases due to the sheer size of the two nations in terms of population, but also how central sectors coordinate drives toward computerization in these societies. Here, now some 20 years removed from the early initiatives on the part of India and China, they still lag far behind the First Tier of societies in terms of not only computerization but other indicators of connectedness such as TVs, Radios, and Phones.

In Table 9.7 below we compare India and China as one slice of the world, and at 1/3ʳᵈ of the world population, it is a very significant slice of the world. Internet Usage for these two giants only averages at 70 Internet Users per 1000 Persons. Other communication technologies faired slightly better. For example, the rate for Televisions and Radios for these societies was roughly in the 200 per 1000 Persons range. If we compare China and India to the rest of the World from all Five Tiers, we find both these societies lagging far behind the global means and medians despite their computerization initiatives begun in the mid-1980s. Comparing India to China we find China ahead and almost doubling connectedness experienced by India. For example while China's Internet Use per 1000 Persons was under 100 at 84, India's total barely reached 54. In terms of Televisions and Radios per 1000 Persons, China again topped in at 291 and 342 correlative to India's rate at 75 and 120, respectively. Finally, though, based on GDP Ranking, both societies, while varying with each other, are still both situated in the 3rd Tier.

Table 9.7
Connectedness Indicators: Ranked by China/India and The Rest of the Globe

Descriptive Statistics: URBAN, LIFE, UNEM, INFL, LITERACY, GDP, TVPER, ... (1 = China&India; 0 = The Globe)

Variable	chindia	N	N*	Mean	SE Mean	StDev	Median
URBAN	0	188	1	54.40	1.72	23.63	54.90
	1	2	0	33.45	5.15	7.28	33.45
LIFE	0	189	0	66.595	0.890	12.236	70.850
	1	2	0	68.65	3.94	5.56	68.65
UNEM	0	158	31	14.71	1.23	15.49	9.80
	1	2	0	8.9500	0.0500	0.0707	8.9500
INFL	0	187	2	7.21	1.45	19.81	4.00
	1	2	0	3.00	1.20	1.70	3.00
LITERACY	0	187	2	81.26	1.51	20.64	90.00
	1	2	0	72.8	13.3	18.7	72.8
GDP	0	189	0	10615	866	11909	5300
	1	2	0	5100	1700	2404	5100
TVPER	0	187	2	241.6	16.2	221.2	191.0
	1	2	0	183	108	153	183
RADIOPER	0	188	1	440.1	25.1	344.2	353.0
	1	2	0	231	111	157	231
INTPER	0	189	0	193.1	16.4	225.7	90.9
	1	2	0	69.6	14.8	21.0	69.6
NEWS	0	168	21	101.33	9.83	127.36	45.50
	1	2	0	219	158	223	219
LANDPER	0	188	1	203.0	15.3	210.2	129.4
	1	2	0	156	111	156	156
CELLPER	0	187	2	420.6	27.6	377.8	323.6
	1	2	0	181	118	167	181

A comparative analysis of China and India on one hand reveals computerization essentially out of reach for the masses, and yet, if we center ourselves in the sectors in those societies, in that particular focus we find these technologies, from computers to televisions to cell phones, highly valued in the less developed world. True, such technologies may be only possessed by the elite or the scientific-technical classes, but here too, connectedness is held in high esteem. Hence, despite computerization's low

141

diffusion across the population of societies like India and China, and throughout the less developed world, computerization as well as its brother and sister technologies are highly valued and becoming increasingly necessary in the drives toward modernity in these societies.

Part 5: Visualizing Societal Computerization

In Part 3 we examined the influence of a 5-Tier or what we might more commonly call a 5-Worlds perspective upon various empirical variables of technological connectedness. To be sure, until this point we have viewed the relationship of basic developmental and connectedness variables from the standpoint of descriptive statistics such as Means, Medians, Modes as well as Standard Deviations. From here, however, we will examine the data in scatter- and box-plot format through which the relationship between the variables can be graphically portrayed. This particularized way of presenting data allows us to visually conceptualize and pinpoint the relationship of (x) and (y), or in terms of causality, between independent and dependent variables.

As we found in "State of the Worlds" earlier in this chapter, there are strong positive relationships between GDPRANK and the developmental variables. What is needed at this point, however, is an understanding of how GDP RANKING affects and influences the variables of connectedness such as Televisions and Radios per 1000 Persons.

The first task at hand is to visualize the associations of independent variables such as GDP with dependent variables of connectivity such as Internet Usage per 1000 persons and other variables. In Tables 9.8, 9.9 and 9.10 we examine the associations between Televisions per 1000 persons, Internet Usage per 1000 persons, and Cell Phones per 1000 persons with economic factors such as raw GDP. One will note the strong influence of the economic factor and the dependent variables. Also note the significant clustering of low connectedness in less developed societal systems.

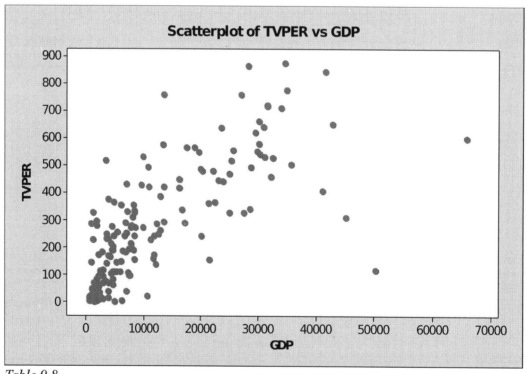

Table 9.8

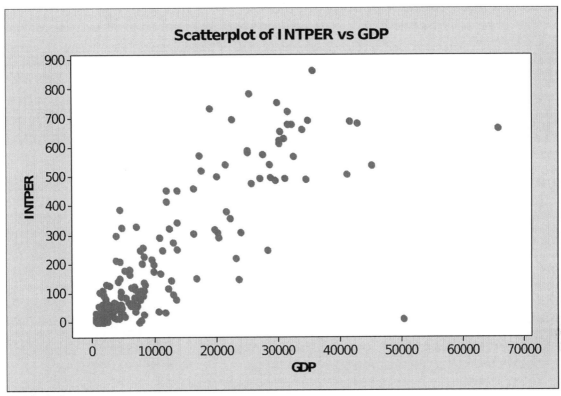

Table 9.9

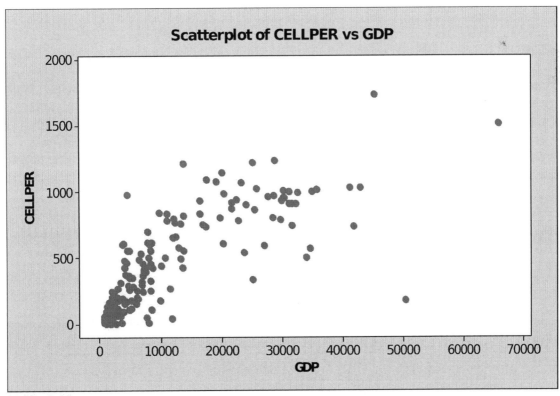

Table 9.10

Joseph J. Matvey, III

Toward a Techno-Connectivity Index

The Number of Radios per 1000 persons in a society or the number of Internet Users in that same society are not merely technological toys or symbols of material wealth, but rather, they are indicators, on the most empirical of levels, of both inter- and intra-societal connectivity or connectedness. On the one hand, in measuring these we are grasping at understanding global connectivity, particularly in terms of computerization across the system of societies. On the other hand, though, we are also looking at individual societal systems and not only their communications-connectivity but cultural-connectivity as well. A society with poor intra-societal connectivity will most likely follow suit in terms of its global connectivity, particularly with reference to communications technology.

As we saw before, many of these connectivity variables are not only influenced by GDP, but exist in association to each other. Hence, higher amounts of access to Televisions in a society are also associated with higher levels of Internet Connectedness or access to radios. It will prove useful in this particular line of thought, to assemble what we might call a "connectivity index" based on a composite of various empirical indicators of technological connectedness. For our purposes here, the TCI is comprised of six connectivity indicators:

TELPER	Televisions per 1000 persons
RADPER	Radios per 1000 persons
INTPER	Internet per 1000 persons
NEWS	News Circ. per 1000 persons
LANDPER	Land Phones per 1000 persons
CELLPER	Cell Phones per 1000 persons

First the various connectedness indicators were categorized in ranks of 5 Tiers similar to the way GDP per capita was rank ordered. In GDP ranking the First World represented the highest rates of raw GDP per capita, while societies like Zambia and Afghanistan were grouped into the 5th Tier. Hence economic rank was sorted from 1 to 5 in descending order. However, in all of the technological connectedness indicators, rank was sorted with (1) representing the highest level of connectedness for a given variable while (5) represented the least connected in the connectivity measure. Hence, the composite score for all six indicators of connectedness ranged from (6) with a society ranking in the highest degree of connectedness in all six indicators, versus a society marked at (30) which would designate a society that had scored at the lowest possible level of connectivity for each of the connectivity indicators.

In examining correlations between these indicators and the Connectivity Index in Table 9.11, we find strong and significant relationships among all of the variables and not only with the TCI but again, in association with each other. Consider the correlation of Internet Usage Per 1000 persons with the TCI at -0.860. Finding like this are common across the board of the indicators and the TCI.

144

Table 9.11
Correlations: TCI, INTPER, NEWS, RADIOPER, TVPER, CELLPER, LANDPER

	TCI	INTPER	NEWS	RADIOPER	TVPER	CELLPER
INTPER	-0.860					
	0.000					
NEWS	-0.696	0.740				
	0.000	0.000				
RADIOPER	-0.765	0.734	0.630			
	0.000	0.000	0.000			
TVPER	-0.839	0.789	0.648	0.748		
	0.000	0.000	0.000	0.000		
CELLPER	-0.842	0.831	0.610	0.578	0.744	
	0.000	0.000	0.000	0.000	0.000	
LANDPER	-0.864	0.867	0.674	0.736	0.819	0.750
	0.000	0.000	0.000	0.000	0.000	0.000

The following graphical summary in Table 9.12 gives one a portrait of some statistics such as Histograms and Medians. One will note in the histogram the distribution of connectedness (TCI) spread across the board, but with clustering in the lower levels on inter- and intra-societal connectivity.

Let us now visualize the association between the Index on the one hand, and raw GDP on the other and again we find in Table 9.13 strong and significant relationships between the economic rank order of the 5 worlds and their corresponding rates of Connectivity. Note the clustered configuration around the 20-degree mark in the TCI and their corresponding rate of Societal GDP—well below $5,000.00.

One final area of concern with regard to the TCI represents where the medians are situated when we boxplot TCI by GDP Rank Order (the 5 Worlds model) Aside from the outliers, a strong and vibrant relationship can be discerned on the basis of economic worlds and TCI in Table 9.14.

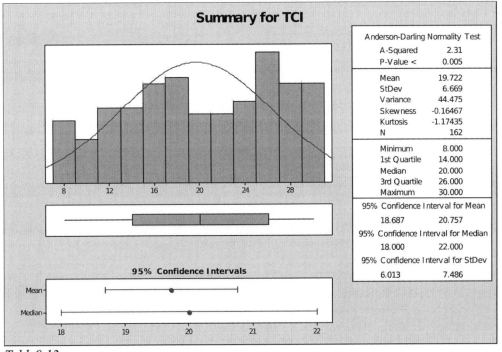

Table9.12

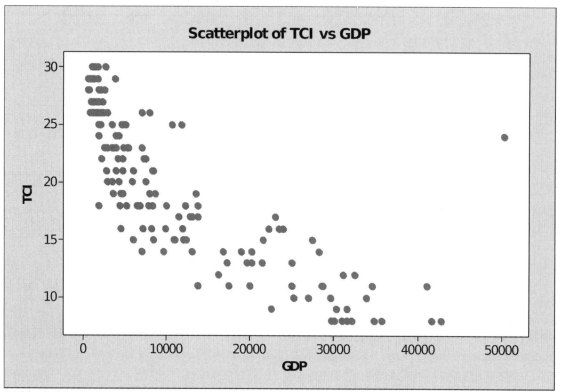

Table 9.13

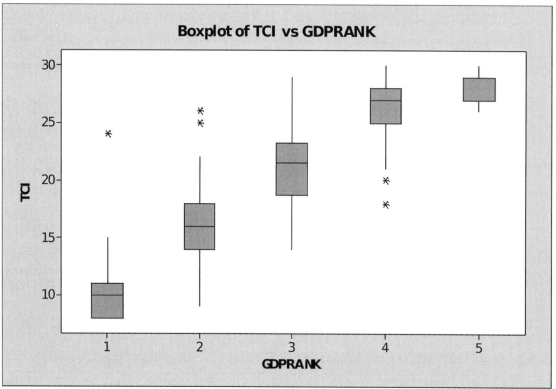

Table 9.14

Part 6: Techno-Connectedness through Historical Time

Let us turn now to a second Global Database comprised of data from 2005 and 2008 and examine what changes, if any, are occurring with respect to the development of computerization in the global system of societies. Is there, in other words, even within a short period of time (such as a three year period) increases in the level or rate of computerization in societal systems irrespective of economic ranking? This Global Database represents 200+ societies, including territories and possessions, and data was gathered for all societies from several sources including World Almanacs, World Almanacs Online, and The CIA Factbook of Nations Online. MiniTab was the preferred statistical package engaging the database and provided the output for the tables in this chapter. The scope of this database is more limited—we could only gauge changes in rates of Internet Use, Cell Phone Use and Land Phone Use. There were also limited developmental variable data from 2005 and 2008—particularly what we utilized included Literacy and Life Expectancy rates.

As an orientation to the tables, let us begin with a look at two developmental dependent variables in Table 9.15, Literacy and Life Expectancy for the year 2008. The data is filtered through the same economic Worlds model utilized for the original database. Literacy rates are presented first, followed by Life Expectancy. The economic factor, as a critical Independent Variable exerts a strong influence upon both Literacy and Life Expectancy.

Note in both sets of boxplots, with the horizontal line within the box representing the median, a steady drop in both Literacy and Life Expectancy by World. Literacy rates, for instance, approximate 100% in the First World, but fall sharply to a 30% level in the Fifth World. Similarly, Life Expectancy rates from slightly above 80% in the First World to near 40% in the Fifth World.

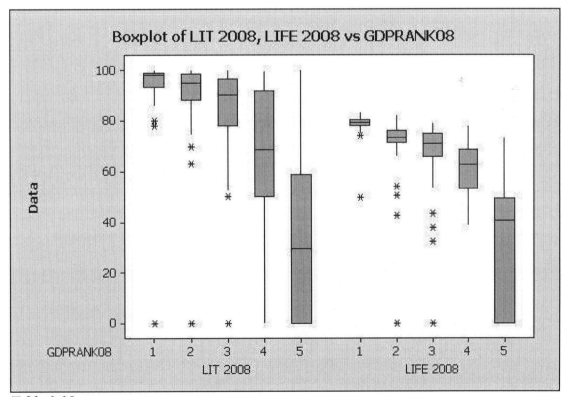

Table 9.15

Visualizing Changes in Technological Connectedness

Now let's consider data from computerization and its brother technology, the cell phone. Consider the histograms in Tables 9.16 and 9.17 for both Internet Users per 1000 persons and Cell Phones per 1000 persons for both 2005 and 2008. Note that in Internet User there has been a slightly pronounced shift in the measure of central tendency from 2005 to 2008. This shift is greater and more statistically significant with regard to the diffusion of cell phones from 2005 to 2008.

Table 9.18 is an alternative way of visualizing the increases and shifts in Internet Users and Cell Phones during this three year time period. Note in Internet Users per 1000 persons an inching upward of the more developed societies in terms of the sheer numbers of Internet Users. For instance, the highest numbers of Internet Users per 1000 persons in 2005 was less than 750, but by 2008 this rate had increased to nearly 1000. In Cell Phone technology, the shift again is more pronounced with the upper tier societies increasing from around 1200 Cell Phones per 1000 persons to over 1500!

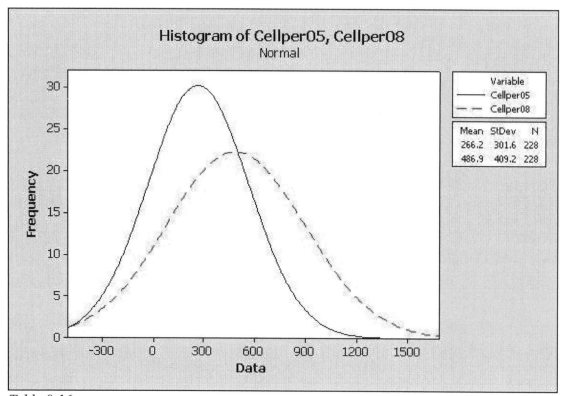

Table 9.16

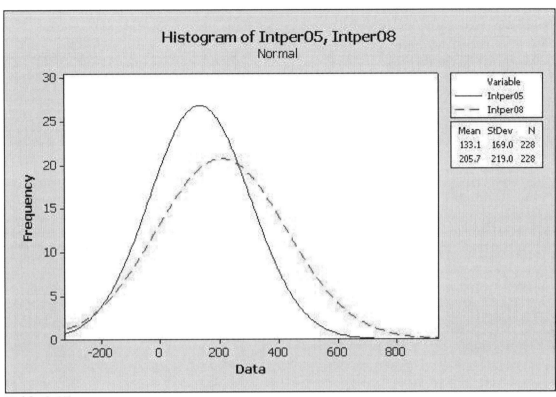

Table 9.17

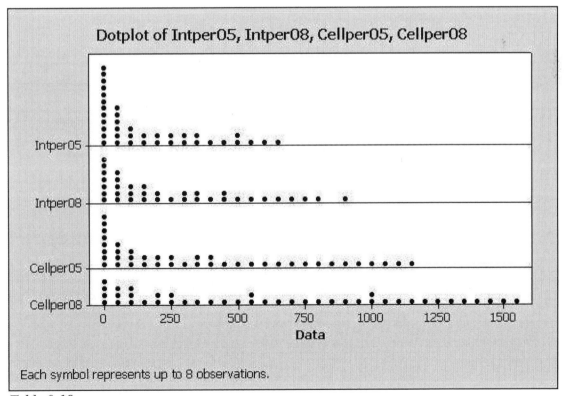

Table 9.18

At the heart of measuring rates of technological connectedness, from Internet Users to Cell Phone Users, is the strong and overwhelming presence of the influence of the economic factor. While it is true, as was earlier noted, that while computerization may be out of the reach of the masses in the less developed worlds, its significance in sectors is evident and may account from the bulk of the increases in computerization for poorer societies. Tables 9.19 and 9.20 reveal the strength of a Worlds Model. Note in Figure 9.19 and 9.20, the steady drop in both 2005 and 2008, of the median number of Internet Users by World. The asterisks represent outliers from the normal population. Note in the Fifth World, the medians are clustered around zero both for 2005 and 2008, although there was a tiny improvement from 2005 to 2008 in both the Fourth and Fifth worlds.

Cell phone diffusion is more pronounced from 2005 to 2008, particularly in the Second and Third Worlds where the median has shifted from close to 300 in the Second World in 2005 to over 600 in the same World in 2008 (compare cell phones from Figures 9.19 with 9.20). In the Third World, similarly, the medians jumped from levels near 100 to 200!

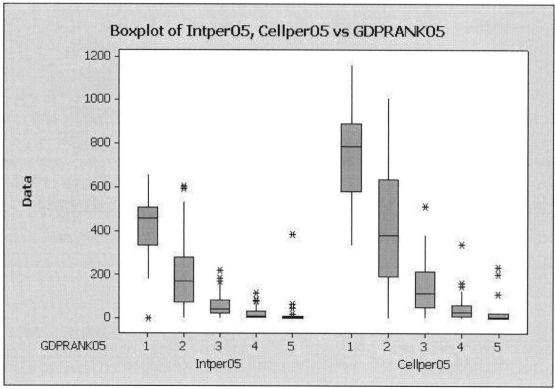

Table 9.19

150

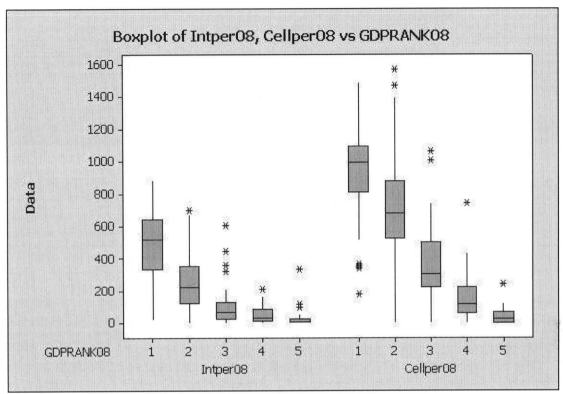

Table 9.20

A final visual example is the Interval Plot where a sample mean and its confidence interval at 95% is given for a particular dependent variable. In other words, if the intervals of, let's say, Internet Users per 1000 persons overlap between 2005 and 2008 it basically means the samples are not statistically significant or statistically differentiated from each other. This being said, we should note we are not dealing with samples here, but the actual population of the global system of societies. Hence, if Intervals do not overlap our argument and case that the populations are statistically significant only grows stronger!

In Figure 9.21, consider Land Phone diffusion from 2005 to 2008—the intervals around the means overlap to the degree that there has almost been no shift at all in 3 years. But compare these means and their corresponding intervals with Cell Phone diffusion—what a radical and progressive shift from 2005 to 2008! This shift is much less pronounced in Internet Users per 100 persons, but it is also statistically significant in that both populations are differentiated.

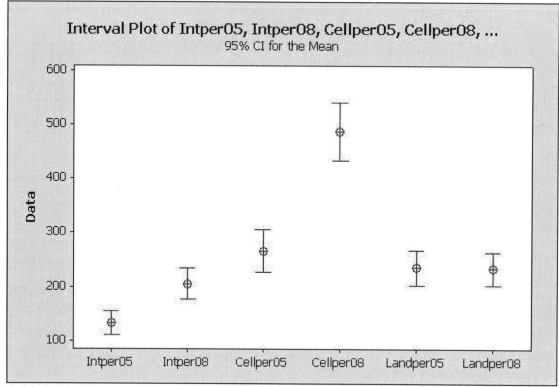

Table 9.21

Part 7: Summary of Study

At the outset, we explored computerization and the globalization process and discovered several findings.

First, we have found that classifying the world in 5 Tiers instead of 3 is a fruitful endeavor. Not taking anything away from a Core-Periphery or a First, Second and Third Worlds categorization, the 5 Tier model allows us to pinpoint subtle to overt distinctions between these nation-state groupings. What we have found in the data, from the 1st Tier to the 5th Tier is a regressing and steady drop of socioeconomic and developmental statistics; hence, the 3rd Tier can be statistically distinguished from the 4th and 5th Tiers. A distinction between the 4th and 5th Tiers is less compelling, but there is a difference in where data points cluster with respect to those societal systems on the bottom rungs.

Further, in examining the global database we are immediately presented with a great disparity in communications and computer technology between the top and bottom of the world. In the First World, computers are not only workstations, but also multidimensional household items integrating Television, Music, Video, and Communication Technology. The disparity continues across the board as much of this technology is out of reach for those beyond the doorstep of the First World.

Second, computerization is embryonic in the 3rd Tier and nearly non-existent in the 4th and 5th Tiers. In the 1st Tier computerization is manifested throughout the entire structural and cultural fabric of those nations and in those societies technological culture is primary. However, as was stressed in the introduction to this chapter, while computerization may be out of reach for the masses, it is also significant, even in the Fifth World nations to sectors and social spheres in the sociological definitions of those terms. It should also be noted that while a computer might not mean much to a village farmer and his family in rural Thailand, its existence at this point is in the hands of a tiny scientific and economic elite of that nation.

Third, Internet Users, Radios, Televisions, Cell and Land Phones and Newspapers are not merely technological culture and items of communications technology, but they represent indicators and dependent variables of globalization. We specifically call them indicators of global connectedness, but they also indicate the multidimensional and entire globalization process including global moral density (increased global interaction) and global institutionalization such as international sectors and global institutions.

Following from three, a fourth finding reveals that all of these items of global connectedness are strongly related to Gross Domestic Product per Capita, and in turn all of these indicators strongly correlated with one another. The greater the number of Televisions per 1000 Persons will also reveal a greater number of Internet Use as well as a greater number of Radios per 1000 Persons. Spikes and subsequent increases in these variables suggest reverberations and feedback to other indicators of connectedness, and all reflect life and light on the globalization process.

Finally, we found that technological connectedness or connectivity is on the move and can be adequately measured even with a period as close as three years. Cell Phone Diffusion is explosive, particularly in the developed First World and developing Second and Third Worlds, while the Fourth and Fifth World still cluster at extraordinarily low rates and levels. Internet Use is on the other hand, while significantly differentiated by World, shows somewhat less of a rate of change from 2005 to 2008. Dotplot analysis also showed some significant increases in the Developed World, and we also see this change in Interval Plots, but boxplots reveal little change in the medians from 2005 to 2008 for this particular economic group of societies.

Four Year Utopia

Afternoon.
I find myself leafing through a dust covered
bound periodical of Poetry.

Images suspended

in time now reawaken in my thoughts:
college will soon become another yearbook

Memory.
[that girl's pen is writing secret love notes
to her professor (disguised in physics equations) and

for a long time my vision began diffusing.
Even after I bought the new pair
atoms floated about lacking permanency.

I was asking myself what had happened to my values.
At breakfast she caught me wading into her breasts
but seemed infatuated.

It was three p.m. when I woke: the plants
struggle unwatered and I

writing reams of poetical ideas
hoping for beauty
amidst hundreds of fraternity parties
sociology tests and ninety-five cent cheeseburgers.

The Human Experiment. Christ this is like a disease
hanging suspended from a tree of absurdity. Wait!

You're telling me the particles comprising my brain
are billions of years old? Transitory matter?

Well
What matters is the fact I'm alive. Touch the scars
in my side and

Where is modern man?]

At least I left with a soul still awake
partly older and rusting gradually but knowing
truth finds itself

in love's gentle arms reassured and
resting in its proper place. Unnoticed as hell.

CHAPTER TEN

Globalization and Glocalization in Internet Chat Systems: The Case of the Pittsburgh Region

Introduction

Roland Robertson, perhaps the foremost sociological theorist on the paradigm of Globalization, has suggested that the process of Globalization is not necessarily a one-way avenue with macro and global processes restructuring every nook and cranny of local human communities, but it also involves what he advances as "glocalization." Glocalization is the interpretive cultural reflex of the local. Upon its contact and interaction with globalization, there is a response, an adaptation, reorganization, and redevelopment of these social responses whose outcome becomes part of what Robertson terms the "glocal."

In several respects this work is about the global. It is also about the local. And in this dynamic interplay between the two, we find a "glocalized" outcome as the cultural change and condition that results. Let us turn now to the historical emergence and development of Internet Chat Systems as one crucial part of both computerization and the Internet Experience. The methodology of this study was direct participant observation in the chat process by the author over a period from 1995-2005.

The Emergence of Chat Systems

Since 1990 there has been a steady development and expansion of Internet Chat. Before the early 1990s the closest thing to real time chat was the "online bulletin board" where people posted threaded messages to a variety of topic-driven boards and waited for replies to their posts. At this time, while real time Internet chat was embryonic, there was a large and diverse community of Bulletin Board Systems (BBS). These were launched and operated by grass roots folks who happened to have a desktop PC and modem along with enough entrepreneurial gumption to run, manage, and maintain a full service BBS.

Essentially, cyber visitors would dial into a particular BB service, wander about in the "files" lists, perhaps read and then post messages on a variety of topics, and then return later to view the ongoing message thread. Those with a larger hard disk might also sport a "pics" section where one could download pictures from the BB to their home computers. The closest thing to real time chat was if the BB owner would initiate a chat with a visitor who might be online at any given time. This chat would be one-to-one between the BB owner and visitor.

The limitation, of course, was the fact that with one phone line on the BB service, visitors couldn't type in a many-to-many chat format. One was stuck in a Bulletin Board format. Despite this, there was an explosion of BBs in the early 1990s. The BB software was easy to download and set up, and the ownership of a BB ranged from high school teens to more adult oriented sites. Hence at this particular time, Bulletin Board Systems were heavily localized and competitive, and offered primarily an avenue for message posting and pic retrieval.

What emerged in the early1990s, however, was the development of nation spanning Internet Service Providers such as Prodigy, CompuServe, and AOL. In the early years these providers offered a wide variety of services from email accounts, to bulletin boards, news, and the Web. The bulletin boards were national in scope and offered a sophisticated look and maturity as opposed to the localized BBS. Prodigy, for instance had its own nation spanning bulletin boards, as was the case with Compuserve. These boards allowed a national area network (NAN) to manifest.

Dimensions of Real Time Chat

Chat from the early 1990s developed along two prongs. The first was the development of the **Chat Room** that allowed for a many-to-many chat format. Chat rooms could not only hold many people at one time, but within the chat room there was an option for private messaging, one on one, to another person in the chat room. There was also the option to "ignore" a person if they became a bother or abused the system. Chat rooms took off on Prodigy, Compuserve, AOL, and other Internet oriented ISPs. Yahoo and MSN also developed free chat service. Stretching back before 1990 the IRC, an Internet chat client, also developed. We will explore that particular chat protocol shortly.

As chat began to develop, two major services, Yahoo (Yahoo.com) and MSN (Hotmail) emerged and offered free email and chat services to members, as opposed to pay nets such as Prodigy, CompuServe, and AOL.

Another dimension of the chat room was the development of particularized chat formats that evolved alongside "games" rooms such as poker, slots, backgammon, blackjack, pool, and many other gaming venues. In addition, Gay.com also emerged as a premier chat site for the gay community, and boasted a national area network of chat rooms.

A second manifestation of "chat" was the **Instant Messenger** carried by both Yahoo and MSN. Messenger chat was real time, but unlike the chat room format, messenger chat was one-on-one. Technological developments increased and in time one could utilize "Talk Chat" in instant messaging or even in Yahoo's chat room format. Along with this came the web-cam giving folks multidimensional avenues for the connectedness of parties.

In the Messenger format, a person would typically have a "buddy" or "friends" list of other members on the user's system. So if I was on AOL and had several folks on my buddy list, if any one of those buddies were on line, I had the option of starting a conversation with them through the use of Instant Messenger.

The evolution of Messenger saw several developments over the last 15 years. First, the system allowed the operator to create mini chat rooms comprised of a list of buddies or friends who might be online at any given time. Thus, if I was Messaging Arlene, and saw that our mutual friend, Dana, was on line, I had the option of inviting Dana into my conversation with Arlene, hence creating a mini chat room. Other developments over the years included the use of the web cam to actually see, in real time, your chat partner.

The major Messengers included Yahoo, MSN and ICQ, and also AOL. What has emerged very recently is the ability to communicate beyond sectarian lines. Here, a person with WindowsLive, an offshoot of MSN, can communicate with folks not only on MSN, but AOL's AIM and Yahoo Messenger. There is also Gaim that became Pidgin, a free service that is sort of a meta-chat system that allows one to connect on a variety of chat protocols and manage instant chat as well as chat rooms.

A Case Study: The Internet's Classic Chat Years in the Pittsburgh Region

In the early 1990s in the Pittsburgh region there was only one ISP for quite a time. This service, **Telerama**, offered a wide array of Internet services as a provider. Basically the 20 dollar a month package included Unix shell access, with an email account, web access, chat access, gopher, usenet newsgroups, telnet, ftp, and pico editing services. It was an all in one package offering unlimited access to the Internet.

Telerama enjoyed regional Internet supremacy for quite a number of years. Not only was it the only provider in the Pittsburgh region, it became a threat to the large number of Bulletin Boards in the region as well. At this time, improvements in modems allowed one to connect at 56K and rendered many a BB service as obsolete. Telerama also carried usenet newsgroups that operated like massive bulletin board systems. At that particular time there were 20,000 some newsgroups users could post upon. The other lucrative thing about usenet is the fact that one could post a new comment or a reply on a particular bulletin board, then log into another feature such as FTP or Gopher or Email, and return to Usenet at a later point and find replies to their original posts. This process was far less hassle then having to phone into a BBS service throughout the day to see if there were replies to one's posts.

Telerama offered chat access in those early days of Internet, termed "IRC," Internet Relay Chat. IRC was a sophisticated chat system, and essentially a network of hubs and servers offering connectivity to individual accounts. Figure 10.1 reveals the network structure of servers including hubs and their servers, and individual users to those servers. This network runs far beyond the RAN (regional area network) of a BBS in a given metropolitan area. It also spans beyond the "NAN" (national area network) due to the fact that the servers jump societal lines with the nodes strategically placed in the US, Canada, and Europe. One should also note that not all hubs are located in the U.S., but also in England and Europe.

IRC was also a collection of real time chat rooms, called "chat channels" running in the thousands that anyone could connect to with IRC access. As Wikipedia notes, it provided 'many to many" chat formats. In addition, it also provided PM or private messages between any two connected users on the IRC.

Primarily, Telerama's format was as follows: An individual had to sign in to the shell account, then log onto the IRC client. At this point one would be placed in a chat channel on the IRC called "#Telerama," and from here one would type in /join #channel to choose whatever chat channel the person preferred to join. Hence, channel #Telerama was a gateway or portal to enter the IRC world of chat. All chat channels began with the # symbol, and as we discuss "Telerama," the channel, we will refer to it as #Telerama.

Channels varied, as there were thousands to choose from on any given day. China, gayfriendly, depression, thirtysomething, newyork, pittsburgh, haystack, newbies, chat central, etc., etc. If one could think of a chat name, one could probably find a channel for it. Channels also varied in size from a channel like Chinese with 40 or 50 regulars, to smaller, and/or more specialized channels.

People signed on with "nicks" or screen-names, and many times one would have to alter their nick if another user took it. Hence, I am trying to sign on as Joe, but IRC notes that "Joe" is already taken, so I choose "Joe__" or "Joe7" and keep going until I find an opening.

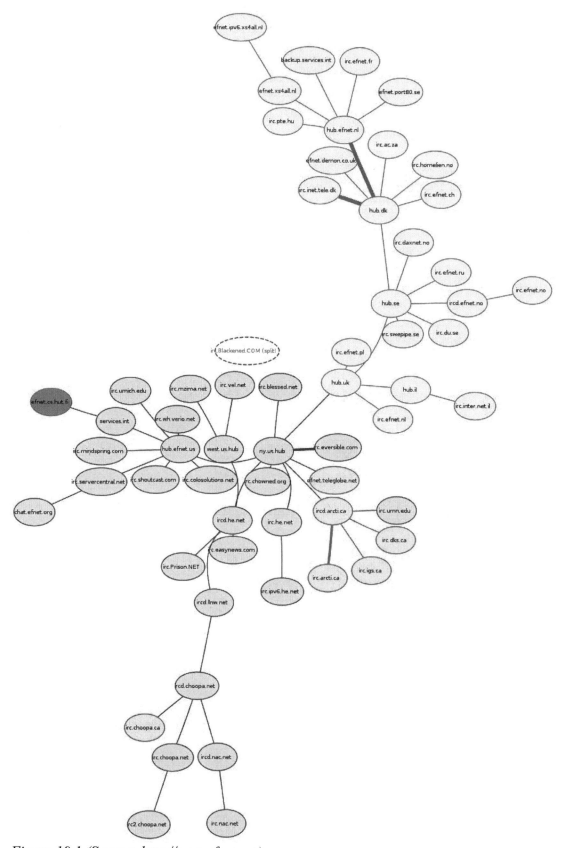

Figure 10.1 (Source: http://map.efnet.net)

The IRC Network

Returning to the Map, Figure 10.1 represents the server network of the IRC chat system. Here we find several hubs of servers, often university systems that individuals would connect to in joining the IRC. Into these hubs are smaller, connected servers. Individuals, desiring connectivity would log on to one of these servers and thus connect to the IRC.

Individuals could connect to IRC from any server. If I lived in Atlanta I could not only connect to IRC through Atlanta's server, but New York or LA's server. Once I logged into the server, I was instantly connected to a cyber cosmos with servers and hubs as nodes connecting between 50 to 100,000 individuals, who in turn, were aboard the individual servers.

Although servers were primarily located in the U.S., Europe and Canada, the network was truly a global area network (GAN). Joining a channel such as Taiwan, one would not only find Taiwanese located in the U.S. at major universities, but also folk from and in Taiwan who were also connected to one of the many servers. The same pattern rang true with Japan or Nippon, England, Scotland, Poland, etc. Not all channels were English speaking as well, adding to the global flavor of IRC.

The IRC network was not without its problems and glitches. Several basic reoccurring situations emerged in trying to manage a truly global social network.

The Network's Woes: Lag and Netsplits

The one annoying problem was lag. Lag occurred when a server or servers, like a lazy eye, grew out of sync with the rest of the system. For example, irc.igs.ca and its closest servers may become lagged with other hubs such as hub.uk or ny.us.hub. If I was on irc.igs.ca when it was lagged and said something to the channel such as "Hi everyone!" they might not receive that message for several dozen seconds if they were all logged into other unaffected servers.

Lag wasn't the only problem for the network. Sometimes servers, and in fact, hubs, split off from the rest of the net. Figure 10.2, from Wikipedia, reveals this process. When a split occurs, those on split servers can no longer "see" or "communicate" with each other. There are several dimensions to this ranging from one lagged server finally splitting from the rest of the net, to larger splits involving two hubs such as hub.uk and ny.us.hub. One must wait out the split until the hub and its server's return. Figure 10.2 provides a simplified graphic of this process. The bottom figure is only one example of a split, due to the fact that splits can sometimes be major, with several hub servers splitting from each other.

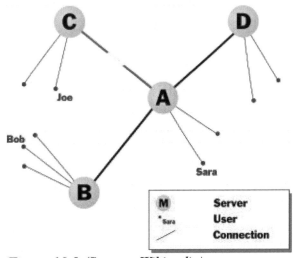

Figure 10.2 (Source: Wikipedia)

The Social Relations of Chat

What is a chat room, sociologically speaking? Is it just an aggregation of nicknames with no structure or form? Or an association of folk: people coming and going, saying their hi's and hello's and manifesting chit chat and then moving on?

In sociology we note that not only are there aggregations and associations of beings, but in some cases there are highly structured communities with norms and roles and institutions binding those individuals together. Hence, walking down Fifth Avenue in NYC during lunchtime is merely an aggregation of people, but a junior high school football team represents something much more ordered and structured with roles, rules, and social relations governing the team.

What I advance now is the notion of IRC as an ordered social community with a definite social structure. There are several structures in IRC Chat that allow us to jump above definitions such as aggregations and associations to the concept of a structured chat community. These features include, the power of "ops", "kicks" and "bans." Along with these, Private Messaging for one-on-one linkages continued to bind users in friendships, romantic and platonic. Finally the power of "bots" as part of the social structure, solidified power and authority relationships in the channel.

At first, a look at a particular channel on IRC reveals a room with dozens of users (nicknames) listed on the channel but there is also a social structure underlying the chat channel. An IRC chat channel is not merely an association or connection of individuals on a particular chat space, be it a room or channel. These chat channels have technological features that encourage the development of a particularized social structure across the entire board of channels.

The first feature is the creation of Private Chat along with Group Chat. Primarily I can be in a room of 30 people, but private message another member of the channel to start a one-on-one conversation. There is at once, the creation of a group community with the ability for numerous one-on-one chat interactions to manifest. Private Messages, in some cases, allow for the development of numerous online friendships. It can also be a tool to harass individuals, and what developed to combat these particular problems was the evolution of the "Ignore" feature on IRC.

A second device, perhaps the key feature that creates and maintains authority relations in chat channels, is a device called "ops". Let us return to the image of our chat channel with 30 users. Ops show up next to a nickname and utilizes the @ sign to designate a user "holding"ops. There are two ways to receive ops---one must be the first person in the channel to automatically receive ops, or someone who has ops must give a person ops.

Ops allow one to politically control a channel. With ops, I can kick someone who is also on the channel and abusing the system or other regulars on the channel. Or, I can kick persons that I don't want on the channel for whatever reason. When one is kicked off the channel, one is left in dead cyberspace unless they rejoin the channel.

To "kick" a person or several persons, one must have ops. Oftentime in channels, alliances form and you'll find that one subgroup will only "op" their own clique. Channel wars have evolved from these alliances, and ownership of the channel changes hands, sometimes many times.

Following from Ops and Kicks, are "Bans." With a "ban" one can flat out terminate an individual from the channel. Once an individual is kicked and banned, the only option is to submit to the authority of the channel or find another channel. Bans target the users IP address and once an individual is banned he can only re-enter if the Ban is lifted.

The Political Economy of the Bot

The social structure, in the form of the stabilization of power and authority relations is brought about by the addition of a "Bot" on a chat channel. A bot is simply a script that follows a series of commands that were before preformed by individuals, but now are automated. A bot is logged into the IRC in a similar fashion that Internet Users sign on to IRC.

For instance, on channel #Telerama is a bot called Tel. As a script, Tel is not only granted ops by the regulars, but also programmed to give ops to anyone on the bot's op list. Not only that, but there is also a kick and ban list and anyone banned from #Telerama will automatically be kicked and banned if they try to join the channel. Hence, I am free to come and go without worrying about how I will obtain "ops." Tel has my nick and IP address and will automatically grant ops.

Bots help stabilize the authority structure, but such is not always a good thing. If a channel was hijacked in a takeover by channel hackers, often we find that the hackers bring their own bots to the channel and set up shop. These bots in turn restrict ops from the regulars, and kick and ban anyone who challenges the new power structure. Other times as a show of force, channel hacks will mass kick and ban anyone who was part of the old authority structure.

Generally, one finds several bots on an IRC channel. There is good reason for this due to takeovers and channel wars. If I run one bot named Tel and Tel is connected to IRC via a particular server—if that server splits, the chances of a takeover increases. While the split occurs, channel hacks could wrest control of the channel through a number of different techniques and means. If, however, several bots are up and running and existing on different servers, in a netsplit there would still be a number of bots with ops on a number of servers. Hence, the takeover threat diminishes.

Takeovers and Channel Wars

Channel wars developed in many ways. In some cases there were two or more factions or cliques in the channel. While individuals from each sect had bots and obtained ops, sometimes what would occur was a skirmish where Group A would de-op Group B and Group B's bots. This basically sounded the horn for an all out channel war. When there happened to be a netsplit Group B often took command and were quick to de-op the opposing alliance when those users or bots rejoined the channel.

Another problem for folk that just wanted a chat home with regulars was the outside takeover. One or two channel hacks might join the channel and pose as newbies. They would gain trust and in time were put on the bot's op list. When the opportunity arose, these hacks were quick to de-op not only all bots in the channel, but all users as well. The next step found the hacks bringing in their own bots along with their own clique of associates. There was basically nothing one could do.

The Power Elite: Linux and the Ability to NUKE

In addition to bots, takeovers and channel wars, those folks who ran "Linux" systems had the ability to subjugate and control any channel "at will." These amateur "Black Hats," had the power to a) knock anyone off line at any given time regardless of whether the user had ops or not, and b) actually cause a major "netsplit" during which time the Black Hats would wrest control from the regular bots and ops.

The power to knock anyone off line at any time came to be known as "nuking"—a user was literally deleted and knocked off the Internet relay chat system. This power, however, vaulted the Black Hats to prestige and prominence in any given channel. The power elite was usually structured with Black Hats at the pinnacle, their associates and bots below them, and the frustrated regulars who saw normal authority relations reorganized.

It was not always dim, however. The "White Hats," a group of Linux Users also wielding such power often became the Robin Hoods, coming to aid of the poor and humble IRC masses. They battled

161

for control of the channel with all the chivalry of the Knights of the Good Kingdom. The trouble, however, was "White Hats" were few and far between in relation to the Black Hats.

From Globalization to Localization: How we found ourselves.

The attraction of the IRC to the many that became addicted to it over the last 20 years, is that IRC has the technological power to put you on an overseas channel with people from that particular channel. Oftentimes, folks from foreign countries who were studying in the US used the IRC as a way to maintain homeland contact while they were overseas. In the early days, I found a home in #Chinese and enjoyed chatting with two students originally from Taiwan who now were attending college in Boston.

There was something very "global" about IRC, especially in the early days with channels like Chinese, Taiwan, Hong Kong, England, Germany, etc. In the early 1990s if one didn't have a home channel along the lines of a foreign county, one might have a home in a special interest such as "depression support" or "twentysomething" or "teen chat" to name a few.

The process of logging on to the IRC from Telerama's shell account would place users on the internet relay chat system on the Channel #Telerama. As users surfaced onto #Telerama, most would type /join #(Channel) to be transported to one's home channel. Very little time was spent in channel #Telerama and those who met in passing gave a sort of wave to the others and then joined their own channel. One might say that chat in the early days was very "global" in nature. In my own experience I spent much time on #Chinese or #HongKong.

And then came the Great Split!

What occurred in the mid 1990s, often termed the Great Split, was a political split between a number of European and U.S. servers. Some issues revolved around control and structure of the IRC but the net was sorely divided for a time between these groups. If memory serves, it was around Christmas time when Telerama lost global connectivity. One logged on and was dumped onto channel #Telerama without the ability to join any other channel.

I can remember most people bitterly complained about not being able to get to their regular channels, and would often end by coming and going to check and double-check if the system was finally up. This default "#Telerama" channel would just not suffice!

Then a funny thing began to happen for roughly 15-20 of us locals. Clustered on channel #Telerama for several weeks we began to discover each other and realized that we, too, were interesting people. Those two weeks became a very interesting and intense process of getting to know the local Telerama users. Even when global connectivity was restored, most of us remained on #Telerama getting to know each other and solidify friend and fellowships. The channel began to develop as well, and a schematic of the channel regulars is provided in Figure 10.3.

As #Telerama developed one of the members, whose nick escapes me, wrote up a bot-script and termed it "Tel" and this became our first working bot on newly emerging #Telerama. Basically it was a simple script used primarily for opping the regulars on the channel, but it was also used for ban lists.

#Telerama and the "Great Split" both emerged and represented a shift from Globalization to Localization or "glocalization." From Global Area Networks (GAN) (international channels) to National Area Networks (NAN) (#HotTub, #Twenty Something, #Chat special interest channels) to Regional Area Networks (RAN) (#PA, #KY, #Cincinnati) the process of localization opened new doors for chat. In time #Telerama began averaging some 25-30 regulars, including folks from other states and societies as well.

Figure 10.3

Core Group	Location	Migration to Undernet
Flirt	Local	Yes
Pensfan	Local	Yes
Candy	Local	Yes
Shari_	Local	No
Skeets	Local	Yes
SP	Local	No
CK	Local	Yes
Magus	Local	No
Parrotthead	Local	No
Maduro	Local	Yes
NightHawk	Local	Yes
Jake	Local	Yes
ACE	Local	Yes
Entropy	Local	No
Brainstrm	Local	No
Harry	Local	No
Mo	Local	Yes
Shinya	Local	Yes
Tigga	Local	Yes
Lesley	Nebraska	No
Emily	Nebraska	No
Tiff	Local/Philippines	No
Ceb	Boston	No
Weatherman	Wisconsin	No
Funny	Seattle	No
Soliel	France	No
yyz	Michigan	No

At some point folks began to meet each other on a one on one for lunches. But the group, at 20 or so folks was hankering to have a larger and more inclusive event that would bring all of us together. Enter Shari__ who suggested a birthday party for Skeets at a popular neighborhood bar and grill in late May. At least 15 showed up and conversation flourished. People could finally put faces to "nicknames" and for the most part the Telerama crew really enjoyed the evening together. Later that August, Skeets organized a pool and picnic party for the group who were at the birthday party along with all others frequenting the channel. This event proved to go even better with roughly 25 people in attendance.

Following form those two events, Darla took the lead, and organized several small group lunches that took place and later evolved, over the years, to everything from bowling get togethers to dinner meets at local restaurants.

The Demise of Channel Telerama

#Telerama remained a central chatting point in the mid 1990s, but several changes began to emerge that would signal the downfall of the chat community. First, new members who began to join

#Telerama were often out of state hacking-oriented folks who took control of the channel a number of times. They also brought their bots and many times one found #Telerama with hackers and their bots opped with the rest of the regulars restricted from ops. One couldn't challenge the hacks because they would just kick and ban and tighten their control. On might ask, why not leave and begin a new channel, but we tried that approach and found the hacks found us and the takeover and channel wars continued.

Second, during the time of the takeovers, many regulars began to rekindle their relationships with their original home channels before the birth of #Telerama. Some went back to TwentySomething, some found new homes.

Third, Telerama itself was now facing competition from other ISPs that had emerged in the vicinity such as Nauticom and NB.net. Many of Telerama's customers migrated to newer ISPs and also a large number of newbies emerged from other ISPs. Basically Telerama lost some of its initial customers. Many who left as well as the newbies from other ISPs weren't bound to channel Telerama any more. #Nauticom had its own channel now, and it rivaled Telerama.

Fourth, #Haystack, a breakaway channel from #Telerama, emerged and attracted a number of folks, all in response to what was happening on #Telerama. Haystack was short lived and was attacked by not only some members of #Telerama, but also subject to takeover wars from channel #Texas. The reason for the Texas takeover I never quite learned, but they did a pretty good job of destroying the channel. The #Texas folks were well equipped—I believe one regular had several dozen bots he brought to the table. In the end, people just stopped visiting and the channel died.

Fifth and finally, Darla, our maternal IRC Queen, suggested the creation of #PGH to solve the Telerama/Nauticom/NB NET split. It was about this time that Telerama Administration changed its home channel from #Telerama on the IRC Efnet to #Telerama on the Undernet. The Undernet was a breakaway "net" from Efnet, the original network on IRC that became quite successful. Hence, when those of us from Telerama logged on to IRC we were now dumped onto #Telerama but the channel was now on the Undernet. #Telerama, as a Pittsburgh channel, didn't last long on the Undernet.

The Rise of the Undernet

Speaking in terms of "net," The IRC network known as Efnet can be conceptualized as the original net. The Undernet developed in the mid to late 1990s, and represented an entirely new net with new servers, new channels, and a flavor all its own. Over the years it has surpassed the Efnet in terms of user population. #Pgh emerged as the central location for localized chat in the Pittsburgh region. Darla continued to sponsor parties and lunches and dinners and the community evolved from an Internet chat community to a reality-based community in real time and real life.

The Undernet also solved the Takeover and Channel Wars problems that plagued the Efnet. Undernet developed one bot, X, placed on all registered channels. One applied for ownership of "X" and if granted, X was placed on the particular channel and the channel owner would add members to an op list on X. If one de-opped the X bot, irccops were notified in a flash and such tampering with X could bring about the user's termination from the Undernet. Hence, a group of channel hacks could no longer hack an X-based channel. To do so would mean de-opping X and this was not tolerated.

In addition, the tighter and more comprehensive control of "X" over the Undernet put an end to the threat and power elite status of the Linux "Nuker." Nuking was deemed a DoS or "denial of service" and "X" had the power to ban any given Nuker on any given chat channel.

IRC, of course, is merely one empirical example of real-time many-to-many chat systems. Quite heavily developed in the past decade, are Yahoo and MSN chat along with specialty chats such as chats in gaming venues, like Pogo and Poker Stars, or gay.com chat. The IRC has lost users since the early

1990s due to the expansion and growing popularity of the Yahoo and MSN chat nets. In addition, while at one time the Efnet and Undernet were the two principal nets on the IRC, today there are 100+ nets such as Dalnet, global-IRC, Chatnet, Malaynet, total-IRC, etc. Competition from these nets has cut into Efnet's and Undernet's base but these original nets still remain popular venues for chat. As we have seen in this chapter, chat is more than an aggregation of individuals but *how* the channel is configured (kicks, bans, ops, bots, etc.) itself determines the formation and how highly structured the chat group will develop. Finally, while the IRC represents a GAN, there is substantial glocalization within this chat network.

Kings.

These are not representatives
and presidents.
They are kings.
They like the juice of swine
adore the romance of dominance and conquest.
They have prize horses
bet on sports affairs
and trade weapons of war.
But at night they dream
of a different kind of Kingship
with dominion over perhaps all the world
perhaps with a single unifying voice.
Their own undoubtedly and of course.
They pretend for the Great Peace I suppose.

These are kings
in funny looking clothes.

CHAPTER ELEVEN

Global Sociology, Culture, and The Presentation of the Sociological Enterprise

Introduction

Sociological theory was born amidst and partly in response to the Great Shift. From Durkheim's mechanical to organic, Weber's traditional forms to rational legal forms, Tonnies' Gemeinschaft to Gesellschaft, Marx's feudal peasantry to capitalistic free labor, and in the migrations from the hinterlands to the urban mosaic, radical social change was on the doorstep of the globe. Fueling the heart of such change and upheaval was the Industrial Revolution; however, many situate the prime mover further back, perhaps in the 16th century. In the 20th century, just when the core of sociological theorists had thought they had mapped out the necessary framework for the study of modern societies, along come two vibrant processes, post-industrialism and globalization that in turn became the fuel-injection system making the Industrial Revolution pale in comparison to the qualitative and quantitative kinds of technological changes occurring in the past 30 years.

The Great Shift, however, was a "singularity" so completely overwhelming, it provided the substance of sentimentality and nostalgia for generations of both past and present sociologists in the formulation of both social theory and social research strategies in the discipline. To be sure, Sociology began as an intellectual reflexivity toward the massive social reorganization of the Great Shift, but now knocking on the door are, *first*, the intensifications in the evolution and maturity of this Great Shift (urbanization rates, information society, computerization, etc.) also commonly referred to as "hyper or post industrial" society. Whether one accepts Post Industrialism as a new social formation, historical epoch or an extensive evolution of Industrial Capitalism, one must reckon with the fact that it is a sweeping process and an agent of social change in the present era. "Hyper-Industrial" might be a better term for we are talking about "intensifications" in industrialism but not changes in the mode or social relations of production. Be that as it may, the *second* dominant process, subsuming and theoretically ordering Hyper Industrial, Post Industrial and Information Society, is this thorny process termed "Globalization."

Theoretical globalization goes back and reorders and restructures the established concepts of sociological theory, particularly the unit of analysis which was once the "societal" but now the "global." Now not only do we deal with the system of social stratification in one society, but beyond the borders of the national society we can also map a "global" stratification system resulting from the system of global social relationships. All things once considered as societally situated independent variables and "causes," now become seen as dependent variables to the process of Globalization.

Earlier, we examined the societal division of labor as a class based social set of relations between owner and laborer. That has not disappeared, but with the intensification of Globalization we need to refocus economic concerns on the global stage. Hence, we can speak of a global capitalist class and global technical class and global manufacturing class, all spatially expressed in either core or peripheral economic zones. Sometimes these economic zones correspond with national societies, but other times they cut across those societies. Appalachia, for instance, may be considered an internal periphery in the core country of the U.S., while other peripheral systems may sweep across Latin America or Southeast Asia. One central problem with the globalization, particularly economic globalization, is that while core-to-peripheral systems, as one property of the globalization process, establish and evolve across the globe, we have the problem of "uneven development" across core and peripheral zones. The fact that globalization developed *where* it did and *how* it did eventually gave some sociocultural systems a head start or push as in the case of the development of capitalism in Europe. Since that time, there has been an evolution of capitalism through colonialism, conquering every nook and cranny of the social, rendering it a commodity to be bought and sold on the market, or as some have called "the universalization of the market," but the entirety of this process, was in fact, Globalization. The marketization of social life, like core to peripheral economic systems, is another property of Globalization and its evolution.

Again, not only did some societies enjoy core positions, but also through slave, peasant and colonialism these societies structured the eventual peripheralization of other societies. Some of these peripheral societies were advanced horticultural and agrarian systems—some not embedded in wider trade relations or what Wallerstein has called "mini systems," but as capitalism developed wider and broader areas of the social were brought within the world division of labor.

So where does Sociology stand? After all the work of theorists of The Shift, along with their subsumption by Parson's model of the social system, where do we go from here? As one commercial suggests Tacos over Burgers, "think outside the bun (box)." With Sociology we find ourselves at a crossroads…do we merely tack on a global "focus" to our introductory texts or give ourselves over to a comprehensive understanding of the globalization process, seeing the world through clearer, newer lenses.

It is not a joke to recommend that *Introductory to-* and *Principles of-* Sociology texts need to be rethought, reorganized and rewritten. Precisely because of ongoing evolution of The Shift, and also the evolution of societal and global differentiation as properties of Globalization, we need to refocus from within the paradigm of Globalization. To some extent, as the body of this paper suggests we are moving toward that end, which itself is a new beginning for the direction of the sociological enterprise. I will explain in upcoming sections, the need for a system wide development of "Global Sociology."

I remember my first Sociology course in undergraduate school. The teacher, Alan Banks was an Assistant Professor of Sociology at Union College a few years removed from graduate school and not only teaching but also pursuing research on class and labor in the coalfields of eastern Kentucky. Banks was a friendly sort, and considered himself a "democratic socialist" reading his weekly issues of *In These Times* and *Mother Jones*, sipping from a mug of *Sleepy Time* herbal tea in his office. Not only a democratic socialist, but also academically a committed Marxian Sociologist, many of the concepts we discussed appealed to me, a product of the inner city streets and underclass of Appalachian Pittsburgh, Pennsylvania.

In any event, I still can remember the first Sociology text Banks used: D. Stanley Eitzen's *In Conflict and Order,* 1978. I recently took it from the bookshelf and dusted it off and paged through it. I thought it odd that many of the chapters were about Sociology as an American Enterprise with an American focus. For instance, instead of a chapter on culture, the corresponding title was "American Values." In the chapters discussing social inequality consider the following titles: "The American System of Social Stratification, The Distribution of Power in American Society, and Poverty in the

United States." Further, in the section on social institutions we find "The American Family, Religion in America, American Education, and The American Economy."

On reflection of the increased awareness and perception of the global age, along with changes in how we present the "sociological enterprise" rests with the fact that we have moved away from titles and topics such as "The **American** System of Social Stratification." In its place are the terms Social Stratification, Racial and Ethnic Stratification, and now increasingly chapters called "Global Stratification." We will speak more to Global Stratification at a later point, and while Eitzen's book is not representative of all Sociology texts in the 1970-80s, it does portray a discipline whose content structure was clearly within "the box" some 30 years ago.

The Study of...

In many texts we find convergence in the central thrust of the sociological enterprise. In Macionis' *Society: The Basics*, Sociology is defined as:

"Sociology is the systematic study of human society" (Macionis: 1)

Similarly, Anderson and Taylor in *Sociology: Understanding a Diverse Society*, note that

"Sociology is the study of human behavior in society" (Anderson and Taylor: 2)

Primarily in a content analysis of introductory texts we find terms like "scientific study of society," "systematic study of society," scientific study of social behavior." Some texts leaning toward a social psychological theme might utilize phrases like "The Individual in Society," while Macro oriented texts may simply emphasize "study of societies and social systems."

Sociology, it should be pointed out, is only one of a number of enterprises immersed in the study of social behavior. From Political Science to Economics, many disciplines focus on parts of the social system. But primarily for our purposes here, we define five central disciplines or sub-disciplines closely related to the heart of Sociology. These include:

1. Sociology Proper
2. Cultural Anthropology
3. Cultural Geography
4. Macro Sociology
5. Global Sociology

Consider, for instance, Marvin Harris' definition of Cultural Anthropology:

"Cultural Anthropology deals with the description and analysis of cultures—the socially learned traditions of past and present ages" (Harris: 2).

Lenski and Nolan, Macro-sociologists who borrow heavily from Sociology and Anthropology, speak on the commonalities of the fields:

"The study of human societies has never been exclusively a sociological concern... Only Sociology and Anthropology have been concerned with human societies per se. That is to say, only these two disciplines have interested themselves in the full range of social phenomena, from the family to the nation and from technology to religion. And only these two have sought to understand societies in their own right." (Lenski and Nolan: 21)

Lenski and Nolan go on to point out

> "In matters of research there once was a fairly well-established division of labor between Sociology and Anthropology. Sociologists studied industrial societies, Anthropologists studied preliterate societies. This division of labor made good sense, since the skills needed to study a remote tribe in the mountains of New Guinea are very different from those needed to study a modern industrial society." (Lenski and Nolan: 21)

They further note in "teaching and the development of theory" the "separation of Sociology and Anthropology has been far less satisfactory".... "As a consequence, there has been a long tradition of intellectual "borrowing" between Sociology and Anthropology, and this volume stands in that tradition." (Ibid: 21)

Like Sociology and Anthropology, there tends to be convergence in the aims of Cultural Geography:

> "Cultural Geography, then is the study of spatial variations among cultural groups and the spatial functioning of society. It focuses on describing and analyzing the ways language, religion, economy, government, and other cultural phenomena....a celebration of human diversity." (Jordan-Bychkov and Domash: 4)

Enter Culture

Perhaps more than any other topic, the study of culture is given high premium in the sociological field. We will not only examine its importance in *In Conflict and Order*, but in the present era texts as well. Primarily in Sociology texts "Culture" as a chapter heading is essentially situated as the first **true** topic of sociological study. Usually the opening two chapters of Sociology texts deal with "The Sociological Perspective" or "The Origins of Sociology." A chapter, in turn, follows this on both Theory and Methods of Sociology. There are varying combinations but these generally characterize the introductory chapters in Sociology texts. The third chapter, however, is often simply called "Culture."

In returning to Eitzen's volume, he lists 4 central elements for consideration in building a working definition of culture:

1. Culture is an emergent process.
2. Culture is learned behavior.
3. Culture channels human behavior.
4. Culture is boundary maintaining

There is a factual strength that resonates with Eitzen's dimensions of culture. Imagine the power of culture from the guidelines he has provided. Consider a Malaysian woman at age 30 not only living but reared and socialized in the northern Italian city of Udine with a foster family since birth. Although biologically she shares all of the racial features of the population of Malay folk, and indeed, may look "out of place" in the heartland of this Italian society, she nonetheless speaks fluent Italian, utilizes a fork and knife for eating, and has grown up loving lasagna and spaghetti. She is also most likely a Roman Catholic and participates in attending Mass and saying the rosary.

Here, in this case, consider biology as the "hardware" of the system while culture is the software of the human experience. I can wipe my hard drive clean of that annoying operating system known as Windows Vista, and instead install the latest version of Ubuntu Linux as an operating system. In the same sense we can socialize a human from birth into one of the many hundreds of social and ethnic cultures in the world today. It shows that culture is emergent, learned, channeling, and boundary maintaining. Eitzen's notion of culture is strong and still crisp in the present era.

Now jump ahead some 25 years and examine Anderson and Taylor's definition of culture:

> "Culture is the complex system of meaning and behavior that defines a way of life for a given group or society. It includes beliefs, values, knowledge, art, morals, laws, customs, habits, language and dress. Culture includes ways of thinking as well as patterns of behavior." (Anderson and Taylor: 58)

Macionis, in *Society: The Basics*, echoes the assertions of Anderson and Taylor:

> "Culture is the values, beliefs, behavior and material objects that together form a people's way of life." (Macionis: 35)

Now ahead some 30 years after Eitzen, and from the global paradigm, Cohen and Kennedy note in *Global Sociology*:

> "…Most sociologists see culture as the repertoire of learned ideas, values, knowledge, aesthetic preferences, rules and customs shared by a particular collectivity of social actors." (Cohen and Kennedy: 47)

Hence, there is not a lot of qualitative variance in the definition of culture employed by sociologists. It is on the one hand, central to the study of society, and on the other, fairly refined over the ages.

There is also convergence across the social-scientific disciplines with regard to culture. In *Cultural Geography*, Jordan-Bychokov and Domash (2001) note that:

> "…culture as learned, collective human behavior, as opposed to instinctive, or inborn behavior. These learned traits form a way of life held in common by a group of people…" (2001: 4)

In revisiting Sociology's closest relative, Cultural Anthropology, we can also view the similarities with respect to culture:

> "Culture refers to the learned, socially acquired traditions of thought and behavior found in human societies. It is a socially acquired lifestyle that includes patterned, repetitive ways of thinking, feeling, and acting." (Harris: 10)

The Presentation of Culture

In studies of culture, keep in mind that socio-cultural systems do not neatly end at the borders of a given nation state. We might do better in a study of culture, to speak of "socio-cultural" systems rather than national societies. And although individual texts vary, most central to the study of culture are *values, beliefs, and norms. Symbol systems* and *language* or *linguistics* closely follow.

In addition, many texts make the distinction between *material* and *non-material* culture. While non-material is grounded in the study of thought processes and symbol systems, material culture opens the door for a study of the "technology" of a society and its mode of subsistence, be it hunting and gathering, simple and advanced agrarian, industrial and/or post-industrial societies.

Subcultures and *counter cultures* are also part of the staple of discussions of cultures. Here again material and non-material culture is important. If we look at the 1960s sub or youth counter culture we find not only the values, beliefs, and norms of the Youth movement (peace, right on brother,

171

make love not war) but a vast array of material culture from bell bottom jeans to tie dye t-shirts, roach clips for the use of reefer along with vans or Volkswagen bugs. This material culture is not the exclusive domain of the movement for even today we find the bell bottoms and tie dye shirts making a fashion comeback, but it is important to note that these were the cultural artifacts of this particular youth movement. The youth movement was a vast counter cultural formation that spawned several subcultures. Hence, with the youth movement as the umbrella, we find within its boundaries subcultural groups such as the anti-war wing, youth of the Feminist and Black movements, the gay movement, the environmental movement, the Sexual Revolution subculture, the "Hippie and Drug" wing, the folk music followers, and finally, the rock music wing of the Beatles, Jimi Hendrix, Jefferson Airplane, and the Rolling Stones. The youth movement was, of course, all of these combined and there was considerable overlap, but clearly, each subculture could be seen as a specific intensification of the youth movement centered on a particular cause or symbol.

In continuing, we find the following two concepts in many basic introductory texts. *Ethnocentrism* and *cultural relativism* are variables in the study of culture that refer to presuppositional notions regarding the universalism and particularization of culture. Ethnocentrism deals with our viewing of another racial or ethnic group as inferior to our own, or the superiority of one's own culture over the vast array of others. Cultural relativism centers more on matters of objectivity/subjectivity and the relation between subject and object. Macionis notes that cultural relativism is the "logical alternative to ethnocentrism." (Macionis: 51). Here, all societies are placed on the level playing field and we look at each from its own standpoint of values, beliefs, customs and norms and then draw comparisons and conclusions.

Multiculturalism is yet another subject in chapters on culture. Particularly this term is increasingly addressed even more so in light of objective Globalization and the growing "awareness" of the global in everyday life. Objective Globalization here deals with everything from increases in study aboard for college students to rates of international tourism. Here we find more global density as the world is brought into contact with itself. Universities and their immediate domestic neighborhoods are themselves multicultural wonderlands of folk from all over the world—a truly global mosaic. Multiculturalism also deals with "promoting the equality of all cultural traditions" (Macionis: 48) and this equality is grounded in social diversity, but there are many ways and forms that multiculturalism is made manifest, and increasingly made manifest in the present era.

Finally, and more will be said about this at a later point, there is an attempt in the so-called age of Globalization to take into account "the global" or "global culture" in the overarching study of culture. Far short of writing the chapter on culture from a "global" perspective, many sociologists are adding "the global" to the end of chapters on either culture or social change. There are two levels of global concerns increasingly appearing in sociological texts. First, toward the end of the chapters on culture, we find a blurb, or perhaps a blog, dealing with notions of "A Global Culture," in Macionis (2004: 53), while Anderson and Taylor (2004: 74) devote a section called "The Globalization of Culture."

As we have noted the drop in terms and themes of "America" in introductory texts, and the addition in some cases of chapters dealing with global stratification, we are now starting to see Globalization or the "global" emerge and seep into what were once strictly "societal" thematic domains. At this embryonic stage, however, much of our notions of the global are "tacked on" sections at the end of sociological chapters or lumped into later chapters such as "social change and social movements."

As a footnote to the study of culture in Sociology, and across the basic sociological texts we find the entire thematic of religion relegated to a subsidiary role in Sociology. Most place religion at the end of introductory texts, and often in combination with the Family and Aging. It is somewhat odd, I think, that while the cultural is elevated to such a prominent position, religion is pushed to the wayside. Yet isn't religion at the core of the study of such cultural "properties" such as values, beliefs, norms, habits, customs and rituals? There is a scramble to greet these characteristics under the umbrella of culture, however if they are embedded in religious forms we brush them aside.

The Study of Society: A Typology

The following study, methodologically speaking, was drawn and based upon a small sample of Introductory Sociology texts found in the stacks of the popular and growing bookseller, "Half-Price Books." Half-Price Books stocks it shelves from a variety of sources. The most common source are customers who re-sell their books to the store for a fraction of what they paid for them. While this sample does in no way constitute a true representative sample of the population of all Introduction to Sociology texts, it does represent a study population of resold texts in the Pittsburgh metropolitan area. To increase the legitimacy of this study population, we further sampled texts for their TOC (Table of Contents) listed and defined on Amazon.com. In most cases we were able to access the TOC for a content analysis from these online listings. In some cases after the particular text was selected and no TOC was available, we then visited various textbook sites and were able to retrieve TOC documentation.

In addition to a random sample of introductory sociology texts, we employed a purposive or judgmental sampling technique to select texts that fell in the category of either Macro or Global Sociology. In continuing with the purposive sampling we selected two popular texts from Cultural Anthropology and Cultural Geography. The late Marvin Harris, was a power horse in Anthropology and his Introduction to *Cultural Anthropology* was selected as one representation of that field. By the same token, The *Human Mosaic*, by Jordan-Bychkov and Domosh, was also purposively sampled to gain a flavor of Cultural Geography.

All in all, we sampled 5 basic Introductory Sociology texts, purposively sampled 3 Global Oriented Sociology texts, and purposively sampled 2 texts representing Cultural Anthropology and Cultural Geography.

Figure 11.1 (figure at end of Chapter) represents a typology of a very small sample of texts in the social sciences and primarily in the field of Sociology. The horizontal axis moves from a focus on the Individual in Society to The Society as the Unit of Analysis to the Global as fundamental organizing social force. On the vertical axis we look at Sociology from the standpoint of its Micro vs. Macro orientation.

Consider, for instance, the relationships and interactions generated in a social dyad or triad at various age groups. Here we not only examine the individual personality characteristics, but also the social dynamics of the group interactions. Rightly, we may place these studies as grounded in the Individual/Societal relationship. If instead we speak of the effect of social class, ethnicity or race in limiting or opening social mobility, we are dealing with societal forces as central influences acting upon the individuals. If we continue to proceed toward the global we will come to perhaps an analysis of core-to-peripheral economic systems or the growing "awareness" of the global as global properties impacting upon 1) societies 2) social groups and organizations, and 3) individuals. At the horizontal level, each move to the right opens up a deeper and more subsuming theme with the societal subsuming the individual and the global subsuming the societal. In turn, each move from the top to bottom takes us from studies of individuals and small groups to larger social and sociocultural organizations.

At first sight can we not say the move from the Individual to the Global is a move from the Micro to the Macro? In some instances yes, but consider a study of a social triad as an example. On the one hand we can analyze the triad from an individualist perspective, but on the other, we can take the triad and speak about how social class orders and regulates the nature and character of their triadic social relationships. Here we have jumped to a "societal" groundedness but kept the Micro focus. Socialization as a topic is also a good example. Here we examine the enculturation of the young into the social system and its values, beliefs and norms. If, however, I analyzed peripheral nations and the literacy or life expectancy rates across these societal types, the unit of focus has jumped to emergent global properties such as core and periphery systems. Here it is not each society dictating what those rates will be, but rather an emergent globalizational property, the core-to-periphery economic system, that in turn, through its systemization, creates and patterns those differences in literacy and life expectancy.

Hence, we have a horizontal continuum of Individual to Societal to Global intersecting with a vertical axis ranging from a Micro to Macro focus. In referring the Figure 11.1 (see figures at end of chapter) we can plot the structural contents of various texts from the social sciences. Where would one expect to find Sociology made manifest on the typology? Clearly while the "social" and "culture" as meta-conditioning forces in the diversity of social life across the globe, many texts fall alongside the "societal" as the appropriate of unit of analysis. Perhaps it rests with a social versus psychological determinism? Clearly both basic Introductory Psychology and Social Psychology texts cluster in both the Individual/Societal and Micro Orientations.

Much of Sociology is situated just south of the Micro and Macro fault with most clustered on the Macro orientation. There are several chapters in most Introductory Sociology texts that deal with social interaction that exclusively focus on the Micro rather than the Macro. However, the discussion of cultures along with social inequalities and the vast array of social groups, organizations and institutions give the sociological a much deeper rootedness in the societal field versus the more psychological Micro orientation.

Why are Macionis and Anderson and Taylor not situated closer to the global? Primarily the reason here is that as a reflection of the sociological enterprise in the present era, attention to the global and the Globalization process is either embryonic in representation or neatly "tacked on" to the end of basic sociological chapters.

Before we speak of Macro and global oriented sociologies and sociological texts, it is fruitful for analysis to consider Cultural Anthropology and Cultural Geography. Note that they are positioned down and much further embedded in a "Macro" orientation than their sociological cousins. What is the reason for this particular plotted arrangement? First, both Cultural Geography and Anthropology focus on societies either as socio-cultural systems, or societies and/or cultures. The unit of analysis is clearly the societal whether we are dealing with small Hunting and Gathering Tribes, Horticultural groups, advanced Agrarian systems, Industrial and Post Industrial systems or hybrid Industrial-Agrarian systems.

One distinguishing feature is that while a majority of Sociology concentrates heavily on the modern, industrial, and post industrial societies, much attention is also given to some Micro oriented analysis. Cultural Anthropology and Geography are centered not only on modern societies, but two other social formations: past and present pre-literate societies. Present day preliterate societies are crucially endangered due to emerging and extensive contact with core-peripheral economies of the global economic system. But the important point here is Anthropology and Geography deal with these socio-cultural systems as valid and analyzable entities in discussing the mosaic of human societies. We will have more to say on these societies soon, but important for now is that both Cultural Geography and Anthropology take the unit of analysis to be the "society," and are more concerned with making comparisons within and across all these social formations rather than just a part of them.

Enter Global Sociology

Building on the "societal" focus of both Cultural Anthropology and Geography is a field we might loosely term "Global Sociology." Here are some considerations regarding the composition of this group: First, short of a sweeping global perspective, we will consider texts that present a strong and "grounded internationalization" as part of this field called Global Sociology. Second, Global Sociology is home to texts that borrow from both the Sociological and Anthropological traditions. Third, the unit of analysis hangs in the balance of the both the societal and global condition and hence the "global" is considered a primary organizing force of social life. In addition to these requirements we find several other modes of focus in a truly Global Sociology that we must consider:

1) Past societies are crucial in Global Sociology as they reveal the history and diversity of human societies.
2) Present day preliterate societies such as Hunters and Gatherers, Horticultural and Agrarian social systems that have had little contact with the modern world are also crucial. These are living arrangements precious for the study of present day social and cultural diversity.
3) Hybrid Societies, generally speaking, advanced agrarian social systems that have been impacted upon by global trade and global capitalist patterns of ownership. Much of the Third World or the Peripheral systems fall into this category.
4) The Global system of societies as defined by the UN, 191 nation states and/or national societies.

Structural Content: Social Science Texts

If we turn to Figure 11.2 and 11.3 (see figures at the end of chapter), we find the content analysis for both those texts in the sociological discipline and its cousins in Cultural Anthropology and Geography. At first glance consider the convergence and similarity between the two Sociological texts. With very little variation we find the two almost mirror images of themselves. Both spot Culture in a prominent place in the arrangement of contents, and both have some global orientation with not only "global" blurbs and maps throughout their texts as we noted earlier, some of the "global" here is tacked on to the standard sociological chapters. We also should note, with great zeal at the development of an entire chapter on "Global Stratification."

As we leave the "Sociology proper" note the variation in content in Figures 11.2 and 11.3, among both Cultural Geography and Anthropology. There is not only variation between these two basic texts, but across the board. In examining the sociological and anthropological, in particular, we do indeed find some overlap. In other words, there seems some convergence in Harris' *Cultural Anthropology* when we pit it against Macionis and Anderson and Taylor. Consider for instance the overlap in Race, Ethnicity, Class and Caste, Economic organization, and Religions. Also, in Harris' text note the chapter at the very end entitled "globalization." While we are a long way from the strategic priority of globalization in Cultural Anthropology, the blows against the empire are more frequent and coming with growing intensity.

A Global Perspective?

You'll note a few things in examining Figure 11.1 with Figures 11.2 and 11.3: Ferrante's *Sociology: A Global Perspective*, Lenski and Nolan's *Human Societies* and Cohen and Kennedy's *Global Sociology*, are strategically positioned in the lower right quadrant. All three are closer to a "global" rather than an "individual/societal" focus. They are also more deeply Macro oriented than both the basic Sociology texts or their anthropological/geographical cousins. Why is this so?

In Figure 11.4 (chapter's end), we find the content structure for Ferrante's "*Society: A Global Perspective*." This text was situated closer to the global than the basic social scientific texts in Sociology, Anthropology and Geography. They were also plotted south of these same texts with regard to the Macro-orientation. We can see that Macro-oriented Global Sociology is manifest in the lower right quadrant of our typology.

First, note the lack of variation in Ferrante's chapter structure in comparison with both Macionis' and Anderson and Taylor's texts. Again, a mirror image is presented. In a sense, and we will qualify this at a later point, Ferrante is working "within the box," or more appropriately the sociological "box" in building up to a global analysis.

Ferrante's work, to be sure, is located in the loose knit category of Global Sociology, but what she has done is internationalized her chapters while keeping the basic structural content of standard sociological texts. In each chapter this is an international focus by utilizing one country or social organization or phenomenon as the major field of study. Hence in the chapter on deviance, the international focus is on the Republic of China, while the chapter on culture focuses on South Korea. India is the spotlight for the chapter on Population, while Mexico is highlighted in the chapter on Methods.

Ferrante's global focus highlights various societies and analyzes them in each chapter. The problem is that there are, by nature, about 20 chapters in a basic Sociology text. That means while we would get a good education on 20 societies, what about the other 171 societies or national societies? Here is the problem as we've yet to get out of the "societal" box. Why not start from the Global?

Macro Global Sociology: Lenski and Nolan and Cohen and Kennedy

In Figure 11.5 (chapter's end), note the distinctiveness of structural content between Lenski and Nolan's *Human Societies* and Cohen and Kennedy's *Global Sociology*. Actually Lenski and Nolan, Cohen and Kennedy, and Ferrante can all be cast as variants, to a greater or lesser extent, of Global Sociology. While we already discussed the similarities of Ferrante with Macionis and Anderson and Taylor in respect to structural content, the commitment to internationalization by Ferrante places her work in the field of Global Sociology. Still, however, the global rootedness is more readily apparent in either Lenski and Nolan or Cohen and Kennedy.

Lenski and Nolan open their volume with a discussion of "The Human Condition," that humanity, in itself, is a "global-orientation" for the discussion of human societies and the evolution of human societies. Once the human condition and evolution of socio-cultural systems are presented, we find a description and analysis of the following societies:

Hunting and Gathering Societies
Horticultural Societies (simple and advanced)
Pastoral Societies
Fishing Societies
Maritime Societies
Agrarian Societies
Industrial Societies
Industrializing Societies (Hybrid)

The strength of Lenski and Nolan's approach is the focus not only upon societies in the modern age (both literate and preliterate) but the store of knowledge on "past" societies that match the definitions of one of the societies mentioned above. The approach is thus historical and ecological-evolutionary.

Central to Lenski and Nolan's thematic is the *mode of subsistence*, how it differs in various societies, and also the commonalities and contrasts of societies both within and across various modes of subsistence. Hence, we can find more commonalities in comparing *past* H&G societies with today's dwindling number of H&G tribes, while stark contrasts are found in a comparative analysis of present day societies with differing modes of subsistence.

Make no mistake, societies in Lenski and Nolan's scheme are equally weighted in comparative analysis, and this is one of the main factors designating *Human Societies* as a global Macro sociological work rather than another run of the mill Introduction to Sociology text. Here too, it goes without saying; we are comparing societies, or rather, the global system of societies rather than individual or individual societal behavior. This is another reason for plotting Lenski and Nolan in the area of global-Macro Sociology.

Cohen and Kennedy, in *Global Sociology*, make a remarkable move toward situating the "global as the primary" organizing force of social life. On this level, Cohen and Kennedy's structural content differ from not only basic sociological texts, or Cultural Anthropology and Geography, but also distinctively different in organization from Lenski and Nolan's *Human Societies*.

In Figure 11.5, consider the chapter headings: nation states, modernity, world society, uneven development, tourism, consuming culture, global media, global religion, population and migration. Along with these global variables are discussions of global actors, and not merely nation states, but growing transnational actors such as TNCs (transnational corporations), IGOs (international government organizations), and INGO's (international non-governmental organizations). (Cohen and Kennedy: 2007).

Cohen and Kennedy diverge from Lenski and Nolan however, as their main focus is upon the modern global system of societies—hence, mainstream national societies holding the bulk of the globe's 6 billion people. The unit of analysis is the globe and emergent global properties ordering and structuring its constituent parts (nations, institutions, organizations and individuals). We also find longstanding sociological concepts like "social movements" rejuvenated with analysis of global oriented social movements such as the explosion of International Non Governmental Organizations or the growth in Trans National Corporations as current social organizations.

There is some overlap as well. For instance, in Ferrante, Lenski and Nolan, and Cohen and Kennedy there are extensive studies of social inequalities to be found in chapters on "global stratification." In Cohen and Kennedy, this also includes chapters dealing with race, ethnic and gender inequalities at the global level that can also be found in Ferrante and Lenski and Nolan.

As we move further into the realm of the global through the media, the computer, the economy, multiculturalism, and global stratification we find ourselves faced with new organizing forces. Or perhaps they are not "new?" Perhaps they were embryonic forces emerging with the first proto-state formations before the development of industrial capitalism, which now have "de-cloaked" to use a term from Star Trek, as we can now see these naked forces operating on the global stage, the national stage, among institutions and organization and finally among the real being of "individuals."

Toward a Global Sociology

The works of the global sociologists along with Harris' Cultural Anthropology heavily influenced Figure 11.6. Here we find a number of properties. First, T1 to T7 is a rough draft of seven or so timepieces in the long haul of the evolution of the global system of societies. T1 for instance lasted from 100,000 to 12,000 BC and was marked by hunting and gathering organization. This particular mode of subsistence gave way to forms of Horticulture, simple to advanced agrarian, emerging industrial to industrial, to hyper industrial and post industrial arriving at T7.

This of course is the evolutionary trajectory of the system of societies through historical time under varying modes of subsistence and production.

Above this trajectory, though, we flesh out the Macro social formations through plotting various political economies and their respective evolutions and rise and declines of these formations. Hence H&G was often characterized as communal equalitarian even though there was often a headman or tribal chief. These forms gave way to chiefdoms to early pre-state formations manifesting themselves in slave and peasant systems. As the "state" emerged we find also the era of colonialism emerging from Europe to the rest the global system. In the demise of colonialism we found an era of independent statehoods guided by neo colonialism and core-to-peripheral economic systems. Advanced states continued to evolve through the present era of a democratic global system of societies. What of the future? Perhaps it is a sort of global federationalism with global actors, global cities, and nation states all ordering and structuring social life. We actually have an emergent form of global federationalism now, but perhaps in several dozen to hundred years we will see the evolution of a world polity?

These questions lend themselves to developing a Presentation of the Sociological Enterprise where the "globe" and/or the global system of societies is the base unit of analysis with a host of emergent properties impacting upon social groups, organizations, individuals. Political systems, or rather the configuration and development of universal and particular political systems is but one dimension of the globalization process. Consider everything from socialist to hybrid to advanced capitalist economies as the wide variety of modes of subsistence that Lenski speaks about, along with matching ownership scenarios at the economic level of the global system of societies.

As a note of conclusion, I would like to emphasize that the author holds no grudge against texts and disciplines where either the individual or individual-in-society is the unit of analysis. I do, however, have very definite ideas of what "Sociology" as a socio-scientific discipline should look like and how it should be organized. The global in many sociological texts is still embryonic, but being pushed forward by writers such as Ferrante, Lenski and Cohen and Kennedy. We are at the doorstep and some, such as Lenski and Cohen, have entered the party festivities while many others line up for their turn to turn to the global.

(Figure 11.1)

Micro-Sociology

Basic   *Basic*
Psychology   *Social Psychology*
Texts   *Texts*

Ind/Society_____Societal_____ Global

Basic Sociology
Texts. 2 Examples:

Macionis'   *Anderson & Taylor*
Society: The *Sociology: Understanding*
Basics   *a Diverse Society*

Basic Anthro/
Cultural Geography
Texts. 2 Examples:
The Human Mosaic   *Harris'*
Cultural Geography   *Cultural Anthropology*

Ferrante's
Sociology:
A Global Perspective.

Lenski's Human
Societies

Cohen's
Global
Sociology

Macro-Sociology

178

(Figure 11.2)

THE INDIVIDUAL AND SOCIETY

Society: The Basics. Seventh Edition. John J. Macionis	Sociology: Understanding a Diverse Society. Third Edition. Anderson and Taylor.
Sociology: Perspective Theory and Method	Sociology Perspective
	Doing Sociological Research
Culture	
Socialization	Culture
Social Interaction	Socialization
Groups and Organizations	Society and Interaction
Deviance	Groups and Organizations
Sexuality	Sexuality
	Deviance
Stratification	Crime
(Social, Global and Gender)	
Race and Ethnicity	Social Class and Social Stratification
	Global Stratification
Economics and Politics	Race and Ethnicity
Family and Religion	Gender
Education and Medicine	Age and Aging
Population: Urbanization and Environment	Families
Social Change: Modern and Post Modern	Education
Societies	Religion
	Economy and Work
	Power, Politics, and Authority
	Health Care
	Population, Urbanism and Environment
	Collective Behavior and Social Movements
	Social Change in Global Perspective.

(Figure 11.3)

COMPARING SOCIETIES

Cultural Anthropology. Sixth Edition (late) Marvin Harris and Orna Johnson.	**The Human Mosaic: A Thematic Introduction to Cultural Geography. Terry G. Jordan-Bychokov and Mona Domosh.**
Nature of Culture Evolution and Capacity for Culture Language and Culture Production Reproduction Economic Organization Domestic Life Descent, Locality and Kinship Law, Order and War in Non-State Societies Origins of Chiefdoms and the State Class and Caste Ethnicity, Race and Racism Sexuality and Gender Hierarchies Psychological Anthropology Religion Art Applied Anthropology Globalization	The Nature of Cultural Geography People on the Land The Agricultural World Political Patterns The Mosaic of Languages Religious Realms Folk Geography Popular Culture Ethnic Geography The City in Time and Space, The Urban Mosaic Industrial Geography

(Figure 11.4)

THE GLOBALLY GROUNDED

Sociology: A Global Perspective, Sixth Edition. Joan Ferrante	A Global Perspective: With Emphasis on:
The Sociological Imagination Theory and Methods Culture Socialization Social Interaction Social Organizations Deviance	Mexico North Korea and South Korea Israel, the West Bank, and Gaza Democratic Republic of Congo McDonalds People's Republic of China
Social Stratification Race and Ethnic Classification Gender	Global Rich and Poor United States American Samoa
Economics and Politics Family and Aging Population and Urbanization Education Religion Social Change	Iraq Japan India European Union Islamic Republic of Afghanistan Global Interdependence

(Figure 11.5)

Human Societies: An Introduction to Macro Sociology Tenth Edition. Nolan and Lenski	Global Sociology. Second Edition. Cohen and Kennedy. NYU Press.
> Part One: Theoretical Foundations The Human Condition Human Societies as Sociocultural Systems The Evolution of Human Societies Types of Human Societies >Part Two: Preindustrial Societies Hunting and Gathering Societies Agrarian Societies Some Evolutionary Bypaths and a Brief Review >Part Three The Industrial Revolution Industrial Societies: Technologies and Economies Industrial Societies: Ideologies and Politics Industrial Societies: Social Stratification Industrial Societies: Population, Family, Leisure Industrializing Societies Major Social Experiments of the Twentieth Century Retrospect and Prospect	>Interpretations Introduction The Making of Global Sociology Thinking Globally Modernity and the Evolution of World Society The Changing World of Work Nationhood and Nation-States > Divisions Social Inequalities: Gender Race and Class Corporate Power and Social Responsibility Uneven Development: The Victims Crime, Drugs and Terrorism Population and Migration Health Lifestyle and the Body >Experience Tourism: Social and Cultural Effects Consuming Culture Media and the Information Age Sport in a Global Age Global Religion Urban Life > Dynamics and Challenges Global Civil Society Challenging a Gendered World Toward a Sustainable Future Identities and Belonging Contested Futures

(Figure 11.6)

Macro Social Formations

T1   (100,000-8,000 BC)_____**The Global System__T7**

Political Economies   *Present Day*

Communal Egalitarian

    Localized Stratified

        Chiefdoms

                Era of Empires

                Slave and Peasant Systems

                Early States   Modern States

                Era of Colonialism

                        Era of
                        Neocolonialism

                        Independent Polities

                        Global Corporations

                              Global Federationalism

                              Global Polity?

T1_____**Societal Evolutionary Trajectory**_____**Globalization__T7**
Hunting & Gather Horti   Simple Agrarian   Adv-Agri   Industrial Hyper-Ind Post-Ind
    Fishing   Maritime   Industrializing
    Pastoral   Pastoral

T1_____**T2**_____**T3**_____**T4**_____**T5**_____**T6**_____**T7**

100,000-- 8,000 BC ---3,000BC----------- 1.000BC----------1,800AD----2,000AD ---- 2,100 AD

Political Authority

Headman   Chief   Kingship   Emperor   Early State Modern State Global Fed
                                            Republic

remembering

they were words. perhaps
only words.
yet words charged with the
fervor of youth
the passion of dreams.

god how he made the heart feel.

they were heartwords for
our emotional anthems still in cocoon
and sent us soaring on eagle wingtips

and
crushed before butterfly.
god how many faces collapsed

routines frozen like icicles.
candles burned.
prayers thrown up above
an ocean of tears.

they were words. Words
that became our worlds

CHAPTER TWELVE

How is Global Space Possible?
Revisiting Robertson's Paradigm of the Global Field

Global Spaces from the Local

As I sat in my living room on an early Sunday evening amidst the shadowed sunlight of a mid February in southwestern Pennsylvania, my consciousness was overcome with a growing perceptual awareness. Here I was relaxing with cool bottle of French sparkling mineral water, enjoying the remainder of a tray of sushi, with the closing ceremonies of the 2010 Winter Olympics on the television about to commence—all while skimming through Lechner and Boli's *World Culture.* If you haven't already guessed I had become aware that I was having a "global" moment.

Yet it went deeper. Although not initially conscious of each choice I made, I had in fact made several decisions that Sunday evening that created a sort of *Personal Global Space* within and around myself. This wasn't merely cosmopolitan culture—I don't enjoy all of these things together on a regular basis. No. It was deeper, perhaps signaled by the global ritual of the Games, enticing me to be drawn to a more global orientation and richness of global culture in my own personal time & space. I had, in fact, created for myself a global space. But was there such a thing?

Well think about it? Globalization. Where is it? If there is such a thing there must be a space for it? In *World Culture,* Lechner and Boli (2005) speak about the unique space of airlines and airspace being "global" in nature—not connected to any native ground. And native ground is "local" is it not? I mean unless one is physically inside the UN building, all is local? Or is it? Can the local also be global? Had not I witnessed such a transformation of the local to the global that Sunday evening? Perhaps, I was in a global state of mind since we cannot truly rid ourselves of the local. On further reflection, even the UN building is in fact, in New York. The Local permeates our existence then, but it may be possible to create other spaces, or collective states of mind attached to particular spaces that give us a glimpse of more than the local. We have in fact been doing such since the beginning of civilization and its very localization.

The Glocalization of Space and Culture

Roland Robertson speaks of what he has coined "glocalization" (2009: 43-7). Now at the outset, be aware glocalization differs from the more popularized term, "globalization," but involves both the local and the global. Culturally, and oft times, globalization or more accurately, forces of globalization

185

act upon the local. Consider an example of a Walmart coming to a small town in America. While we are dealing strictly with American culture here, an accurate example nevertheless in the sense of "scale" where a huge intruding monolith comes upon the quaint local suburban/rural village and threatens to reorganize, restructure and redevelop every aspect of culture the town had ever known.

One would not dismiss events like these as both culturally damaging and facts of life in global capitalism, yet, at the same time glocalization gives local cultures more credit, resourcefulness, and creativity in dealing with what appears to be a cultural Godzilla about to trample all that is scared to a town and community. The response, or outcome is "glocalized" --a process leading to an output that is arrived at through not only the will of the global monolith, but upon the reaction of the native culture to such global forces on local ground. It is also clear that local communities, particularly local planning and development boards exert considerable power in exactly the ways in which a Walmart will enter a community, let alone if it will enter the community at all.

Hence on one level, my Pittsburgh suburban living room had not changed over the course of the past two week Olympic period, but it had been somewhat re-oriented due to the emergence of the Olympic games as a global fact or impending global force upon the local, and my localized reaction in the creation of what we might term a ***glocalized*** *Personal Global Space*. I would resist the term *State of Mind* here primarily due to the fact that there has become some transformation of public or private space. Had I had several friends over to watch the local Pitt Panthers' basketball game with Iron City Beer, Pittsburgh Pirogies, laptops tuned to Pitt basketball websites along with the local Sunday paper sport pages, one could equally argue that "space", heavily grounded in local themes and localized, had been also "transformed"--only in this case what had been created was *Personal Sport Space* or more accurately *Localized Sport Space*, in that it involved more than a single individual.

A Paradigmatic Model of the Global Field

Before we depart on a discussion of *Global Space* we would do well to introduce a theoretical research tradition broad enough to embed rich meaning to these cultural empirical observations we uncover. At one time in my intellectual career I thought a core-periphery model offered the solution to every concern or problem of global and social life, but even unique matters of cultural significance such as the notion of "personal" space, the transformation of space, collective states of mind regarding space, and the devotion to and of space, are not appropriate methodological or empirical material for a core/periphery model. Please, do not misread my own personal research tradition, as I spent the better part of my career applying a core/periphery model to the Appalachian case. But the fact is new empirical directions have rendered core and periphery rather inadequate in tackling these cultural questions in social/global scientific research.

For example, in a straightforward criticism leveled against the economistic axis of the World System Perspective, Robertson (1987: 3) contended that "the economic factor is only one of the facets of the making of the modern international system, which itself is, in turn, but one of a number of dimensions of globalization." The multidimensionality of globalization was accurately fleshed out initially in the early to mid 1980s at the University of Pittsburgh when Robertson (1985) developed a four dimensional theory encompassing themes of individual selves, societies, the system of societies, and mankind. As an example of the sheer magnitude of Robertson's theoretical tradition, core and peripheral matters would find their expression or rather, witness their subsumption within the system of societies axis, and further specified in the economic axis of that system under the rubric of problematics of regionalism.

Before returning to notions of space and time in global context, we should also point out here that Robertson's theoretical and research tradition not only subsumes core and peripheral conceptualizations, but the Boli-Bennett and Meyer World Integrationist Perspective as well. While I've noted elsewhere (Matvey 2005) that the Integrationist model involved adding State power and centrality of the State to Wallerestein's economic foundation in a similar way that Weber added power and prestige to Marx's constricted economic dimension of social class, it can also be said here that Robertson's multidimensional schema subsumes Meyer and Boli-Bennett in the sense that here too the political and economic dimensions are two aspects of the system of societies which in turn is but one of the multidimensional features of Robertson's model.

Robertson's theoretical model is complex and the first comprehensive schematization of it emerged in a paper he and Chirco authored in 1985 entitled "Humanity, Globalization, and Worldwide Religious Resurgence: A Theoretical Exploration," in *Sociological Analysis*. The basic schema involves a four-component grid including individual selves, societies, the system of societies, and mankind. Essentially, Robertson and Chirco globalized Simmel's basic question of "*how is society possible*" and asked instead "*how is the globe possible*," and also a related implicit question of how is *humanity* possible? What's most fascinating theoretically about Robertson's scheme is not merely the quad-dimesnional model but the linkages and interpenetration of each processual component with the three other dimensions of the model. Hence,

> ...The linkages of which we have just spoken involves four processes of relativization, two having to do with the relativization of societies (trans-socialization) and two having to do with the relativization of persons (trans-personalization). By relativization we mean a process involving the placing of sociocultural or psychic entities in larger categorical contexts, such that the relativized entities are constrained to be more self-reflexive relative to other entities in the larger context..

> ...The relativization of selves involves, along one dimension, the situating of selfhood in the more inclusive and fundamental frame of what it means to be of mankind; while the relativization of societies—along another, parallel dimension—involves the situating of concrete societies in the context of a world complex of societies... (Robertson and Chirco, 1985: 234)

Robertson goes on to point out that in addition to these trajectories, there "branches from each a secondary process of relativization, one having to do with the relationship between concrete societies and the category of man, the other involving a connection between selves and the global complex of societies" (Ibid).

The system of modern societies, then, is but one dimension in the overall schema, and in its broad scope the variety of intersections and interpenetrations possible with the four processual dimensions, socio-scientific exploration can proceed not only along the lines and from a multidimensional and multiplicity of axes and nexus points, but we also begin to gain the flavor of the answer to the initial questions of how the globe, globalization, and humanity are all possible in concrete as well as theoretical terms. While Robertson has spoken of these dimensions and their respective links in what he has coined as the "crystallization" of the "thematization of humanity," these very questions his model successfully answers all reveal how each processual theme or dimension leads into and mutually reinforces the other in answering those fundamental themes.

In 1992, with the publication of Robertson's *Globalization: Social Theory and Global Culture*, the theoretical schema continued to develop. While humanity as a theme remained a central issue, Robertson also kept the four component grid in the fore in terms of the "individual thematizations of societies, individual selves, international relations and humankind" (1992:28) in what was more broadly theoretically cast as "***the global field***" (Ibid:27). Figure 12.1 represents a diagram of the 1992 version of the global field. The global field represented an upgrading over Robertson's 1985 model with Chirco, where he redefined a number of key linkages in the revised paradigm including what he terms the individual-society problematic in the selves/national societies axis, and the realpolitik-humanity problematic in the world system of societies/humankind axis (Ibid: 27). Additionally are four relativizations in the linkages: a) the relativization of self-identities in the selves/humankind axis; b) the relativization of societies in the national society/world system of societies axis; c) the relativization of societal reference in the selves/world system of societies axis; and d) the relativization of citizenship in the national societies/humankind axis (see Figure 12.1). Although Robertson has yet again upgraded the global field in his forthcoming book on Globalization, the 1992 global field model is still very much on the cutting edge as a paradigmatic shift along with its corresponding theoretics within the social sciences milieu.[8]

In Robertson's research tradition thus, it becomes possible at one and the same moment to speak of the global system of modern societies in its evolutionary history as it intersects with bio-psychic developments in our individual human conceptual apparatus for increasingly understanding and intellectually grasping our own humanity. We see psychic and sociocultural evolution in a "systems" sense the way Parsonian (1977) imagery had intended, only within a richer and broader global and humanitic context. We not only see ourselves as individuals, members of societies, brothers and sisters in a humankind that transcends our societal identity, but also as having a unique and moral relationship with the globe in an analogous manner that we hold a relationship with our own respective societies. The important point here is the multidimensionality of Robertson's schema. It is culturally and structurally comprehensive and also allows us to move flexibly and fluidly between each. Hence as we proceed here, we will make reference to Robertson's model in our empirical observations.

Devotion and the Sacredization of Space

We start with the proposition that space can be transformed, perhaps never really eliminating local space, but rather "devoting" that space to something other than the mundane local. Consider now the notion of devotion as it relates to space. Remember in fact it was The Christ, who noted "When two or more will gather in my name, there I will be in their midst." (Matthew 18.20) Here we are given the notion that "space" itself can become sacred, and we can thus devote "geography" to sacred or holy space. Religion as a moral force has perhaps the longest history of creating, making, constructing, transforming and transcending the mundane local into *Sacred* space. We not only devoted ourselves to deities such as the Buddha, or the Christ, or even to teachings such as Biblical treasures and Sutras but to sacred spaces such as holy lands, head temples, historical birthplaces, and other sacred geographic markers.

---

8   Why I refer to Robertson's Theoretical Research Tradition as a Paradigm extends beyond his schema of the Global Humanitic. There are several other crucial developments in the research tradition with the advent of *Globalization: Social Theory and Global Culture* and henceforth that lead one to conclude this theory as a paradigmatic shift in thinking. Also developed in *Globalization (1992: 78-9)* are several Images of World Order that also constitute a viable research orientation entitled Global Gemeinschaft and Gesellschaft I and II that hinge on eight conceptions of global social order increasingly held by psychic entities and sociocultural systems. This theory continued to develop from *Globalization* in 1992 through *Globalization and Football* in 2009. Five other key theoretical tools in Robertson's paradigm include the Universalism/Particularism fault line (1992: 97-114; 2009: 32-5); The Five Historical Phases of Globalization (2009: 3-29); The Homogenization-Heterogenization issue (2009: 38-43); The Global/Local nexus as manifested in the previously discussed concept of Glocalization (2009: 43-47); and finally, the Nostalgia or Nostalgic Paradigm (1992: 146-164; 2009: 60-2). It should be noted these are wide ranging theoretical tools surrounding the initial schematization of the Global Humanitic and allow one to fine-tune a methodological research approach for a variety of problematics in socio-scientific investigation.

Sacred space is a not just space but a dimension of our identity and humanity. Native American Sacred burial grounds, and Japanese Shinto *Torii* Gates sacredizing vast territories are two additional examples. In the same way, then, a *Personal Global Space,* even as the one I unconsciously created that Sunday night, relates in fact, to Robertson's model. It touches upon the individual/global dimensions as expressed in the selves/world system of societies nexus and relationship.

Robertson's *Global Field* Paradigm

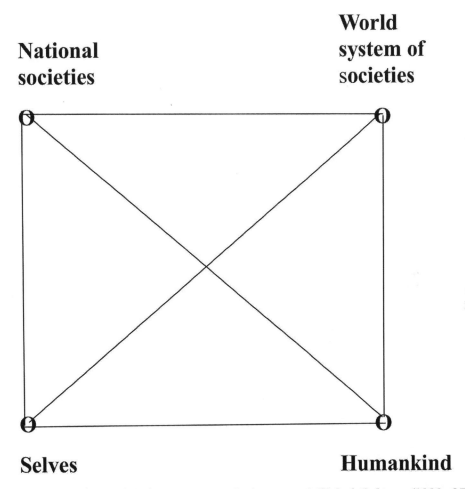

Figure 12.1: from Globalization: Social Theory and Global Culture. (1992: 27)

We have already touched upon Sport Space, but additionally noteworthy is here in southwestern Pennsylvania culture, is a more intensified version of sport space--what we might call *Hunter's Space* where local space is transformed into quasi-sacred hunters' grounds. The success of the movie *The Deer Hunter,* brought many themes in western Pennsylvania together from the Vietnam War to east European Culture, but it also touched part of a deeper humanitic of man as hunter—notions found in the Individual/Mankind nexus.

Consider also, the opening and closing ceremonies of the Olympic games. The games in fact take place in "local" space. But might not we say one of the purposes or functions of the opening and closing ceremonies of the games is to globalize and de-globalize what might be considered for two weeks as a *Public Global Environment*. As *Torri* gates announce and demarcate sacred space, so do the opening Ceremonies announce the creation of global time & space—hence transcending the local.

The Computer, Internet and Global Space

Solitary relational space should be considered human space in solitude yet devoted to the social. An example here is a teen in her room after school until supper, lost in internet chat rooms. Why does this work? Why has it become popular and why does it persist? Primarily it touches on the individual-social humanitic---it allows us to touch both individual and social dimensions of our humanity at one and the same moment. The internet has led to an explosion of *solitary relational space and time* in the last few decades so much so it was reported on the news that less teens today are getting their driver's licenses at 16 not only due to economic constraints on parents (ie: insurance costs) but due to the fact that many teens today remark "I can see my friend on the internet" rather than in person. Collectively, the internet has created not only an upward push on *solitary relational space* but a downward push on *face to face interpersonal space*

There is also in cyber lore the story of a man and woman who meet on the internet and fall in love over a period of many months yet when they meet in person they find they are a bundle of nerves and only resolve the problem by getting on two different computers in the same house and proceeding to interact in the way they know best. Eventually they calm down and proceed in person.

Hence we return to the concept of *Global Space* as a growing cultural trend that part of our personal, living, group or solitary space is increasingly devoted to a global orientation. In my anecdote at the outset of this essay, all of my choices lent themselves that Sunday evening to *Personal Global Space* in that these activities and objects were in and of themselves transsocietal or global in character.

It is also clear that the computer is not merely a "technological" item or commodity, or even disposable technology in the First World where the Ghz race is alive and well and keeps product turnover at an all time high. Additionally, the computer, may be viewed as a commodity of connectivity, an item of globalization, a gateway or *Torii* gate for *Cyber Global Space*. In other words, take the concept of *Solitary Relational Space* and globalize it in the sense that the computer user is involved in any of a number of global oriented activities from international chat spaces, to global research, global cyber tours, international touristry, global web surfing, and among other pursuits, economic transactions across societal lines. Perhaps much of Internet related activity occurs within national boundaries. Yet the door is open to enter Cyber Global Space at any point merely by attending to an internet-ready computer.

Global Inequality and Access to Global Space

Do the urbanized have greater access to *Personal Global Space* than rural? Does the first world have greater access as opposed to the 3rd --5th Worlds? On one level rurality might be considered a factor until you look in the back yard of a resident of rural Pennsylvania and find a full blown Satellite system. Yet what of the rural farmer in Malaysia who might be deeply entrenched in *Personal Local Space*? There is a wonderfully thought provoking picture on the cover of Robertson and Giulianotti's *Globalization and Football (2009)* of a small African child in front of his 5th world rural village of huts, and one might be tempted to give the odds in favor of a completely ruralized localization, except for the fact that this child is there playing with a soccer ball. Can we say such a village is without the global? To be sure, the poignant scene is a blending of the local, glocal, and global.

Calhoun (1987), however, even back in the 1980s documented the fact that societal systems at the bottom of the world (ie: 5th World GDP) might appear to be very localized, but scratch beneath the surface and you find these governments and societal sectors heavily involved in grants and fund raising activities with not only the 1st World, but with IGO's and INGO's as well. Hence we might say these societies, sectors, institutions and organizations exist part of their time in not so much the local, but in what Matvey and Chan (2005) coined as states of *Orientational Fluency* with the Global Field

A global IGO or INGO exists as a global entity in a state of *Orientational Primacy*. At the distinctly global level they exist in the cultural global core, while social units such as nations, sectors, institutions, and organizations (and individuals) exist in relation to the cultural global core---in states of orientational fluency.

While the Malaysian example may be the rule rather than the exception, it is clear that global and international markets, religious missionary movements (including Christian and Buddhist), dealings with IGOs and INGOs all bring the local into various states of orientational fluency with the Global Field. Both orientational primacy and orientational fluency have increased historically, particularly as the result of the growing technological compression and computerization the globe. In terms of primacy look at the explosion in the last century of not only IGOs, but INGOs as well.

The Internet is not the only dynamic factor increasing fluency, but televisions, radios, land and cell phones and news media in all its outlets all work to mutually reinforce connectivity. In addition, as noted earlier, the web of interactions occurring among states, sectors, institutions, organizations, and individuals all bring the world objectively speaking, into greater levels of fluency. It should be noted however, that the inequality in access to technological items of connectivity is astounding between the 1st and 5th Worlds. Clearly technological culture favors a) the economic and political core b) the urbanized, c) the literate, d) advanced techno-infrastructures, e) the highly educated, and f) the technologically adept.

Concluding Remaks

Global Space, or rather *Personal Global Space* along with increasing states of *Orientational Fluency* between the local and global should be seen as embryonic at this point in that such trends are merely beginning to unfold at this particular historical juncture. Consider the Olympic games. The fact is that both the Summer and Winter games, as an ongoing global ritual, only meet once every four years. True, they do dominate the media during that two-week period every four years, but long term evolution of the Games will see the increasing frequency in regards to how often they meet at a particular "local" space. Other events too, such as the emerging gathering of religious elites at Assisi which has taken place now roughly once a decade, also has a long way to go before such an emerging tradition is fully ritualized and perhaps institutionalized as an aspect of the human condition. The question this brief essay has attempted to answer is not only how is "global space" possible across the vast territorial expanse of the local, but also why it is on the increase. The answer to both questions I have suggested is such "global" space touches upon individual, organizational, institutional, local, global and glocal dimensions of our lives—our humanitic condition. *Solitary Relational Space* is both possible and popular because it emerges in the individual/societal nexus, while *Personal Global Space* increasingly becomes possible as individual/global themes emerge in the present day civilizational history.

The idea here for further consideration and research is not only is *Global Space* embryonic at this point, but the trajectory necessarily increases over historical time. As we have seen with the computer as not merely a technological item but an item of globalization, *Global Space* has become commonplace in the First World. As the rest of the world experiences such technological compression, so too will *Global Space* be increasingly accessible to the rest of the world.

Department Store

She fills balloons
with compressed feelings
dazzling colors given to children
floating above what pushbrooms
sweep away as useless.

He paints walls
in superficial gloss
with a worn roller
and covers many sins
immaculate
--a fresh soul
sold to lonely-eyed
mannequins.

The elevator stalled
between floors
momentarily
and still
only a glance was given
at most.

CHAPTER THIRTEEN

Culture, Globalization, Bob Dylan and "The Christ"

A Changing of the Guard

> …Then you better start swimmin'
> Or you'll sink like a stone
> For the times they are a-changin'…
> (From "The Times They Are a Changin'," Dylan: 1963)

Bob Dylan wrote "The Times They are a-Changin" in 1963, five years before the assassinations of Martin Luther King and Robert F. Kennedy and the subsequent explosion of dissent and mass protest across college campuses and in the streets of African American communities.

Some have called Dylan a prophet, a leader of a generation, the prince of the protest movement, and among other titles, a hero of the outcast and downtrodden. In numerous interviews Dylan has rejected being placed on such a pedestal and has plainly called himself nothing more than a songwriter.

What is clear in "The Times They are a-Changin" however, is the notion of social change, and not just gradual evolutionary change but a rapid social upheaval along with a "changing of the guard" in the social and political order. The words resonate--almost biblically: "For the loser now will be later to win," "the slow one now will later be fast" and "the present now will later be past." "The order is rapidly fading" as sons and daughters are pitted against mothers and fathers—and parents are to "get out of the new one" if they can't lend a hand.

Dylan in some respects represents a John the Baptist figure, appearing and heralding the unfolding of a new social order. He is an announcer, a bearer of the news, the one who watches from the rafters and reports the changes unfolding. Dylan understands the changes are not fully upon us yet, and though embryonic in form, are rapidly maturing and materializing. The question is though—what is this new social formation? One can gain some inkling of this order if we visit other Dylan songs, most notably, "Chimes of Freedom," (Dylan: 1964) written one year after "The Times They are a-Changin," where Dylan speaks of justice "chiming" for the downtrodden, outcast, poor, victims, "warriors whose strength is not to fight," refugees, "mistitled prostitutes," rebels, and among other categories, the forsaken.

Long before Dylan became a born-again Christian in the late 1970s his poetic works and songs were filled with the logic and compassion of the Beatitudes. Dylan's notion of a just social order ministers to and ordains the peaceful, meek, humble, and poor. It represents a revolution unfolding for the plight of the underclass.

Jesus said much the same things nearly 2000 years ago. In the new order he envisioned and presented, blessed were the lame, sick, mentally afflicted, poor, homeless, outcast, downtrodden, mute, deaf, dumb, and lame. It was also a social formation where if one wished to lead, he and she would lead by serving. His peace was made perfect in weakness. St. Francis, Mother Theresa, Billy Graham--all would become his peaceful warriors. The logic of this type of compassionate love was at the heart of the Kingdom of Heaven and that Kingdom existed within the hearts of all.

Jesus' Revolution would not only rock the foundations of existing social establishments but strike at nearly every social sphere of human life and its social institutions. Consider what Jesus said about the social institution of the family in Matthew 10:34-42:

> [34]Do not suppose that I have come to bring peace to the earth. I did not come to bring peace, but a sword. [35] For I have come to turn
> a man against his father,
> a daughter against her mother,
> a daughter-in-law against her motherinlaw—[36]
> a man's enemies will be the members of his own household.
>
> [37]Anyone who loves his father or mother more than me is not worthy of me; anyone who loves his son or daughter more than me is not worthy of me; [38]and anyone who does not take his cross and follow me is not worthy of me. [39]Whoever finds his life will lose it, and whoever loses his life for my sake will find it.
>
> [40]He who receives you receives me, and he who receives me receives the one who sent me. [41]Anyone who receives a prophet because he is a prophet will receive a prophet's reward, and anyone who receives a righteous man because he is a righteous man will receive a righteous man's reward. [42]And if anyone gives even a cup of cold water to one of these little ones because he is my disciple, I tell you the truth, he will certainly not lose his reward. (NIV, Matthew 10:34-42)

Jesus represented the heralding of a new human formation, not built on economics, politics, or military regimes but rather, grounded in kindness and love. It is a comprehensively compassionate love that we find in the essence of the words of the Beatitudes. Sometimes it requires a son or daughter to discern and shatter the embeddedness of existing traditions and laws—even within a core institution such as the human family, and hence, The Christ came not to bring peace but "a sword."

Some forty years have passed since Dylan authored "The Times They are a-Changing" and we find ourselves, once again, on the threshold of rapid social change. The essence of this social change is not merely technological or institutional but a global change that defines our human family above and beyond the limits and boundaries of national origin and cultural ethnicity. In the face of globalization, we are moved to confront our own humanity binding us all to each other—and as John Lennon so eloquently called it "a brotherhood of man."

Globalization and The Family of Humanity

Robertson has ceaselessly emphasized the "growing perception and fact" of the world as a "single place" in referring to the globalization process. Again, as noted in the Introduction, this does not necessarily represent the withering away of national societies or the end of the nation states as much as it does indicate a growing and expanding global field or arena of consciousness. In Chapter Seven we examined the concept of "humanity" as one referent point or dimension of global culture. In other words, as the world grows more compact and smaller, global notions of humanity, humankind and the human family necessarily expand and enlarge.

We are entering a point in human societal evolution where new generations grow up not only asking, "Who am I?" but also pondering the question "Who is my society?" I may be Malaysian, and this man may be Canadian, but on another level we are brothers in the broader family of humanity. Hence, appealing to the humanity in us as a referent point, we are no longer strangers but neighbors, both in the system of national societies as well as in the human family across those societies. Appealing to humanity allows us to jump over social and cultural fences previously separating us.

Again we return to Jesus. In the parable of the Good Samaritan we find the compassionate logic of kindheartedness and loving-kindness. Jesus hurled such parables at the established order and presented a radically alternate view of our social roots and roles—that all men were neighbors. 2000 years before all the talk of globalization and humanity The Christ recognized the singularity of the human family. The Christ used examples like the Samaritan to pulverize deeply ingrained notions of "untouchable castes or classes," and to reveal the humanity in all races, ethnicities, cultures, or societal origins.

The Transformation of the Human Heart

In another Gospel (Luke 19) is the story of Zacchaeus, the tax collector with whom Jesus ate lunch:

> [1]Jesus entered Jericho and was passing through. [2]A man was there by the name of Zacchaeus; he was a chief tax collector and was wealthy. [3]He wanted to see who Jesus was, but being a short man he could not, because of the crowd. [4]So he ran ahead and climbed a sycamore-fig tree to see him, since Jesus was coming that way.
>
> [5]When Jesus reached the spot, he looked up and said to him, "Zacchaeus, come down immediately. I must stay at your house today." [6]So he came down at once and welcomed him gladly.
>
> [7]All the people saw this and began to mutter, "He has gone to be the guest of a 'sinner.'"
>
> [8]But Zacchaeus stood up and said to the Lord, "Look, Lord! Here and now I give half of my possessions to the poor, and if I have cheated anybody out of anything, I will pay back four times the amount."
>
> [9]Jesus said to him, "Today salvation has come to this house, because this man, too, is a son of Abraham. [10]For the Son of Man came to seek and to save what was lost." (NIV, Luke 19)

Overwhelmed by the presence of The Christ, Zacchaeus proclaimed that he would return all monies he swindled from the poor, and give half his wealth to charities. Jesus response was simple, yet direct: "Salvation has come to this house today." Was Jesus more interested here in "works" such as Zacchaeus donating money to charity? On one level yes, but a deeper more fundamental interpretation was the change of heart experienced by Zacchaeus. Here is the kernel and the chief concern of Jesus— the human heart undergoing a transformation from greed to giving, self-centered to other-centered, passion-filled to compassionate, apathetic to empathetic, slothful to value-creating, and finally, from anger to love. In short, a renewal or rebirth.

This then is the "global" human heart and its capacity for transformation—existing in the meek, humble, outcast, poor in spirit, downtrodden, sick, suffering, victim, and prisoner. It further exists as a heart in all people, transcending culture, race, ethnicity, and societal origin. Social Change in

Jesus' schema emerges not from a top-down political or economic revolution, but rather a revolution starting in the human heart. This transformed human heart, would, in turn and in time, shatter old social codes and socially imposed stigmas by emphasizing the humanity in all of us.

Who is my neighbor?

Consider the problem of and responses to poverty and human disaster. Many baby boomers reading this book will remember hearing about the "poor hillbilly" of Appalachia, the poor African American in the inner city ghettos and the reservation-bound Native Americans. Mission movements appealed to our sense of family as Americans to help out the less fortunate. These groups were part of our societal family and hence, our neighbors. Now however, wired and connected to the world through the global media, global computerization and increases in global moral density, we find the human family expands to include not only the poor in U.S. society, but the earthquake victims in Haiti, China, Pakistan, and Iran, along with the refugees in Africa, tsunami victims in Indonesia, and finally to the desperately poor, homeless and starving of the Third, Fourth, and Fifth Worlds.

In a globalized world, human disasters, from earthquakes to tsunamis, become global events requiring a global response from individuals, societies, global institutions such as the UN, and International Non Profit Organizations (INPOs). Further, in a globalized world, the poverty of the Appalachian in southern West Virginia is but one dimension of human hardship as the field necessarily expands to encompass the poverty and hurt in the Third and Fourth Worlds.

Concluding Note

Globalization, we have found, represents rapid social change in such spheres as religion, education, global institutions and organizations, and in the more technological aspects such as societal and global computerization. Much of the core/peripheral model utilized to explain regional underdevelopment in Appalachia can and has been applied to Third and Fourth World societies in a sociology of the development of underdevelopment. World Systems Theory and Dependency Theory are two such examples. In some respects Appalachia shares the subsidiary-dominated economic structures found in the Third and Fourth World periphery. Here we follow Walls' insights on viewing central Appalachia as an "internal periphery" in a core society.

By way of a conclusion I put forth the question "what does globalization mean for us as a human family?" In some respects globalization represents intensified underdevelopment in the periphery from Appalachia to the Third and Fourth Worlds, but on the other hand globalization has enabled most of us to view the peoples of the globe as our brothers and sisters. We feel the empathy of humanity upon us as globalization proceeds. As tens of thousands die in earthquakes our hearts feel the hurt suffered thousands of miles away. We are connected instantly to the tragic scenes through the global media and witness the suffering of our brothers and sisters. In a globalizing world, our family has broadened to encompass the whole of humanity. What is our role, not only in our communities, nations, and cultures but also in our human family? How can we contribute value to our humanity? How can we "serve" to lead? What can we do to promote global justice, freedom, and liberty? At some point the "global" heart will reach a critical mass, and what appear as "valued ideals" will manifest upon the real world.

For Bob Dylan

hands in your pockets
new york 1961
with a song to woody.
harmonica piercing through
ice
and thoughts in your eyes.
we flocked to you like sheep.
like a poem blowing in the wind
your odyssey became our conscience.
They say you've changed...

but years later
you spoke for Rubin Carter
Lenny Bruce
and provided thoughts for us
of the Jokermen.

Somehow
after hard rains
and hurricane
you're still here, Bob
behind sunglasses from the sixties
still making heroes out of outlaws
hands in your pockets
thoughts in your eyes.

CHAPTER FOURTEEN

Epilogue

Blows Against the Empire: Globalization, The MS Windows Monopoly and The Linux Challenge

"Microsoft became rich, and maintains its wealth, by a virtual monopoly over PC manufacturers....you usually have little choice to buy Windows with a new PC. Try it now. Phone your favorite big-name computer retailer. Say that you want a PC but you *don't* want Windows installed. Then listen as the salesperson on the other end of the phone struggles to understand." (Thomas, 2006)

"Welcome to the world of Linux, the operating system developed by thousands of people around the world." (LeBlanc, 2004)

An epilogue generally signifies a finalizing, an ending, a reviewing and wrapping up of loose ends, a seeking of closure after the body of the text has been presented. This chapter, however, is offered not only as a sociological and economic analysis, but more in the form of a social and political editorial, while also inter-mixed with a degree of social forecasting.

Discovering Linux

In 2008, the first time I booted and logged into a Linux desktop I was greeted by a spectacular background wallpaper portrait of a coastal shoreline with the word GNOME across the picture. Gnome stands for **GNU Network Object Model Environment.** It was exciting and inviting at one and the same moment. This looked somewhat different than Windows, somewhat new and enlightening. The desktop icons also reflected this sense of "new uniqueness." Instead of "IE" was a browser called "Mozilla Firefox" with the graphic of a globe aflame as the icon. Upon further investigation, I found not only Firefox but also another browser entitled "Konqueror." Konqueror was an eye-opener in that it sported functions other than just web browsing—it also acted as a file system, network system, and starting point for all the system's applications.

The email client I found with a graphic of an "envelope" and called "Evolution" also did not disappoint. It was close to Outlook Express. As a hobby, I "chat" in both (global, national, local and special interest) chat rooms along with chatting over several Instant Messengers such as Yahoo, Windows Live, AOL, ICQ, etc. What I found in GNOME pleasantly surprised me as it sported a Messaging Client called Pidgin that essentially allowed you to connect to the wide variety of separate messaging protocols. No need to spend all my time exiting out of Yahoo, and signing into MSN. Pidgin put "chat" in the easy chair.

What about office needs? Again, here we find an integrated system called Open Office, which in many respects is a mirror image of Microsoft Office with spreadsheets, word processor, database, and presentation software. Are you noticing a pattern here? What I was finding was a whole new world of software under the Linux umbrella that worked just as good, if not better, than Windows oriented software. The brightest benefit, however, was the software on the Linux distribution CD/DVD: free, open source, and upgradeable.

Some months later, I continued to explore Open Suse Linux (which is a distribution of Linux, and we will have much more to say about distributions at a later point, but for now all that needs to be known is that a distro is like a dialect in the language of English). What I found was not only one desktop orientation such as GNOME, but also another titled KDE. About this time, Linux was upgrading its package from 10.3 to 11.0, so while I had the opportunity to download this software for free on the Open Suse Internet site, I went ahead and purchased the boxed version that came with several months of free technical support. At this point I did a clean install of 11 and went with KDE instead of Gnome.

Much to my surprise I found several goodies. First, all of my favorites continued to be offered on KDE such as Pidgin, Open Office, Konqueror and Mozilla Firefox, however, I also gave KDE's mail client a try, known as Kmail, and I actually grew to prefer Kmail over Outlook Express in Windows.

There were also additional forms of software from CD and DVD burners, to Media Players, CD and Video Players, Photo Management Systems, Dolphin File Manager, Web Page Creation, and several dozen other programs that work comparably and in some instances, better than Windows oriented software.

On the Nature of Linux

Historically, Linux was developed in 1991 and was based largely upon the Unix System that had its origins at "Bell Laboratories in the early 1970s." (Leblanc p. 11). Common to Unix is the "shell environment which holds the root, directory, and file structure" as well as text command line where commands are entered to start applications, internet and/or task oriented, such as pico, vi, emacs, pine, usenet, tin, gopher, lynx, links, irc, ircII, html, and dozens of other programs and applications. In 1991, more than 20 years after the development of the Unix mainframe system found at many universities and colleges, Linus Torvalds (Leblanc, p. 11) developed the Linux Kernel which would become the historical starting point for the development of what are essentially today's Desktop and Laptop "shells"--a kind of mini mirror of the Unix system on a personal PC.

Return to the opening quotes at the top of this chapter. Notice any difference in the essence of the two operating systems?

Globally, according to Thomas, "Windows is used on 91% of the world's desktop computers" (p. 6). Linux has also existed since 1991; 20 years of development, then, at still less than a 10% share of the global market points to the monopoly environment quoted from Keir Thomas above. Thomas (p. 8-9) goes on to mention several benefits of the Linux Operating System over Windows.

First, viruses, worms, security holes, and glitches bewilder Windows, while Linux sees little or no problem with viral attacks. Second, the system is crash free. Third, the security of the Linux system out-competes, by far, the Windows system. Fourth, all of the software on Linux is "free and shareable." A fifth benefit is the latest versions or distributions of Linux are compatible with Older Hardware. While Windows 7 has requirements of 1-2 gig in RAM, I am running the very latest version of Open Suse Linux 11.1 on a back-up 800mhz ½ gig RAM machine and it works perfectly. Finally, Thomas mentions the "Linux Community" that is at its essence a huge support group that acts like the one room schoolhouse days where those further along share their knowledge with newer Linux users.

Leblanc lists nearly a dozen reasons the collaborative effort of Linux wanted it to succeed. This list includes "multiuser orientation, multiprocess, multiplatform, interoperable, scalable, portable, flexible, stable (it doesn't crash), efficient, and free." (Leblanc, p. 12) Leblanc goes on to ask the question, "Who's in charge of Linux anyway," in that we find a vast difference between the top-down MS Windows organization whose boss is the billionaire Bill Gates, to Linux which is a loose knit federation of what are called various "distributions" of Linux. Think of distributions as dialects of the English Language, or a variety of different denominations in a larger religious umbrella such as Christianity. Leblanc lists several distributions of Linux such as Debian, Gentoo, Libranet, TurboLinux, Mandrake (now Mandriva), RedHat and Fedora, Slackware, Open Suse, Ubuntu. As we noted in the previous section of this chapter, there are 2 major desktop environments across the Linux distributions: GNOME and KDE.

Linux users generally support a particular distribution they come to feel comfortable in using. Derek Knaub, a friend and colleague from Ohio State University and also a System/Network Administrator, throws his support behind Mandrake/Mandriva, while I personally utilized the Open Suse system for a time, then gave Mandriva a go, but settled on the Ubuntu Distribution. The systems are generally alike, as when a technical glitch emerged in my system Derek was able to help me primarily from his knowledge of the basic logic embedded the Linux system and across distributions. Generally in this chapter I will refer to Linux in its Open Suse or Ubuntu distributions, but many points made can be applied to all of the other distributions of Linux. Specifically though, Open Suse is what I learned Linux upon, and it "is one of the oldest distributions of Linux available," and "originally a German company, but nowadays it is owned by Novell. (Thomas, p. 22)" Keir Thomas notes "Nowadays, Linux is a thoroughly modern and capable operating system, considered cutting-edge by many. It also runs on many different types of computer hardware, including Apple Macintosh computers, Sun SPARC machines, and the ubiquitous desktop PCs equipped with Intel or AMD processors." (Ibid, p.17)

The Models of Desktop Operating Systems: Windows and Linux

Computerization has gotten itself into a pickle. Microsoft and more specifically the Operating System Windows, has come to dominate more than 85% of the U.S. Market in computerization. Apple has tried to challenge, but many say the Macs are overpriced. To be sure, what we have in societal and global computerization today is a Windows System that represents an MCM (*Monopoly Capital Model*). It is corporately owned, integrated, and fed to the masses as a one-way or perhaps only-way to heaven. It is the Bill Gates or Donald Trump top-down orientation. This also echoes the "Colonial" and/or "Neo-Colonial" models of economic development as a process where multinational and transnational corporations penetrate LDCs and essentially set up a subsidiary landscape that is vertically integrated with the core-centered corporate parent firms. The enterprise is reminiscent of the Ma Bell configuration—where the giant corporation dominated every aspect of the land phone system—local and long distance. Computerization's Ma Bell orientation in the manifest form of Windows, to quote Marx, is "Moses and the Prophets."

The top down logic here is the corporate parent firm dictates the operating system and software technology, and whose power to establish what the customer needs is absolute and unchallenged. It is a monopoly of not only the Windows product, but of much of the software embedded in the Windows operating systems.

The other side of the coin, and the opposite of the MCM, is what we will appropriately term the PCCM (*Pioneer-Collaborative-Cooperative- Model*).

Before we delve into the Linux Model and its future, it is important to engage a theoretical construct here that encompasses the Linux Enterprise and allows us to understand why Linux is the way it is in confronting the established Windows giant. This construct is sociologically known as the "Pioneer Ethic," lectured on once at the University of Pittsburgh, but that was many moons ago, however, if memory serves I can dictate the gist of this particular Cultural Ethic, along with the move toward an application of this theory to the case of Linux.

Briefly stated, while the 9-5 routines of life, the daily structures of domestic life, the social routines of social interaction, and the repetition of tasks and chores all represent the mundane and established social order--these then signify the normal social reality we confront on a daily basis. However, when a society, or perhaps a social group or organization or a segment of the population delve on the "cutting edge" of a new experience, a new direction, a new invention or investigation, or a new journey the resulting exploration and expansion into the new sphere creates what will be termed a vibrant cultural "Pioneer Ethic." The ethic, in turn, operates and exerts a multidimensional influence on social interaction and behavior. First and foremost, the pioneer ethic is comprised of several behavior-guiding orientations such as collaborations, cooperativeness, togetherness, other-oriented behavior, selfless as opposed to selfish traits, collective altruism, helpfulness, friendliness, social cohesion, mutual aid and assistance, and interdependence. Along the cutting edge of this pioneer space are dangers, real and imagined, that reverberate back to the social group and promote this kind of helpful cooperation as a means to confront and overcome the dangers. Where an individual might clearly perish in the danger, it can be overcome with collective cooperation.

One major application of this theoretical construct is the Westward Expansion and settlement of the West. Here we found the "pioneer" ethic operating in the cohesion of families, related and unrelated, in pulling together for both the trek and settlement of the West. There were many threats along the journey and in the settlement process, and those orientations of togetherness and expressive helpfulness dominated social behavior more often when folks confronted the "cutting edge."

In pulling this construct of the "Pioneer Ethic" along, and reapplying it to today, we find that in the age of Globalization, expanding societal computerization and even global computerization represents the cutting edge with respect to scientific and technological developments. We are in fact pioneering into Globalization and find the development of the computer and its dissemination across societies represents this doorstep of social change regarding our future.

In the official and unofficial Linux Enterprise we find all the elements of the PCCM theoretic. It represents the pioneering into new or unknown space---and interestingly enough, one of the dangers or perceived threats here is the monolithic Windows or Microsoft Multinational dominating between 80 and 90 percent of the market, swallowing up all newcomers or threats, in a top down monopoly technological schema. Windows exists as Godzilla existed in Japanese films of the 50s and 60s at a time when Japan was busy rebuilding after WWII and charting into pioneer territory of its own in terms of its emerging economic and political development and expansion in the modern system of societies. How did they defeat the beast? The Danger? The Unknown? How did they pave into the future? Only through cooperation and collaboration among themselves and also among the victorious Allies now stationed on their shores.

As computerization proceeds, there is a strong spirit of collaboration in Linux. First, it is "open source" that is unlike the top down technological model of Windows. Folks are allowed to input their skill, knowledge and talent into the software, adding and developing and redeveloping the software. Hence software development, and also "desktop" development is a concerted and collaborative effort, not only among Americans, but globally situated across societal lines. There are also longstanding user support forums among almost every distribution of Linux. This is "free" help, and "status" in the forums is often determined by who can offer the most expert advice, another indicator of the ripe Pioneer Ethic at work in the heart of the Linux Enterprise.

As we mentioned earlier, all of the developments in the Linux enterprise are embryonic at this point, but once it reaches a "take-off" stage, a long-term prediction is that it will overcome Windows as the dominant protocol for everything from software to the Desktop environment. Several distributions of Linux have developed, most notably being Open Suse, which originated in Germany and now is backed by corporations such as Novell and Dell. In returning to our model, not only do we witness computerization as a pioneering effort, or even a collaborative and cooperative effort, but also as it grows it begins to mirror "competitive capital" rather than the monopoly model of Windows. Right now, there is already "friendly competition" among several distributions such as Ubuntu, Open Suse, Mandriva (formerly Mandrake), Redhat, and about a half dozen other distros in the mix. But the real competition will emerge when Linux distros come to compete against the monolithic Windows as well as Apple (which represents another enterprise thrown into the soup). Hence we will witness "competition" between the Windows Giant, its corporate competitor Apple, and not one, but several dozen Linux distributions—some backed corporately and some remaining independent.

The Case Against Monopoly and Oligopoly Capital

In this era of globalization and the universalization of the market, computers, particularly laptop and desktop PCs, have been geared to become "disposable technology." Consider the following scenario when newer technological upgrades become available on the market. 1.2 ghz replaces 800 mhz, along with 1 gig of RAM replacing ½ gig of RAM. What occurs during this interval, we find a new Windows OS released, and it is found to work better with 2 ghz speed and 2 gig of RAM. Hence, hardware manufacturers are forever in pursuit to "kick it up a notch." And in a few months faster and more efficient hardware will be released and the middle class will discard their 2 ghz machines for something faster.

The MS Windows Enterprise, as the dominant monopolistic OS producer, is deeply entwined with an oligarchy of hardware producers, and together have created a market atmosphere that not only turns computers into "disposable technology," but creates an illusion of new invention and innovation and pits customers with a market anxiety that they forever need a faster, more efficient, greater hard drive holding desktop or laptop or netbook.

A central criticism to be leveled against the hardware oligopoly is that these firms now possess the technology far, far in advance of what is presently being released. For example, while 1.2 ghz emerges on the market in January, then 1.4 in May, then 1.8 in September—these hardware manufacturers in January have the knowledge and possess the skill to not only make a 1.8 ghz at that time, but far beyond that to perhaps 3.0 to 5.0 ghz. By releasing newer technologies in small increments, however, customers are drawn into the Best Buys or computer outlets more often, in search of the so-called newer innovations.

However, the corporate goal is to keep the product moving and keep the turnover at high rates of speed. I would also suggest that MS Windows works hand in hand with the hardware oligopoly timing its releases of Operating Systems that require the masses to purchase newer and faster computers to run the new Operating Systems. To be sure, all versions of Windows 7 **require** XP users to perform a **custom clean install**, while users of **some versions** of Vista may **upgrade** to Windows 7. Windows Vista, they further note, should be a smooth transition to Windows 7. Ideally however, the fact that "Buy a new PC" ads are heavily featured on MS sites offering advice on upgrading and custom clean installs, acts to promote a market environment suggestive of as well as edging people toward the purchase of new PCs rather than dealing with the potential hassle and confusion in either the upgrade or clean install.

Why did I refer to MS Windows earlier as akin to "Godzilla"? Precisely because the monopolistic and oligopolistic conditions of the market have corrupted and destroyed the Pioneer Ethic from operating in that particular kind of market environment. In other words, like Ma Bell, what drives the market is not a comprehensive dose of the PCCM model but rather purely the profit rates making things forever a catch-up game in a technological meat market. The PCCM model does exist, however, in the loose knit federation of Linux Distributions and will at some point reach critical mass and with that the stone of David will be hurled at the Goliath, and the giant will come tumbling down.

A Blog Regarding the Linux Experience

This section of the Epilogue represents both a divergence from purely objective sociological analysis and also a social call to action to join the ranks of all those committed to and who support the ideals, goals, orientations, and values embedded in the Linux enterprise and more broadly, the Linux social movement. It can be a commitment on many levels. For instance it can be simply an exploration like the first time I logged into Linux and found the technological wonderland of Open Source Software. Or perhaps you are committed at the next step where you support the overall goals of Linux but are not ready to discard the Windows Operating System. That is fine as well. Ultimately for some of you who chose to explore Linux, like my colleague from OSU, the commitment to Linux is comprehensive as one becomes fully immersed in the cause. At whatever the level you offer your support, you are invited and welcomed and encouraged to participate in the Linux enterprise and experience.

Getting started with Linux is as simple as a few mouse clicks away. Several steps will make your exploration easier. First, visit a used or "Half-Price Bookstore" in your metropolitan area. Go to the Science, Technology and Computers section and scan the shelves for "Linux" or "Unix." Once you've located this zone, look for general books on Linux. Start out slowly by investing in the ***Linux For Dummies*** editions. At Half-Priced Books you may find several "....For Dummies" texts ranging from Linux Redhat to Suse Linux help books. Choose the latest version available. There are also, aside from the Dummies series, several other books you may wish to purchase including Suse or Redhat Bibles for various versions. I list this as a second choice because many of these so-called Bibles contain loads of information that is not very useful for those beginning in Linux. Perhaps a few chapters will contain some necessary information, but much of what's in the Bible are for more advanced users of Linux.

One book I would wholeheartedly recommend is a text entitled ***Beginning SUSE Linux***, by Keir Thomas (Second Edition, 2006: Apress). If you cannot find this volume at Half-Priced books, look online at Amazon.com or Barnes&Nobles. The wonderful thing about this volume is that it is written for us all coming out of the Windows tradition. We know Windows and some of us know Windows very well. This book is written from that perspective, continually comparing the ways of Linux to the ways of Windows. It is well written and an interesting read and not only gives technical advise to Linux beginners but a Linux and Windows history lesson for those of us who are new to the Linux scene. In fact, I learned more from ***Beginning SUSE Linux*** in the first two chapters of Keir's book than all other Linux manuals combined. This is not to suggest the other manuals are useless—far from it. However Keir writes from the standpoint of the Window's user first encountering the new and unique operating system called Linux.

After you have digested some texts on Linux you have a choice to either purchase the boxed set in the price range of 60 to 70 dollars, or you can surf the web and download the latest version for free. The crucial difference with the boxed set is that they usually come with three or more months of technical support. However, as was mentioned earlier Linux is firmly in the grasp of the Pioneer Ethic and there is an extensive support community online that ranges in knowledge from beginner to expert. These communities are extremely helpful as in my case I solved several technical problems through accessing the Open Suse community after my technical support from the boxed set had retired.

As far as downloading Linux from the web is concerned, you have two sub-choices here. First, you can download what is called a LIVE CD (Desktop). These disks contain either KDE or the GNOME desktop operating systems, and they allow you to preview or test-drive Linux before you actually commit to it. The simplicity here is you a) download the LIVE CD, b) burn the ISO file to CD, and c) boot up your computer from the LIVE CD. Simple as that. Furthermore, this method allows you to test Linux, to become familiar with the system and how it differs from the Windows system. When you are finished, simply remove the disk and reboot and your computer is as it was: untouched by the test drive.

The LIVE CD's generally contain ISO files ranging from 600 to 700 MB that can neatly fit on a CD. They also contain and allow for the second sub-choice: the installation of the Linux system on your computer. Here too, everything is made easy and user-friendly. The process is called the "Live Install" option on the test drive's desktop where one can install quickly and easily the Linux OS on your computer. The install process walks you through each step of establishing a Linux foothold on your computer system. What's more amazing is the Live Install will automatically make suggestions regarding the shrinking of the Windows partition and expansion of the Linux partitions, and then goes on to initiate such changes during the Perform Installation process. What does this mean in plain English? That when all is said and done and you have the Linux system installed, it will coexist side by side with Windows, and you will have not one but two operating systems on your computer. Many folks keep Windows and enjoy what is called the "dual boot" capability, but a number of other new users to Linux soon thereafter delete the Windows Operating System and become dedicated Linux users, throwing their economic support behind a particular distribution.

You are probably asking, "where do I find it," and it is as I mentioned earlier, a few mouse clicks away. Google "Linux Live CD," "Ubuntu Live CD," "Open Suse, Live CD" or "Mandriva Live CD" and explore. The official site for Ubuntu can be found at the following:

http://www.ubuntu.com/GetUbuntu/download

The official site for Open Suse site can be found at this location:

http://www.opensuse.org/en/

And the download center, can be located at:

http://software.opensuse.org/111/en

The specific or particular download site may change with regard to continued upgrades such as the development of 11.1 to 11.2 to 11.3 etc. In the Open Suse homepage site, click on "Get it" to download the Beta or Latest release. You also have the option here to either download the LIVE CD for KDE or GNOME desktop versions, or the full 4.3 gig DVD containing all of the free Open Source software that is bundled with Open Suse DVD disk. In addition, at this site you can opt for the boxed version of Open Suse Linux for somewhere in the range of $60 with the added attraction of free technical support for several months. If you opt to download the free version you will want to have the Open Suse Forums site handy. It can be found at:

http://forums.opensuse.org/

Or for Ubuntu,

http://ubuntuforums.org/

In a nutshell, these are the guidelines for opening up a whole new world of computing in the age of globalization. Supporting Linux is not merely a blow against the monopoly empire but a political choice to support the Pioneering-Collaborative-Cooperative-Model in our everyday lives. Will most of us add to or program the Open Source software we use on Linux? Probably not, but the door is not slammed shut as in the case of Windows. There are opportunities for dialogue, discourse, and debate as well as discussion and learning on the Linux forums. The fundamental question becomes "What kind of a computerized future do we want to live in?" Do we want a top down Ma Bell monopoly oriented model that has rendered desktop and laptop PCs as disposable technological and communications items, or do we want a cooperative and collective global support environment that is competitive at its core but not monopolistic or oligopolistic in nature. Do we really want to be duped into buying so-called necessary "systems requirements" upgrades in the purchase of newer computers every several months?

We have presented two models here, and sadly the general model we now predominately live under is a monopoly oriented structure. Linux is an embryo at this time, but the "take off" phase is rapidly approaching. My colleague, Derek Knaub, from Ohio State relayed to me information that billionaire Bill Gates' Foundation donates millions of dollars worth of software and operating systems to poorer public school systems in various city schools across the country. This is quite commendable from one angle, but from Derek's viewpoint this action continues to solidify the Windows Monopoly Model—hence, the children "learn" and are "socialized" into the world of computerization on MS software and Windows Operating Systems. With limited incomes they are at the mercy of the MS Windows market pricing structure for their later software needs. Linux, along with Open Source software, on the other hand, is free and much more conducive to the plight of the poor.

Like a professional hockey game, expect several skirmishes. Windows will not give up one market percentage point without a fight to the degree that we could have an all out operating systems war with several heavy causalities most likely including some Linux distributions. There may, in light of these systems wars, be significant government intervention to the point of the State restructuring the OS market in the same way it intervened in the splitting up and reshaping of the Bell Telephone. This may in fact give everyone a small piece of the pie, but the competitive nature of capital will be given an opportunity to flourish and the spillover will be a better and more innovative operating system in tomorrow's computers.

remnants of the mills.

Years ago sweat poured
from my great grandfather's face:
droplets of dreams.
For more than fifty years
by the waters of the Monongahela
he worked the mills
melting cold iron ore
into burning liquid steel
forging this work of art:
Pittsburgh
city of steel
cast by the hands of my forefathers.

Most of the mills are closed now
left to history and rust:
particles of the finite.
Corporate skyscrapers,
these tall buildings
are their
end product.
And yet
concealed within the columns
of those giant superstructures
are remnants of sweat and pain.
The girders hold aspirations
and in the frameworks rest
forgotten dreams.
They are monuments symbolizing the fire
that once burned in the heart
of the furnace
in the heart of the worker.

sweat poured from his face years ago
gone.
Particles of the finite.
They import steel now--
it's the economy you know.

SOURCES

Sources: Introduction

Bergesen, Albert. 1980. "From Utilitarianism to Globology: The Shift from The Individual to the World as the Primordial Unit of Analysis," in Albert Bergesen, ed., Studies of the Modern World System. New York: Academic Press.

Boli-Bennett, John. 1980. "Global Integration and Universal Increase in State Dominance, 19190-1970," in Albert Bergesen, ed., Studies of the Modern World System. New York: Academic Press.

Braudel, F. (1979a). The Structures of Everyday Life: Civilization and Capitalism, 15th-18th Century. New York: Harper and Row. Volume One.

Braudel, F. (1979b). The Wheels of Commerce: Civilization and Capitalism, 15th-18th Century. New York: Harper and Row

Girvan, N. (1976). Corporate Imperialism: Conflict and Expropriation. New York and London: Monthly Review Press, 1976.

Harms, John B. 1981. "Reason and Change in Durkheim's Thought: The Changing Relationship Between Individuals and Society," in Pacific Sociological Review. 24:4 : 393-410.

Malone, Thomas F. 1986. "Mission to Planet Earth: Integrating Studies of Global Change," in Environment. 28:8 : 6-42.

Meyer, John W. 1980. "The World Polity and the Authority of the Nation State," in Albert Bergesen, ed., Studies in the Modern World System. New York: Academic Press.

Robertson, Roland and Chirico, JoAnn. 1985. "Humanity, Globalization, and Worldwide Religious Resurgence: A Theoretical Exploration," in Sociological Analysis 46:3 : 219-241.

Robertson, Roland. 1987a. "Globalization and Societal Modernization:A Note on Japan and Japanese Religion," Sociological Analysis 47:2 : 35-42.

Robertson, Roland. 1987b. "Globalization, Modernization and Postmodernization: The Ambiguous Position of Religion" presented at New ERA Seminar, October 7-11, St. Martin, French West Indies.

Robertson, Roland. 1989. "Globality, Global Culture and Images of World Order," in Neil Smelser, ed., <u>Modernization and Social Change</u> Berkeley: University of California Press.

Robertson, Roland. (1992) <u>Globalization : Global Culture and Social Theory</u> London: Sage.

Wallerstein, Immanuel. 1979. <u>The Capitalist World Economy</u>. Cambridge: University Press.

Wuthnow, Robert. "The World-Economy and the Institutionalization of Science in Seventeenth-Century Europe," in Albert Bergesen, ed., <u>Studies in the Modern World System</u>. New York: Academic Press.

Sources: Chapter One

BLACKLICK FIELD
http://www.coalcampusa.com/westpa/blacklick/blacklick.htm

Cambria County Pennsylvania Township Maps, Map:
http://www.rootsweb.com/~pacambri/cambrimp/

Carawan and Carawan. (1975) <u>Voices from the Mountains</u>. University of Georgia Press: Athens-London.

Colver HomePage: at http://home.earthlink.net/~hilltj/index.html.

<u>Delano's Domain: A History of Warren Delano's Mining Towns of</u>

<u>Vintondale, Wehrum and Claghorn</u>, Volume I, 1789 – 1930. by Denise Weber reprinted at "A Short History of the Cambria and Indiana Railroad: at http://www.trainweb.org/cambriaindiana/history.htm and http://www.trainweb.org/cambriaindiana/b&yc.htm

Energy Information Administration: EIA Department of Energy.

<u>2003 Annual Coal Report</u>. http://www.eia.doe.gov/cneaf/coal/page/acr/acr_sum.html

Ghost Town Trail at http://cpcug.org/user/warholic/trail.html

Matvey, J, 1987 <u>Central Appalachia: Distortions in Development</u> **Dissertation**. University of Pittsburgh. University Microfilms: Ann Arbor.

Nanty Glo History Timeline, Timeline at http://www.nantyglo.com/frm8.htm

State Coal Profile Index Map http://www.eia.doe.gov/cneaf/coal/statepro/imagemap/usaimagemap.htm

Prine, John. (1971) <u>John Prine</u>. "Paradise." www.jpshrine.org/lyrics/

The University Museum. Indiana University of Pennsylvania. <u>Life in the Valley: Streams of Coal</u>, 2005. The Nanty Glo Tri Area Museum and Historical Society

US 2000 Census: Demographic Profiles. http://censtats.census.gov/pub/Profiles.shtml

USMRA. US Mine Rescue Association. "Worst US Mine Disasters." Online at: http://www.usmra.com/saxsewell/historical.htm .

Zarahoff, Pete. 1977. "No Pretty Song," <u>Emphysema Blues</u>.

Sources: Chapter Three

Appalachain Land Ownership Study. <u>Land Ownership Patterns and Their Impacts on Appalachian Communities. A Survey of 80 Counties</u>. Appalachian State Univ., Boone, NC. Center for Appalachian Studies.; Highlander Research and Education Center, New Market, TN. (Sponsered by: ARC)

ARC Regional Data and Research. <u>www.arc.gov</u> Data based on 1990 and 2000 Census.

Arnett, D. A. (1982) <u>Eastern Kentucky: The Politics of Dependency and Underdevelopment</u> Thesis. Ann Arbor and London:University Microfilms International.

Braudel, F. (1979b). <u>The Wheels of Commerce: Civilization and Capitalism</u>, <u>15th-18th Century</u>. New York: Harper and Row.

Caudill, H. (1963) <u>Night Comes to the Cumberlands</u>. Boston: Atlantic-Little and Brown.

Coogan, M.H. (1980). "Appalachian Views: A West Virginia Banker Speaks."<u>Appalachia:</u> Journal of the Appalachian Regional Commission May/June.Washington DC: Government Printing Office.

Dylan, B. (2006) *Workingman's Blues #2*. <u>Modern Times</u>. Columbia: New York.

Garrett, R. "Absentee Owners Hold Much Coal Land, Pay Low Taxes in East Kentucky, Study Says," and "Study Blames Many of Appalachia's Woes on Land Ownership," in <u>Louisville Courier Journal</u>. Louisville: April 2, 1981.

Girvan, N. (1976). <u>Corporate Imperialism: Conflict and Expropriation</u>. New York and London: Monthly Review Press,1976.

Kentucky Department of Mines and Minerals, <u>Annual Report</u>, 2002.

Lewis, H., edited by. 1978. <u>Colonialism in Modern America: The Appalachian Case</u>. Boone, NC: Appalachian Consortium Press and within:
Primack. "Hidden Traps of Regionalism."
Walls, D. "Internal Colony or Internal Periphery."

Matvey, J. 1987. <u>Central Appalachia: Distortions in Development, 1750-1987</u>. Thesis. University Microfilms: Ann Arbor.

Matvey, J. 2005. <u>Regionalism and Globalization</u>: Essays on Appalachia, Globalization and Global Computerization. Iuniverse: Lincoln-New York-Shanghai.
Global Computerization. IUniverse: Lincoln-New York-Shanghai

US Census: <u>http://quickfacts.census.gov/qfd/states/00000.html</u>

<u>West Virginia Office of Miners' Health Safety and Training</u> "2000 Coal Production by County"

Sources: Chapter Four

Conti, E. A. (1979). "The Cultural Role of Local Elites in the Kentucky Mountains: A Retrospective Analysis. <u>Appalachian Journal</u>. Autumn/Winter 1979-1980.

Jacobs, J. (1984a). "Cities and the Wealth of Nations: A New Theory of Economic Life." <u>Atlantic Monthly</u>. March 1984.

Mutch, R. (1980). "The Cutting Edge: Colonial America and the Debate about the Transition to Capitalism," in <u>Theory and Society</u>. No. 9.

Baldwin, L. (1980). <u>The Keelboat Age on Western Waters.</u> Pittsburgh: University of Pittsburgh Press.

Baldwin, L. (1981). <u>Pittsburgh, The Story of a City</u>. Pittsburgh: University of Pittsburgh Press.

Braudel, F. (1979a). <u>The Structures of Everyday Life: Civilization and Capitalism, 15th-18th Century</u>. New York: Harper and Row. Volume One.

Braudel, F. (1979b). <u>The Wheels of Commerce</u>: <u>Civilization and Capitalism, 15th-18th Century</u>. New York: Harper and Row.

Buck, S. J. and Buck, E.H. (1967). <u>The Planting of Civilization in Western Pennsylvania.</u> Pittsburgh: University of Pittsburgh Press.

Chase-Dunn, C. (1980). "The Development of Core Capitalism in the Antebellum United States," in <u>Studies in the Modern World System</u>, ed. by A. Bergesen. New York: Academic Press.

Eller, R. D. (1978) "Industrialization and Social Change in Appalachia, 1880-1930," in <u>Colonialism in Modern America: The Appalachian Case</u>, ed. by Helen Lewis. Boone, NC: Appalachian Consortium Press.

Eller, R. D. (1982). <u>Miners, Millhands and Mountaineers: Industrialization of the Appalachian South, 1880-1930</u>. Knoxville: University of Tennessee Press, 1982.

Fetterman, J. (1967). <u>Stinking Creek</u>. New York: E.P. Dutton.

<u>Kentucky Gazette and General Advertiser</u>. Lexington, KY: Daniel Bradford, Publisher, September 8, 1807; May 8, 1811.

Lorant, S. (1980). <u>Pittsburgh: Story of an American City</u>. Lenox, MA: Authors Edition, Inc.

Stevens, S. K. (1964). <u>Pennsylvania: Birthplace of a Nation</u>. New York: Random House.

U.S. Bureau of the Census. Selected Reports:
<u>Census of Agriculture</u>. 1860, 1910, 1930.
<u>Census of Manufactories</u>. 1860.

Sources: Chapter Five

Arnett, D. A. (1982) <u>Eastern Kentucky: The Politics of Dependency and Underdevelopment</u>. Ann Arbor and London: University Microfilms International.

Banks, A. (1980a). "The Emergence of a Capitalistic Labor Market in Eastern Kentucky." <u>Appalachian Journal</u>. Spring 1980. Volume 7, No. 3.

Banks, A. (1980b). "Land and Capital in Eastern Kentucky, 1890-1915." <u>Appalachian Journal</u>. Autumn 1980. Volume 8, No. 1.

Banks, A. (1983). "Coal Miners and Firebrick Workers: The Structure of Work Relations in Two Eastern Kentucky Communities." Appalachian Journal. Autumn/Winter 1983-84.

Batteau, A. (1980). "Appalachia and the Concept of Culture: A Theory of Shared Misunderstandings." <u>Appalachian Journal</u>. Autumn/Winter 1979-1980.

Billings and Blee. (2000) <u>The Road to Poverty: The Making of Wealth and Hardship in Appalachia</u>. Cambridge University Press: London. New York.

Braverman, H. (1974). Labor and Monopoly Capital: The Degradation of Work in the Twentieth Century, New York: Monthly Review Press.

Caudill, H. (1963) <u>Night Comes to the Cumberlands</u>. Boston: Atlantic-Little and Brown.

Caudill, H. (1983) <u>Theirs Be The Power:</u> The Moguls of Eastern Kentucky. Urbana: University of Illinois Press.

Conti, E. A. (1979). "The Cultural Role of Local Elites in the Kentucky Mountains: A Retrospective Analysis. <u>Appalachian Journal</u>. Autumn/Winter 1979-1980.

Corbin, D. (1981). <u>Life, Work and Rebellion in the Coal Fields: The Southern West Virginia Miners 1880-1922</u>. Urbana: University of Illinois Press.

Eller, R. D. (1982). <u>Miners, Millhands and Mountaineers: Industrialization of the Appalachian South, 1880-1930</u>. Knoxville: University of Tennessee Press, 1982.

Erikson, K. T. (1976). <u>Everything in its Path</u>: Destruction of Community in the Buffalo Creek Flood. New York: Touchstone Books.

Fetterman, J. (1967). <u>Stinking Creek</u>. New York: E.P. Dutton.

Garkovich, L. (1982). "Kinship and Return Migration in Eastern Kentucky." Appalachian Journal. Autumn 1982.

Gaventa, J. (1980). <u>Power and Powerlessness: Quiescence and Rebellion in an Appalachian Valley</u>. Urbana: University of Illinois Press.

Hevener, J. W. (1978). <u>Which Side Are You On: The Harlan County Coal Miners, 1931-1939</u>. Urbana: University of Illinois Press.

Jackson, M.L., Caudill, R.G., Williams, J., eds. (1975) "The Folks in Wolfe County Hills," by Melvin Profitt, in Recollections: A Journal of the Appalachian Oral History Project at Lees Junior College. Volume 1. No. 4. Jackson, KY: Lees Junior College.

Kentucky Appalachian Development Cabinet. <u>Kentucky AppalachianDevelopment Plan: 1978-1980</u>. Frankfort, KY:1978.

Kentucky Department of Mines and Minerals. <u>Annual Report</u>: Department of Mines and Minerals. 1884-Present. Frankfort, KY: Kentucky Department of Mines and Minerals.

Looff, D. (1971). <u>Appalachia's Children</u>: The Challenge of Mental Health. Lexington: The University Press of Kentucky.

Lewis, H. (1978). ed. by. "The Colonialism Model: The Appalachian Case," <u>Colonialism in Modern America: The Appalachian Case.</u> Boone, NC: Appalachian Consortium Press. See also within: Walls. "Internal Colony or Internal Periphery."

Matvey, J. 1987. <u>Central Appalachia: Distortions in Development, 1750-1987</u>. Thesis. University Microfilms: Ann Arbor.

Matvey, J. 2005. <u>Regionalism and Globalization</u>: Essays on Appalachia, Globalization and Global Computerization. Iuniverse: Lincoln-New York-Shanghai. Global Computerization. IUniverse: Lincoln-New York-Shanghai

Mutch, R. (1980). "The Cutting Edge: Colonial America and the Debate about the Transition to Capitalism," in <u>Theory and Society</u>. No. 9.

Otto, J.S. (1985) "Reconsidering the Southern `Hillbilly' Appalachia and the Ozarks." <u>Appalachian Journal</u>.

Plaut, T. (1979). "Appalachia and Social Change: A Cultural Systems Approach." <u>Appalachian Journal</u>. Summer 1979.

Precourt, W. (1983) "<u>The Image of Appalachian Poverty</u>," in <u>Appalachia and America: Autonomy and Regional Dependence</u>, ed. by Alan Batteau. Lexington: University Press of Kentucky.

Robertson, Roland and Chirico, JoAnn. (1985). "Humanity, Globalization, and Worldwide Religious Resurgence: A Theoretical Exploration," in <u>Sociological Analysis</u> 46:3 : 219-241.

Robertson, Roland. (1987). "Globalization and Societal Modernization: A Note on Japan and Japanese Religion," <u>Sociological Analysis</u> 47:2 : 35-42.

Salstrom, P. (1984). "Subsistence Farming, Capitalism, and the Depression in West Virginia." <u>Appalachian Journal</u>. Summer 1984.

Simon, R. (1981). "Uneven Development and the Case of West Virginia." <u>Appalachian Journal</u>. Spring 1981.

Simon, R. (1983). "Regions and Social Relations: A Research Note." <u>Appalachian Journal</u>. Autumn/ Winter 1983-1984 Southern Mountain Research Collective. (1983).

U.S. Bureau of the Census. U.S. Government Printing Office Washington, D.C. Selected Volumes and Reports:
<u>County City Data Book</u>. 1940, 1947, 1952;
<u>Census of Agriculture</u>. 1910, 1930;
<u>Census of Mines and Quarries</u>. 1929;
<u>Census of Population</u>. 1930.
<u>Census of Housing</u>. 1980.

Wallerstein, Immanuel. (1979). <u>The Capitalist World Economy</u>. Cambridge: University Press.

Weinberg, Daniel H. 1987. "Rural Pockets of Poverty" in <u>Rural Sociology</u>. 52: 3:398-408.

Weller, J. E. (1965). <u>Yesterday's People</u>. Lexington: The University Press of Kentucky.

Wigginton, E. (1972). ed. by. <u>The Foxfire Book</u>. Garden City, NY: Anchor Press/Doubleday.

Sources: Chapter Six

Bloom, Dr. Alfred. Shin Dharma Net Online. http://www.shindharmanet.com/

Boykin, Kim. <u>Zen for Christians</u>. 2003: Jossey Press: San Francisco.

The Buddhist Churches of America. (BCA Web Page: The Beginnings at http://www. buddhistchurchesofamerica.com/aboutus/beginnings.shtml)

The Cleveland Buddhist Temple. (http://samsara.law.cwru.edu/~cbt/ Cleveland Buddhist Temple: History of the Temple)

Habito, Ruben. <u>Living Zen, Loving God</u>. Wisdom Publications: Somerville. MA.

Hanh, Thich Nhat <u>Going Home: Jesus and Buddha as Brothers</u>. 1999: Riverhead Books: New York.

Hanh, Thich Nhat. <u>Living Buddha/Living Christ</u>.

Kasimow, Keenan and Keenan, editors. <u>Beside Still Waters: Jews Christians and the Way of the Buddha.</u> 2003: Wisdom Publications: Somerville: MA.

Lama, Dalai. <u>The Good Heart: A Buddhist Perspective on the Teachings of Jesus</u>. 1996: Wisdom Publications: Somerville MA.

MacPhillamy, Rev<u>. Buddhism from Within</u>. 2003: Shasta Abbey Press. Mount Shasta: California.

Ogui, Sensei<u>. Zen Shin Talks.</u> Compiled and Edited by Mary K. Grove. 1998. Zen Shin Buddhist Publications: Cleveland.

Palmer and Ramsay<u>. Kuan Yin</u>. 1995: Thorsons. London.

Shasta Abbey. (http://www.obcon.org/)

Shin Temples Website: (For a list of Shin Temples please see http://samsara.law.cwru.edu/~cbt/bcadir. html)

Suzuki, Shunryo. <u>Zen Mind: Beginner's Mind</u>. 1970: Weatherhill. New York and Tokyo.

Unno, Taitetsu. <u>Shin Buddhism: Bits of Rubble turn to Gold</u>" 2002. Doubleday: New York.

Unno, Taitetsu. <u>River of Fire/River of Water</u>. 1998. Doubleday: New York.

Watson, Burton<u>. The Lotus Sutra</u> Online. http://www.sgi-usa.org/buddhism/library/Buddhism/LotusSutra/text/Chap16.htm

Yu, Chun Fang. <u>Kuan Yin</u>. 2001: Columbia University Press: New York.

Joseph J. Matvey, III

Sources: Chapter Seven

Bergesen, Albert. 1980. "From Utilitarianism to Globology: The Shift from the Individual to the World as the Primordial Unit of Analysis," in Albert Bergesen, ed., <u>Studies of the Modern World System</u>. New York: Academic Press.

Boli-Bennett, John. 1980. "Global Integration and Universal Increase in State Dominance, 19190-1970," in Albert Bergesen, ed., <u>Studies of the Modern World System.</u> New York: Academic Press.

Calhoun, C., Drummond, W., Whittington, D. 1987. "Computerized Information Management in a System-Poor Environment." <u>TWPR</u> 9 (4) 361-379.

Calhoun, C. 1987. "The Infrastructure of Modernity: Indirect Social Relationships, Information Technology, and Social Integration." in Neil Smelser, ed., <u>Modernization and Social Change</u>, Berkeley: University of California Press.

Food and Agricultural Organization. 1977. <u>The Fourth World Food Survey</u>. Rome: U.N. Food and Agriculture Organization.

The Futurist. 1986. "High-Tech Expansion in China." November- December. 44.

Harms, John B. 1981. "Reason and Change in Durkheim's Thought: The Changing Relationship Between Individuals and Society," in <u>Pacific Sociological Review</u>. 24:4 : 393-410.

Kaye, Lincoln. 1988. "The Brainstorming Way to Success." <u>Far Eastern Economic Review</u>. January. 60-61.

Maier, John H. 1988. "Thirty Years of Computer Science Developments in the People's Republic of China: 1956-1985," in <u>Annals of the History of Computing</u>. 10 (1) 19-34.

Matvey, J. 1988. "Global Connectivity: Theoretical Considerations of its Form and the Role of Societal Differentiation." Presented at ASR Meetings, Atlanta, GA. (Unpublished)

Meyer, J. 1980. "The World Polity and the Authority of the Nation State," in Albert Bergesen, ed., <u>Studies of the Modern World System</u>. New York: Academic Press.

Miller, G.T. 1979. <u>Living in the Environment</u>. Belmont: Wadsworth Publishing Company.

Parsons, Talcott. 1977. <u>Social Systems and the Evolution of Action Theory</u>. New York: The Free Press.

Population Reference Bureau. 1978. World Population Data Sheet. Washington DC: Population Reference Bureau.

Robertson, Roland and Chirico, JoAnn. 1985. "Humanity, Globalization, and Worldwide Religious Resurgence: A Theoretical Exploration," in <u>Sociological Analysis</u> 46:3 : 219-241.

Robertson, Roland. 1987a. "Globality, Global Culture and Images of World Order," in Neil Smelser, ed., <u>Modernization and Social Change</u>, Berkeley: University of California Press.

Robertson, Roland. 1987b. "Globalization, Modernization and Postmodernization: The Ambiguous Position of Religion" presented at New ERA Seminar, October 7-11, St. Martin, French West Indies.

Robertson, Roland. 1987c. "Globalization and Societal Modernization: A Note on Japan and Japanese Religion," Sociological Analysis 47:2 : 35-42.

Rogers, E. 1986. Communication Technology: The New Media in Society. New York: Free Press.

Tate and Maier. 1987. "Dateline Beijing: The China Syndrome." Datamation. 1 September 33-42.

Time, November 10, 1987. "A Summit for Peace in Assisi."

Tombaugh, J.W. 1984. "Evaluation of an International Scientific Computer-Based Conference." Journal of Social Issues. Volume 40, No. 3. 129-44.

UN Chronicle. 1985. 22:4 : 1-72.
UN Chronicle. 1987. "WHO launches world-wide AIDS 'awareness' campaign." 24:8 :74.
UN Chronicle. 1986. "WHO Board reviews 'Health for All by Year 2000' Strategy." 23:3 :88-9.

Universal Almanac. 1991. Kansas City/New York: Andrews and McMeel.

Wallerstein, Immanuel. 1979. The Capitalist World Economy. Cambridge: University Press.

Wuthnow, Robert. "The World-Economy and the Institutionalization of Science in Seventeenth-Century Europe," in Albert Bergesen, ed., Studies in the Modern World System. New York: Academic Press.

Internet Sources Chapter Seven

College View. "The Melting Pot Continues: International Students in America" by John Carter. **http://www.collegeview.com/articles/CV/campuslife/international-students-in-us.html**

Institute of International Education Network (IIEN) **http://opendoors.iienetwork.org/?p=36523**

UIA Volume Six Who's Who in International Organizations. **http://www.uia.be/ybvol6**

UIA Yearbook of International Organizations **http://www.uia.be/node/52**

Sources: Chapter Eight

Bergesen, Albert. 1980. "From Utilitarianism to Globology: The Shift from the Individual to the World as the Primordial Unit of Analysis," in Albert Bergesen, ed., Studies of the Modern World System. New York: Academic Press.

Boli-Bennett, John. 1980. "Global Integration and Universal Increase in State Dominance, 19190-1970," in Albert Bergesen, ed., Studies of the Modern World System. New York: Academic Press.

Calhoun, C., Drummond, W., Whittington, D. 1987. "Computerized Information Management in a System-Poor Environment." TWPR 9 (4) 61-379.

Calhoun, C. 1987. "The Infrastructure of Modernity: Indirect Social Relationships, Information Technology, and Social Integration." in Neil Smelser, ed., Modernization and Social Change, Berkeley: University of California Press.

Food and Agricultural Organization. 1977. The Fourth World Food Survey. Rome: U.N. Food and Agriculture Organization.

The Futurist. 1986. "High-Tech Expansion in China." November- December. 44.

Harms, John B. 1981. "Reason and Change in Durkheim's Thought: The Changing Relationship Between Individuals and Society," in Pacific Sociological Review. 24:4 : 393-410.

Kaye, Lincoln. 1988. "The Brainstorming Way to Success." Far Easter Economic Review. January. 60-61.

Maier, John H. 1988. "Thirty Years of Computer Science Developments in the People's Republic of China: 1956-1985," in Annals of the History of Computing. 10 (1) 19-34.

Matvey, J. 1988. "Global Connectivity: Theoretical Considerations of its Form and the Role of Societal Differentiation." Presented at ASR Meetings, Atlanta, GA. (Unpublished)

Meyer, J. 1980. "The World Polity and the Authority of the Nation State," in Albert Bergesen, ed., Studies of the Modern World System. New York: Academic Press.

Miller, G.T. 1979. Living in the Environment. Belmont: Wadsworth Publishing Company.

Parsons, Talcott. 1977. Social Systems and the Evolution of Action Theory. New York: The Free Press.

Population Reference Bureau. 1978. World Population Data Sheet. Washington DC: Population Reference Bureau.

Robertson, Roland and Chirico, JoAnn. 1985. "Humanity, Globalization, and Worldwide Religious Resurgence: A Theoretical Exploration," in Sociological Analysis 46:3 : 219-241.

Robertson, Roland. 1987a. "Globality, Global Culture and Images of World Order," in Neil Smelser, ed., Modernization and Social Change, Berkeley: University of California Press.

Robertson, Roland. 1987b. "Globalization, Modernization and Postmodernization: The Ambiguous Position of Religion" presented at New ERA Seminar, October 7-11, St. Martin, French West Indies.

Robertson, Roland. 1987c. "Globalization and Societal Modernization: A Note on Japan and Japanese Religion," Sociological Analysis 47:2 : 35-42.

Rogers, E. 1986. Communication Technology: The New Media in Society. New York: Free Press.

Tate and Maier. 1987. "Dateline Beijing: The China Syndrome." Datamation. 1 September 33-42.

Time, November 10, 1987. "A Summit for Peace in Assisi."

Tombaugh, J.W. 1984. "Evaluation of an International Scientific Computer-Based Conference." Journal of Social Issues. Volume 40, No. 3. 129-44.

UN Chronicle. 1985. 22:4 : 1-72.
UN Chronicle. 1987. "WHO launches world-wide AIDS 'awareness' campaign." 24:8 :74.
UN Chronicle. 1986. "WHO Board reviews 'Health for All by Year 2000' Strategy." 23:3 :88-9.

US Department of Commerce, Bureau of the Census. 1988. "First Report on Computer Use: Glimpsing the Dawn of the Microcomputer Age,"in Census and You: Monthly News From The

US Bureau of the Census. 23 (7) 8-9.

US Department of Commerce, Bureau of the Census. 1988. Computer Use in the United States: 1984. (Robert Kominski) Current Population Reports: Special Studies, Series P-23 No. 155. March.

Universal Almanac. 1991. Kansas City/New York: Andrews and McMeel.

Wallerstein, Immanuel. 1979. The Capitalist World Economy. Cambridge: University Press.

Wuthnow, Robert. "The World-Economy and the Institutionalization of Science in Seventeenth-Century Europe," in Albert Bergesen, ed., Studies in the Modern World System. New York: Academic Press.

Sources: Chapter Nine

Universal Almanac. 1991. Kansas City/New York: Andrews and McMeel.

DATA SOURCES for Chapter Nine: Database. 191 UN Defined Nations. Minitab, SPSS and Stata Database Programs Engaged.

CIA World Factbook. 2007.Yahoo Education: Countries and Country Comparisons. http://education.yahoo.com/reference/factbook/

Countries of the World. World Statistics. Country Ranks: 2007. "Communications." www.geographic.org http://www.theodora.com/wfb/abc_world_fact_book.html

New View Almanac. BlackBirch Press, Inc. Information Please. "Computers, Internet" Woodbridge: Conn. p. 526-536.

Time Almanac 2000. "Communications in Selected Countries," "Computers per Capita" p. 160, 554.

World Almanac 2005. World Almanac Books. "Percent of US Households with Internet Access" p.395.

Sources: Chapter Eleven

Anderson and Taylor. *Sociology: Understanding a Diverse Society.* Third Edition. 2004: Wadsworth. United States.

Cohen and Kennedy. *Global Sociology.* Second Edition. 2007: NYU Press: NY.

Eitzen. *In Conflict and Order: Understanding Society.* 1978: Allyn and Bacon: Boston.

Ferrante. *Sociology: A Global Perspective.* 2006: Wadsworth. United States.

Harris (late) and Johnson. *Cultural Anthropology.* Sixth Edition. 2003: Pearson Education: USA.

Jordan-Bychkov and Domash. *The Human Mosaic: A Thematic Introduction to Cultural Geography.* Eighth Edition. 2001: W.H. Freeman and Company: New York.

Macionis. *Society: The Basics*. Seventh Edition. 2004: Prentice Hall: NJ.

Nolan and Lenski. *Human Societies: An Introduction to Macrosociology*. Tenth Edition. 2006: Paradigm: London.

Sources: Chapter Twelve

Boli-Bennett, John. 1980. "Global Integration and Universal Increase in State Dominance, 19190-1970," in Albert Bergesen, ed., <u>Studies of the Modern World System</u>. New York: Academic Press.

Calhoun, C., Drummond, W., Whittington, D. 1987. "Computerized Information Management in a System-Poor Environment." <u>TWPR</u> 9 (4) 361-379.

Lechner, F and Boli, J. 2005. World Culture. MA: Blackwell.

Matvey, J. 1987. <u>Central Appalachia: Distortions in Development, 1750-1987</u>. Thesis. University Microfilms: Ann Arbor.

Matvey, J. 2005. <u>Regionalism and Globalization</u>: Essays on Appalachia, Globalization and Global Computerization. Iuniverse: Lincoln-New York-Shanghai.
Global Computerization. IUniverse: Lincoln-New York-Shanghai. See within:

Matvey and Chan, "Societal and Global Computerization," Chapter Eight.

Meyer, J. 1980. "The World Polity and the Authority of the Nation State," in Albert Bergesen, ed., <u>Studies of the Modern World System</u>. New York: Academic Press.

Parsons, Talcott. 1977. <u>Social Systems and the Evolution of Action Theory</u>. New York: The Free Press.

Robertson, Roland and Chirico, JoAnn. 1985. "Humanity, Globalization, and Worldwide Religious Resurgence: A Theoretical Exploration," in <u>Sociological Analysis</u> 46:3 : 219-241.

Robertson, Roland. 1987. "Globalization, Modernization and Postmodernization: The Ambiguous Position of Religion" presented at New ERA Seminar, October 7-11, St. Martin, French West Indies.

Robertson, Roland. (1992) <u>Globalization: Global Culture and Social Theory.</u> London: Sage.

Robertson and Giulianotti. (2009) <u>Globalization and Football</u>. London: Sage (TC&S).

Wallerstein, Immanuel. 1979. <u>The Capitalist World Economy.</u> Cambridge: University Press.

Sources: Chapter Thirteen

The Bible (NIV)

Dylan, Bob. (1963) "The Times They Are a-Changing" Columbia Records.

Robertson, Roland. (1992) *Globalization: Global Culture and Social Theory* London: Sage.

Sources: Chapter Fourteen, Epilogue

Davies, Whittaker, van Hagen. *SUSE Linux 10: Bible*. 2006. NJ: Wiley Publishing, Inc.

Leblanc, Dee-Ann. *Linux for Dummies*. 5th Edition, 2004. NJ: Wiley Publishing, Inc.

Thomas, Keir. *Beginning SUSE Linux*. 2nd Edition, 2006. NY: Apress.

Manufactured By: RR Donnelley
                    Momence, IL USA
                    August , 2010